The Roadmap of the 18th CPC National Congress
and
The Chinese Dream

Compiled by **Huang Huaguang and Luan Jianzhang**

First Edition 2013

ISBN 978-7-119-08647-7
©Foreign Languages Press Co. Ltd, Beijing, China, 2013

Published by
Foreign Languages Press Co. Ltd
24 Baiwanzhuang Road, Beijing 100037, China
http://www.flp.com.cn

Printed in the People's Republic of China

Foreword

Thanks to over 90 years of persistent efforts, the Party has rallied and led the people of all ethnic groups of the country in turning the once poor and backward old China into an increasingly prosperous and powerful new China, opening up bright prospects for the great rejuvenation of the Chinese nation.

– Report to the 18th CPC National Congress

I

On November 29, 2012, the 21st day after the conclusion of the 18th CPC National Congress, Xi Jinping, newly-elected general secretary of the CPC Central Committee, led all the members of the Standing Committee of the Political Bureau of the CPC Central Committee to the National Museum of China and visited the exhibition on *The Road to Rejuvenation.* After reviewing the historical progress that the Chinese people have gone through in modern times to realize national rejuvenation, Xi Jinping pointed out: Everybody has an ideal and pursues his or her own dream. Now, people are talking about the Chinese Dream. I believe that realizing the rejuvenation of the Chinese nation has been the greatest dream of the Chinese people since the beginning of the modern era. This dream concentrates a long-cherished expectation of many generations of the Chinese people, and encapsulates the overall interests of the Chinese nation and its people. It is the common aspiration of every Chinese.

This was the first time that top CPC leader had focus on the Chinese Dream. Soon a passionate response rose from the people of China, and the concept attracted wide interest and triggered heated discussions in the international community. Many tried to explore the political meaning of the Chinese Dream and its internal and external ramifications. Others sought to understand the concept. According to China's political logic and conventional practice, people would immediately apply themselves to studying, promoting, and implementing the spirit of the report after the conclusion of the 18th CPC National Congress. How could the Chinese Dream, a new concept which had never appeared in the past report to the congress, be proposed instantly after the congress had just concluded?

A careful assessment of the situation would reveal that it is not unexpected. The proposal of the Chinese Dream is a very reasonable step to take. Although the phrase "Chinese Dream" did not feature in the Report to the 18th CPC National Congress, its synonym "the great rejuvenation of the Chinese nation" appeared at least eight times. The Report began with "opening up bright prospects for the great rejuvenation of the Chinese nation," and concluded with "launching the Chinese nation's irreversible historic march to development and great rejuvenation." The overall task of building socialism with Chinese characteristics is, as the Report emphasized, "to achieve socialist modernization and the great rejuvenation of the Chinese nation." This has been the greatest historical goal for the Chinese people for more than a century.

The Chinese nation would be regarded as "rejuvenated" when the goals determined at the 18th CPC National Congress are achieved – that the construction of a moderately prosperous society be completed at the 100th anniversary of the founding of the Communist Party of China, and that the construction of a prosperous, democratic, harmonious and modernized socialist country be completed at the 100th anniversary of the founding of new China. So the Chinese Dream is simply a summary and a popular expression of the aforementioned goals of the "Two Centennials," and the report to the congress has drawn a roadmap for realizing the Chinese Dream. If people want to understand the meaning of the Chinese Dream, they need to understand the essential spirit and the deep connotations of the 18th CPC National Congress, reflecting upon the political messages conveyed by the congress rather than speculating on what the Chinese Dream is and what it means.

II

There are different views and voices in the international community about the Chinese Dream. Some people recognize and appreciate the idea, while others fail to understand or misinterpreted it, or even link the Chinese Dream with pursuing hegemony and building "peace under the rule of China." President Xi's speech at the First Plenary Session of the 12th National People's Congress on March 17, 2013, offered a more clear and precise interpretation of the Chinese Dream: to realize the goal of completing the construction of a moderately prosperous society and completing the socialist modernization of a prosperous, powerful, democratic, civilized and harmonious society. To realize the Chinese Dream of the great rejuvenation of the Chinese nation means achieving the happiness of the people.

The Chinese Dream is a dream about national development, not about achieving hegemony. At the beginning of the modern era, China was impoverished and weak. The Chinese people sustained a hope in their hearts that one day their country would become prosperous and powerful. The word "prosperous" here refers to a wealth that is both material and spiritual, because neither material scarcity nor a spiritual void accord with socialist principles. The word "powerful" here refers not only to growth in economy, science, and technology but also to progress in other aspects like culture, education, sport, national defense, and ecology. That is to say, the true wealth and strength of a country stem from the realization of the comprehensive, coordinated and sustained scientific development of the country. This has nothing to do with hegemony. At present, China is still far from being wealthy and powerful in many aspects. There is still a very long road to go to meet the requirements of the scientific outlook of development. The "five-in-one" general deployment was proposed in the Report to the 18th CPC National Congress. This is in fact a general deployment to realize the prosperity of the country. To succeed in carrying out the many tasks that accord with this general deployment is the key for China to achieve prosperity, power and strength.

The Chinese Dream is a dream about national dignity, not about empire-building. The Chinese people have deep memories about the past: the gradual decline of the country, the loss of sovereignty, and the humiliations of the nation. They have always expected, and continue to expect, that the day will come when the Chinese nation is rejuvenated and reinvigorated. It means that people will live with a greater degree of fulfillment, and with more dignity. It is not a dream about "returning to the grand Tang Dynasty" or about "building a tributary system centering round China." China wants dignity, and the most important characteristics of this are:

Firstly, it means that China should achieve self-improvement. Backwardness means failure, and self-improvement comes only from development. During more than 30 years of reform and opening up, China has concentrated on building the country and has applied itself wholeheartedly to the pursuit of development, otherwise China would not be where it stands today, and it would not have achieved its current level of respect from so many other countries.

Secondly, it means that China should have self-confidence. How can people achieve self-improvement if they have no confidence in themselves? The 18th CPC National Congress put forward that the path, theory, and system of socialism with Chinese characteristics are the basis for China's self-confidence and strength. The international community need not fear that China will ever seek to export its own path, theory, and system.

The Chinese Dream is a dream about people's happiness, not about constitutionalism. In the final analysis, the Chinese Dream is the dream of the people. Happiness is the core content of the Chinese Dream and also the fundamental values of CPC members. In the view of the CPC, the happiness of the people is inspired more importantly by enjoying more extensive, more satisfactory, and more comprehensive people's democracy, not simply by having a better education, a more stable job, a more satisfactory income, more reliable social security, a higher standard of medical care and service, more comfortable living conditions, and a more beautiful environment, not simply by having the opportunity to achieve a more brilliant career and realize one's dreams, nor simply to grow and progress along with the homeland and the times.

According to Maslow's hierarchy of needs, rule by the people satisfies the need of self-actualization, and it is the highest level of happiness. So the first of the eight basic requirements of building socialism with Chinese characteristics in the Report to the 18th CPC National Congress is that the status of the people must be ensured as the main party, the people's rights and interests guaranteed, and the rule by the people safeguarded. In China, the socialist democratic system with Chinese characteristics is the fundamental guarantee of rule by the people. The so-called "dream of constitutional government," which takes the basic political systems of the West such as the "tripartite" political system and the multi-party system as its orientation, cannot bring real and permanent happiness to the Chinese people because it is not compatible with China's national conditions nor with the cultural psychology of the Chinese people.

III

There are universal concerns in the international community on how China will realize the Chinese Dream. In particular, people want to know what the Chinese Dream implies for the rest of the world. In response to this, when delivering a speech at the First Session of the 12th National People's Congress, Xi Jinping emphasized that to realize the Chinese Dream, we must take the Chinese road, carry forward the Chinese spirit, and pool together the Chinese strength. During the informal meeting with US President Obama at the Annenberg Estate on June 7, 2013, President Xi further deliberated on the Chinese way to realize the Chinese Dream in terms of relations between China and the international community. He emphasized that the Chinese Dream means the realization of the prosperity of the country, the rejuvenation of the nation, and the happiness of the people. It is a dream of peace, development and win-win cooperation. It is connected to the dreams shared by peoples of many other countries, including the American Dream.

To realize the Chinese Dream, we have to adhere to the road of socialism with Chinese characteristics, and keep to the path of peaceful development. The path one takes determines one's fate. The Chinese people always adhere to the principle of "never imposing on others what one would not choose for oneself." China has experienced a century of hardships – of foreign invasion and civil war. It will never seek to realize the Chinese Dream by non-peaceful means. The Chinese people value history as a mirror. As China has witnessed the decline and fall of other countries that have sought hegemony, it will never choose to follow their disastrous examples. The Chinese people value pragmatism. China has already been on the road to realize the Chinese Dream in the past 30 years of reform and opening-up, so there is no need to seek other roads. From the perspective of domestic events in China this road is called the road of socialism with Chinese characteristics, and from the perspective of relations with people in foreign countries it is called the road of peaceful development. In essence, they are interconnected. The key idea is to take economic development as the center while pressing forward the development in politics, culture, society, ecology and other aspects. We should adhere to both reform and opening-up and to the direction of socialism. We should constantly liberate and develop social productivity and gradually realize the common prosperity of the people, and promote all-round development of the people. We should develop China through the efforts for a peaceful international environment and promote joint development of the international community. In this process, China always adheres to independence, openness and win-win cooperation. Its national defense policy is based on non-aggression. It opposes any form of hegemony, colonialism and power politics. It will never engage in arms race, seek hegemony, or indulge in expansionism.

To realize the Chinese Dream, the Chinese people need to carry forward the national spirit with patriotism, reform, and innovation as the core, in a spirit of equality, mutual trust, tolerance, learning from each other, and win-win cooperation in international relations. The realization of the Chinese Dream is, first of all, the task of the Chinese people. Without patriotism, it is impossible for the nation to create the solidarity and agreement of all the people. In realizing the Chinese Dream, which is an unprecedented undertaking, the Chinese people will encounter many new circumstances, problems and challenges. Without reform and innovation, it is impossible to succeed in this historical mission. Due to the historic changes in the relations between China and the rest of the world, whether the Chinese people can realize the Chinese Dream is determined to a large extent by two factors: On the one hand, whether China can take advantage of opportunities elsewhere in the world and help other countries to take advantage of opportunities in China; on the other hand, other countries' attitudes toward the Chinese Dream, namely whether they respond with belief or doubt, understanding or envy, support or obstruction. In essence, the Chinese Dream is connected to the dreams of other people in other countries around the world. The realization of the Chinese Dream will bring peace, cooperation, and opportunities for development to the world. It does not represent any kind of threat. But this needs understanding and support, or at least tolerance, on the part of the international community. If other parties stick to a rigid ideology, a cold war mentality or a zero-sum game, or if they respond with resentment to the sight of others enjoying something positive, there will never be peace in the world and no dreams can be realized, let alone the Chinese Dream.

To realize the Chinese Dream, people need to unite not only the Chinese strength, but also the worlds' strength that support, understand, and sympathize with China. The core of the Chinese strength is the Communist Party of China. The key to doing things well in China lies in the CPC. Whether people can realize the Chinese Dream also depends on the CPC. Since the end of the Cold War, the most thought-provoking phenomenon in party politics around the world is that some large parties, and some parties with a very long history and lengthy period of rule, have lost their power. The change of fate of these parties was caused by either corruption, or lack of solidarity, or confusion in ideology. All these problems come down to one single question: How can a party retain its progressiveness? The CPC is not an exception. At the 18th CPC National Congress, it was proposed that the Party should adhere to the principle of liberating ideas in carrying out reform and innovation, should adhere to the principle that the party exercises self-discipline and runs itself strictly, and should adopt a scientific approach to the construction of the Party, with the aim to retain its progressiveness and ensure that the Party always stands as the strong leading core in the building of socialism with Chinese characteristics.

The key to the world's strength lies in the extensive community of developing countries. Deng Xiaoping pointed out: "China shares the same destiny with all the Third World countries." Without the support of the extensive community of developing countries, it would have been impossible for China to resume its legitimate seat in the United Nations. The Chinese Dream will become unrealistic and empty talks if without the support of the extensive community of developing countries as multi-polarization and economic globalization further progress. Therefore the Report to the 18th CPC National Congress reaffirmed that China's international status as the largest developing country in the world has not changed, that

China would continue to strengthen its solidarity and cooperation with developing countries, and that China would always be a reliable friend and sincere partner of the developing countries.

This is a brief and simple explanation of the relationship between the Chinese Dream and the 18th CPC National Congress. Further study on the roadmap of the report will help understand every aspect of the Chinese Dream. Then you will find that the Chinese Dream is not only for China, but also for the rest of the world. China will not jeopardize the progressive interests of other countries and their peoples in its pursuit of the Chinese Dream. On the contrary, together with the international community it will make relentless efforts to realize the world's dreams of peace, development, and win-win cooperation.

July 2013

Contents

Foreword   I

PART ONE
Where Will the CPC Go Following Its 18th CPC National Congress?   1

Chapter 1	Does the CPC Still Believe in Communism?	5
	Why does the CPC hold high the banner of socialism with Chinese characteristics?	8
	Is socialism with Chinese characteristics still true socialism?	12
	What is the difference between socialism with Chinese characteristics and democratic socialism?	17
	Why are the guiding thoughts of the CPC constantly adjusted?	25
Chapter 2	Who Will Accomplish the Mission of the CPC?	33
	How does the CPC admit new Party members?	35
	How does the CPC select and appoint cadres?	44
	How are the top CPC leaders elected?	49
	What is the policy of personnel management that the CPC pursues?	55

Chapter 3	What If Dissenting Voices Arise Inside the CPC?	63
	What is the organizational principle of the CPC?	65
	How does the CPC develop intra-Party democracy?	74
	Why does the CPC constantly strengthen its discipline?	83
	How does the CPC exercise its leadership?	89
Chapter 4	Where Does the CPC's Advanced Nature Come From?	95
	Once advanced, always advanced?	97
	What factors does the CPC depend on to maintain its advanced nature?	104
	Can the CPC check corruption?	113

PART TWO
Where Will China Go After the 18th CPC National Congress?   123

Chapter 5	Will China's Economy Continue to Grow?	127
	Why can China's economy maintain rapid long-term growth?	129
	Does China's economy still have potential to grow?	136

Contents

	How will China update its economy?	142
Chapter 6	Where Will China Go in Reforming Its Political Structure?	153
	What is "Chinese-style democracy"?	155
	Why does China not adopt the multi-party system?	158
	Why does China not apply the separation of powers?	164
	Is law-based governance compatible with the Party's leadership?	172
	Is elective democracy the only legitimate form?	178
	How do the Chinese people participate in and deliberate on state affairs?	186
Chapter 7	How Should Its People Build China into a Cultural Power?	193
	What kind of a cultural power does China want to become?	195
	Will an emphasis on core values affect cultural diversity?	198
	Can cultural freedom and cultural responsibility be unified?	204
	Will China engage in "exporting its culture"?	212
Chapter 8	Can China Really Build a Harmonious Society?	219

	What kind of changes have occurred in Chinese society?	**221**
	What is the CPC's philosophy for social construction?	**227**
	How does the Communist Party of China resolve the issue of employment?	**233**
	What kind of social insurance system is China to build?	**241**
	Will China really take action to change the current structure of interests?	**245**
Chapter 9	How Can We Make China Beautiful?	**253**
	Focusing on ecological progress: no alternative or strategic choice?	**255**
	Building a beautiful China: lip service, or a real commitment?	**259**
	Fighting climate change: good faith or fake?	**266**

PART THREE
How Should China's Relationship with the Rest of the World Progress After the 18th CPC National Congress?   279

Chapter 10	How Should China Advance on Its Road of Peaceful Development?	**283**

Contents

	Will China genuinely take the road of peaceful development?	285
	Will China continue its commitment to a non-aggressive national defense policy?	292
	Does China's peaceful development have a "bottom line principle"?	300
Chapter 11	Can China Really Achieve Win-Win Results with Other Countries?	309
	Has China slowed down the pace of opening up to the outside world?	311
	What is China's view of trade liberalization?	317
	What would happen in the case of trade friction with other countries?	324
	Why does China attach no conditions to its foreign aid?	329
	Is China engaging in neo-colonialism in Africa?	335
Chapter 12	What Role Will China Play as a New Power?	343
	Will China adjust its policies of "non-interference" and "non-alignment"?	345
	Will all-out confrontation occur between China and the USA?	351

Does China intend to "keep friendly
    relations with distant states and attack
    its neighbors"? 357
Will China continue to speak for developing
    countries? 360
What kind of international order does
    China advocate? 364

Afterword 368

The Roadmap of the 18th CPC National Congress and The Chinese Dream

All Party members must heighten their sense of urgency, their sense of responsibility, and their focus on strengthening the Party's governance skills, development, and integrity. We should continue to free up our minds and carry out reform and innovation, and uphold the principle that the Party should supervise its own conduct and run itself with strict discipline. We should make comprehensive efforts to strengthen the Party theoretically and organizationally and improve its conduct. We should improve our capacity to fight corruption, uphold Party integrity and improve Party rules and regulations. We should enhance our own individual ethical structure, and improve our capacity for self-improvement, self-development and innovation, thereby building an innovative and service-oriented Marxist governing party that constantly strives to learn. By taking these steps we can ensure that the Party always provides the core of firm leadership guiding the cause of socialism with Chinese characteristics.

— Report to the 18th CPC National Congress

PART ONE

Where Will the CPC Go Following Its 18th CPC National Congress?

2

Since China adopted the policy of reform and opening-up in 1978, and especially since the disintegration of the USSR and the end of the Cold War, the question of the future direction of the CPC has been constantly asked, and the international community has frequently debated and speculated on the issue, regularly predicting that the CPC will be the next CPSU and implying that the CPC is a facsimile of the CPSU and that when the "winter" of the CPSU has come the "spring" of the CPC will not be far behind. In fact, anyone who is not completely blind to history and is at all free from prejudice will be clear that the CPC once took the CPSU as its role model but it is today a fundamentally different party. There is a Chinese saying: "The blue that is extracted from the indigo plant is bluer than the plant." In the years of reform and opening-up the CPC continued to rebuild. The CPC has become a modern political party which adheres to its basic principles, remains a Marxist party, and blazes new trails in a pioneering spirit to keep pace with the times. This is as apparent from the history of the CPC as from the policies and propositions proclaimed in the Report to the 18th CPC National Congress.

During the revolutionary period, Mao Zedong said, "At the outbreak of the October Revolution, we were given Marxism-Leninism. To walk the road of the Russian is the conclusion we come to." The CPC, however, basing itself on evolving realities, blazed a new and practical revolutionary path of encircling the cities from the rural areas and seizing power by armed force. This was different from the October Revolution. After the founding of the People's Republic of China in 1949, the CPC held: "The CPSU is our best teacher, and we must learn from it." Mao Zedong even envisioned that "the USSR's today will be our tomorrow," but the CPC did not take the

Soviet model as an absolute truth. When the domestic and international situation changed in 1956, the CPC began to re-examine its road to socialism, and gradually effected a transition from "learning from the Russian," to "drawing lessons from the USSR." It was during this period that the system of people's congresses, the system of multiparty cooperation and political consultation under the leadership of the CPC, and the system of regional ethnic autonomy, were set up.

Since the Third Plenary Session of the 11th CPC Central Committee, the CPC has led the Chinese people on the great road of reform and opening-up, a socialist road with Chinese characteristics which is different from that of the USSR. The present CPC is completely different from the former CPSU, and even different from its own previous incarnation of more than 30 years ago. The 18th CPC National Congress marks the beginning of a new period for the development of the Party, and also gives momentum to the confidence and determination of the Party to continue forging ahead on the road to socialism with Chinese characteristics.

The Third Plenary Session of the 11th CPC Central Committee

The Third Plenary Session of the 11th CPC Central Committee was a meeting of the Central Committee of the CPC held in Beijing, China, from December 18 to 22, 1978. The Third Plenary Session criticized the thought of "Two Whatevers" (that is, "whatever decisions made by Chairman Mao will be firmly upheld; whatever instructions given by Chairman Mao will be faithfully followed."), laid down the guideline of liberating the mind, using the brains, seeking truth from facts, and uniting to look forward, immediately abandoned the slogan of "taking class struggle as the key link," made the strategic policy decision to shift the working focus to the development of socialist modernization, and endorsed the principle of seeking truth from facts and the principle of democratic centralism.

The Roadmap of the 18th CPC National Congress and The Chinese Dream

Chapter 1

Does the CPC Still Believe in Communism?

Through more than 30 years of effort in reform and opening-up, we have brandished the great banner of socialism with Chinese characteristics and rejected both the old and rigid closed-door policy and any attempt to abandon socialism and take a wrong turning. The path of socialism with Chinese characteristics, the system of theories of socialism with Chinese characteristics and the socialist system with Chinese characteristics are the fundamental accomplishments of the Party and people, produced and accumulated over the course of 90 years of arduous struggle. We must cherish these accomplishments, constantly uphold them, and continue to enrich them.

— Report to the 18th CPC National Congress

"Does the CPC still believe in communalism?" This is a question often asked by foreign friends. From their point of view, after 30 years of reform and opening-up, the CPC is no longer the party it once was, and it no longer seems to believe in communism. They also think that the violent revolution and class struggle proclaimed by the CPC run counter to the development trend of the modern world, and also contradict the CPC's ideas of peace, development, cooperation and mutual benefit. Therefore, they conclude that the CPC should abandon communism and turn to believe in other "-isms," such as democratic socialism or liberal democracy. In fact, this is a misunderstanding of communism and the CPC.

Facing the oppression of the "three great mountains" of imperialism, feudalism and bureaucratic-capitalism in the old semi-feudal and semi-colonial China, the CPC had no choice but to use revolutionary means to destroy the old world and create a new one. But you cannot draw the conclusion from this alone that communism demands violent revolution and class struggle. Different goals and tasks naturally require different methods. From this perspective, there is no universal model for communism, and the theories and opinions of the CPSU cannot represent communism as a whole. In essence, communism refers to a society which is more advanced in productive forces and more equitable in society. It represents people's aspiration for a happy life, and is a choice for the fulfillment of the goals and value orientations. Different alternatives should also be allowed for the purpose.

Professor Larry Hsien Ping Lang and Professor Yang Ruihui from the Chinese University of Hong Kong (CUHK) pointed out in their study that the word "communism" is associated with "community." But how do we understand "community"? It can be illustrated by an example. In English, anyone who squabbles and disturbs his neighbors, doesn't participate in neighborhood activities, or is reluctant to make any contribution to the neighborhood will be regarded as a person who lacks "community spirit." Therefore, "community" implies harmony. Some European politicians, shocked by the genocide of the two world wars, proposed to establish a European Community, with the aim of transforming Europe into a harmonious home to divert a third world war. Note that in 1825 Robert Owen, a British philanthropist and an early "utopian communist," established the commune of "New Harmony" in Indiana, America. Karl Marx named the world's first fledgling proletarian regime the Paris Commune. This partially illustrates that, at the very beginning, communism was related to "social harmony." In a period of revolution and war, the communists placed the emphasis on revolution, creating an impression that communism is equivalent to violent revolution. According to textual research, it was mainly through the influence of the Soviet policies of socializing private possessions after the October Revolution that Hu Shi translated communism into "*gong chan zhu yi*" (Chinese for communism). The concept of harmonious society and harmonious world

Hu Shi

Hu Shi (1891–1962), native of Jixi of Anhui, was a well-known Chinese contemporary scholar, poet, historian, literary figure, and philosopher. Hu was the first scholar to advocate the use of written vernacular Chinese. He was chancellor of Peking University between 1946 and 1948, the Republic of China's ambassador to the United States of America between 1938 and 1942, and later (1957) president of the Academia Sinica in Taipei.

later advocated by the CPC actually represented a return to the original meaning of communism, indicating that the CPC is probing the universal value of the social relations of contemporary China and the international relations of the contemporary world.

Why does the CPC hold high the banner of socialism with Chinese characteristics?

Though different people have different interpretation of communism, the Chinese Communists have never wavered from their faith in communism – in building a more beautiful, more equal, more harmonious society – and in taking as their responsibility and mission to help people live a happy life. Reviewing the history of the PRC, we can see that it was faith that brought about the founding of the PRC. Since the CPC was founded, numerous patriots have chosen to sacrifice their lives to attain the goals of the Party. It was this spirit that enabled the Party to defeat all of its enemies, to triumph in adversity, and to establish the PRC.

When commenting on the long and tortuous history of the Party, Deng Xiaoping, the core of the second generation of leadership of the Party, highlighted the point that the Chinese revolution would never have succeeded in reviving the fortunes of China if the Chinese Communists had not pinned such faith in Marxism or combined the fundamental theories of Marxism with the prevailing reality in China to probe its own road. "Faith in communism is a driving force behind the success of the Chinese revolution."

At the beginning of reform and opening-up, Deng Xiaoping repeatedly stressed, "Why were we able to overcome endless prob-

A copy of *Communist Manifesto*, published by China Liberation Press, on display in the former residence of Karl Marx.

lems and achieve revolutionary success in difficult circumstances? Because we had ideals, we had faith in Marxism, and we had faith in communism." It has also been highlighted in the Report to the 18th CPC National Congress that faith in Marxism, socialism and communism is the political soul of the Chinese Communists and the ideological mainstay that helps them to go through and survive all kinds of ordeal. Xi Jinping, the general secretary of the Central Committee of the CPC described it through a metaphor, "Faith is the spiritual calcium of communists. If the faith is lost or frail, they will suffer from 'calcium deficiency' in spirit or become weak-boned."

It is one thing to firmly believe in the communist ideal, but it is another to turn this faith into reality. Just as a mansion is built brick by brick, a more beautiful, equal and harmonious society is established step by step. The CPSU once led the USSR to implement the "catch-up-with-and-surpass" strategy of development; the CPC also launched the "Great Leap Forward" movement. Both encountered serious problems. The root cause of this was that they mistook the communist ideal for the prevailing reality. As communism or socialism was firstly attained in those countries which were less developed in economy and culture, a primary stage of socialism or communism was required, part of an ongoing process. Both the CPSU and the CPC made serious mistakes in trying to bypass the historical process of development, but fortunately the CPC eventually found its way back onto the right road by correcting its mistakes. This is the socialist road with Chinese characteristics. In other words, the advanced stage of communism cannot begin until its primary stage ends. In China, we name the primary stage of communism or socialism as socialism with Chinese characteristics, which at present is the common ideal of the Party members and the people of China. In contemporary China, to develop socialism with Chinese characteristics is truly to adhere to socialism and communism. As is clearly pointed out in the Report to the 18th CPC National Congress, "Socialism with Chinese characteristics represents

---

The Great Leap Forward

The Great Leap Forward refers to the nationwide movement of extreme "Leftist" line led by the CPC from 1958 to 1960. In May, 1958, the Second Plenary Session of the Eighth Central Committee passed the general line of "going all out, aiming high, and achieving greater, faster, better and more economical results in building socialism." Then the Central Committee of the CPC launched the "Great Leap Forward," pursuing high speed in production and large scale in construction. There were diverse slogans of "larges" and "specials" for the CPC and the people to adopt. For example, producing mountains of iron; building thousands of railways and breeding millions of pigs. Stimulated by such goals and slogans, China's investment in basic construction dramatically increased, reaching RMB 100.6 billion within three years, which nearly doubled the total figure of the previous five years. The cumulative rate increased abruptly, reaching 39.1% each year on average. The unrealistic quota system was inevitably followed by chaotic organization and exaggeration. As a consequence, the people endured hardships and the economy suffered serious losses.

the general direction of the development of contemporary China, and only socialism with Chinese characteristics can bring progress to China."

Why do the CPC and the Chinese people take socialism with Chinese characteristics as their common ideal? On the one hand, it systematically and pragmatically replies to the fundamental question of what kind of socialism to develop and how to develop socialism in an oriental country which is populous and impoverished. On the other hand, it is the exclusive option appropriate to the modern history of China, which has been proved by the reform and opening-up of the past 30 years to be the right road, theory and system, and which is in conformity with the interests of the broadest masses.

After the Opium War of 1840, as a result of the incursions of the Western powers and the corruption and impotency of China's feudal rulers, China regressed from a strong oriental power which had retained a superior level of civilization for centuries into a semi-colonial and semi-feudal society. From then on, in order to escape this grim fate, the Chinese people conducted painstaking analysis, trying capitalist systems such as the constitutional monarchy, the cabinet system, the multi-party system and the parliamentary system, but all these systems failed to change the nature of Chinese society and the fortuncs of the Chinese people. Influenced by the October Revolution, the CPC led people onto a socialist path, but many problems arose when the CPC copied the Soviet socialist model. Working from the principle of drawing lessons from past socialist experience, the CPC began to seek its own road to develop. In the process, unlike the USSR or East European countries which abandoned socialism and became completely Westernized, China insisted on combining universal Marxist principles with Chinese realities, creating, adhering to and developing socialism with Chinese characteristics. Thus the CPC avoided retracing the steps of the USSR and East European countries, where the party collapsed and the nation disintegrated; on the contrary China achieved extraordinary success.

This period bears testimony to the fact that China's problems cannot be solved by copying Western capitalist models or any other socialist model; China must tread its own path, building socialism with Chinese characteristics. From this we may draw the conclusion that the common ideal of socialism with Chinese characteristics is the choice of history and the people, and it is in conformity with the general direction of the progress of China and the law of social development. Historically this tendency cannot be reversed. It is for this reason that the Report to the 18th CPC National Congress stressed again holding high the great banner of socialism with Chinese characteristics and walking unswervingly along the road of socialism with Chinese characteristics.

Is socialism with Chinese characteristics still true socialism?

Many people wonder what socialism with Chinese characteristics means. From the analysis above, we can provide the answer that what we call Chinese characteristics take the prevailing reality in China as their foundation, and the most obvious and important reality is that China is still in its primary stage of development. Thus socialism with Chinese characteristics is socialism based on the fact that China is in its primary stage of development.

The theory that China is in the primary stage of socialism was formulated by the CPC, and it is taken by the Report to the 18th CPC National Congress as the general basis on which to build socialism with Chinese characteristics. This conclusion was initially drawn at the 13th CPC National Congress, including two main features: "Firstly, China has become a socialist society, and we must adhere to socialism and not deviate from it. Secondly, China is in the primary stage of socialism, and we must take this as the basis and not try to bypass it."

Though China has made considerable progress and undergone some radical changes since reform and opening-up were introduced, the country remains underdeveloped in terms of productive forces, relations of production, economic base, and superstructure. China, as a whole, remains in its primary stage. This led Deng Xiaoping to conclude: "The basic line of the primary stage will be followed for 100 years, and can't be changed." This means that it is a long-lasting period in history. From the 13th CPC National Congress onwards, each succeeding congress has reiterated the proposition that China is in the primary stage of socialism. As is pointed out in the Report to the 17th CPC National Congress, through the unremitting efforts of the CPC since the founding of the PRC in 1949, particularly since the introduction of reform and opening-up, China has made achievements in development that have attracted international attention. However, the prevailing reality has not changed – China is still in the primary stage of socialism and will remain so for a long time to come. The current features of development in China are a concrete manifestation of that basic reality at this new stage in the new century. Stressing the basic reality is not intended to belittle our achievements, to wallow in backwardness, or to encourage an unrealistic pursuit of quick results. Rather, it will serve as the basis of our endeavor to advance reform and to plan for development. The Report to the 18th CPC National Congress also acknowledged that the Party must bear in mind under any circumstances the paramount reality that China remains in the primary stage of socialism and will remain so for a long time, and that it must recognize this reality in pursuing all of its endeavors of reform and development.

Foreign friends often ask, "Where is the socialism when you retain only Chinese characteristics in your practice?" In fact, this is a misunderstanding. What is socialism? To put it briefly, socialism is a society-oriented system instead of a capital-oriented one. Socialism aims at liberating society from the oppression of capital. However, because China is in such a primary stage of development the function of capital can't be excluded completely, and even greater efforts will be needed to develop the market economy or capital market. Socialism with Chinese characteristics is a set of principles under which efforts are made to keep the balance between efficiency and fairness, between labor and market, and between government and market, on the basis of the China's realities, with the emphasis laid on fairness, society and government. These ideas have been reduced to eight basic requirements. To achieve new success for socialism with Chinese characteristics under new historical conditions, these basic requirements must be adhered to. The "Chinese experience"

The eight requirements:

We must maintain the people's principal position in the country; we must continue to release and develop the productive forces; we must persevere in reform and opening-up; we must safeguard social fairness and justice; we must strive for common prosperity; we must promote social harmony; we must pursue peaceful development; we must uphold the leadership of the Party.

widely discussed by the international community mainly refers to these "eight requirements."

Of the "eight requirements," the second one "we must continue to release and develop the productive forces," and the third one "we must persevere in reform and opening-up" are based on the fact that China is in its primary stage of development. In this primary stage, development is still the key. Therefore, China should continue to release and develop its productive forces, to take economic development as its central task, to adjust the relations of production and superstructure to adapt them to the development of the productive forces, and to press forward with reform and opening-up. Without developing its productive forces, and without reform and opening-up, socialism will be a dead-end. In the semi-colonial and semi-feudal period of the past, it was socialism that saved China. When East Europe changed dramatically and the USSR disintegrated, it was reform and opening-up that saved socialism.

All the other six "requirements" are related to the socialist direction and principles that should be followed in the course of continuing reform and open-up and continuing to release and develop the productive forces. **Maintaining the people's principal position in the country** means that the cause of socialism with Chinese characteristics must be of the people and for the people. The people here do not refer to the minority or the privileged class, but refers to the overwhelming majority of the people.

Realizing social fairness and justice is intimately associated with socialism, and it is also an inherent requirement of socialism with Chinese characteristics. Socialism should perform better than capitalism in coping with problems of social fairness and justice and in ensuring the fairness in rights, opportunities and regulations. But because China is and in the long run will be in the primary stage of socialism, individual differences have to be taken into consideration regarding to fairness and justice, and diversity in living standards and quality of life has to be acknowledged between individuals for their differences in physical strength, intelligence, diligence and family background. Therefore we cannot target "absolute fairness" while ignoring the level of the productive forces, the present economic structure, and the prevailing social conditions.

Poverty is not socialism, nor is polarization. Socialism cannot be distinguished from capitalism until common prosperity is realized. Thus **realizing common prosperity** is a fundamental principle of socialism with Chinese characteristics. As was said by Deng Xiaoping, "To walk the socialist road is to gradually realize common prosperity. If the rich becomes richer and the poor poorer, polarization will appear, but it is necessary and possible for the socialist system to avoid polarization."

As is mentioned above, **social harmony** is innate to communism and to socialism with Chinese characteristics. A society, whatever it is and no matter how happy it is, cannot avoid all contradictions or conflicts. As China is in the primary stage of socialism, the contradictions between the productive forces and the relations of production, between the economic base and the superstructure, are still the fundamental contradictions of Chinese society, but they can be solved peacefully and gradually by way of adjustment or reform.

Socialism consists of patriotism and internationalism, and social harmony refers not only to China but also to the international community. This determines that **peaceful development** is the only option for socialism with Chinese characteristics. Otherwise, it would not be true socialism. Deng Xiaoping constantly stressed that socialism with Chinese characteristics is a "peace-oriented socialism." Because the USSR pursued hegemony in breach of basic socialist requirements and principles, it finally disintegrated. China will certainly not retrace the path of the USSR.

Upholding the leadership of the Party is a fundamental principle of scientific socialism. If the cause of socialism with Chinese characteristics were not led by the CPC, this socialism, I am afraid, would change and the color of China would also change.

Of course, socialism with Chinese characteristics is still not mature or advanced. In the process of its development, it cannot be completely disengaged from Chinese features or traces, from China's realities, from China's capacity for putting into practice the basic principles of scientific socialism.

What is the difference between socialism with Chinese characteristics and democratic socialism?

During more than 30 years of reform and opening-up, the Chinese people of all ethnic groups under the leadership of the CPC have achieved impressive results in development. Many challenges, however, have arisen, such as corruption, widening income gaps, pollution, and moral degeneration. Views on these problems in China and abroad are not consistent. One view is that all these problems result from the market economy or the worship of money. The solution is to reduce market economy or freedom and increase socialism or government interference. Some people have even proposed turning China back to a planned economy. Another view is that these problems culminate from insufficient attention to the market economy and too much interference by the CPC, and they can be solved by strengthening all-round reform and opening-up, especially by accelerating political reform or weakening or even eliminating the leadership of the CPC. Some have proposed changing the name of the Communist Party to the Social Party or the Social Democratic Party, and changing the ideology of the CPC from socialism with Chinese characteristics to "democratic socialism." They see no difference between the economic and social policies of the socialist market economy and those of democratic socialism: various forms of ownership and allocation exist, private enterprise is permitted or even encouraged, exploitation is allowed, and a minority of people are allowed to enrich themselves. Other than terminology, they can find no essential difference between the reform policy of socialism with Chinese characteristics and the reformist policy of democratic socialism. In response to these two questions, the 18th CPC National Congress provides the answer that China will hold high the great banner of socialism with Chinese characteristics, indicating that China will neither repeat its old rigid and reserved policies nor abandon the banner of socialism.

It has been just over 30 years since reform and opening-up were introduced, and just over 20 years since the market economy was kick-started. The achievements have been remarkable in such a short space of time. It is in fact impossible for China to retreat to the past, to isolate itself from the outside world, or to turn back to a rigid planned economy, because even ordinary Chinese would resist such a move. So it is certainly out of the question for the CPC to retrace that road. There is no other alternative for China but to continue to reform and open up. The most important aspect of this

In 1993, a shop assistant in a grain shop registers the cancellation of the last batch of grain coupons.

From 1955, the Chinese needed coupons to purchase grains and food. In 1978 China started implementing reform and opening-up, and a market economy was gradually established. Reform was also carried out on the policy of centralized purchase and sale of grain, which had continued for over 30 years. Canceling the final grain coupons brought an end to the system. *(Photographed by Liu Weibing)*

is to choose the right direction, for the faster you go in the wrong direction, the further away you will be from your destination. In the USSR, Gorbachev was initially reluctant to touch the rigid planned economy, but later he adopted radical measures: an overnight switch to a market economy, voluntarily abandoning the ruling position of the CPSU, and adopting a "democratic and humanitarian" ideology. As a consequence, the USSR disappeared as a great power. The lesson was bitter. As past experience, if not forgotten, serves as a guide for the future, the CPC must not follow the USSR, and especially not blindly transform the Party's banner into democratic socialism. Otherwise, China will be led astray, and end up tasting the same bitter fruit as the USSR.

Why must the CPC never change its banner? A review of the drastic changes in central and eastern European countries reveals that the changes began with the conversion of the ruling parties to social democracy and the ideology of democratic socialism. From October 1989, when the Hungarian Socialist Workers' Party became the Social Party, to June 1991 when the Albanian Party of Labor became the Social Party, all the communist parties in these countries, other than the Romanian Communist Party – which vanished altogether – were transformed into social democratic parties. Of these, the Polish United Workers' Party split into the Social Democracy of Poland and the Polish Social Democratic Union; the Communist League of Yugoslavia split into five parties even before the disintegration of the country, when all the constituent republics changed their parties into social democratic parties with nationalist characteristics. This phenomenon happened because the traditional socialism upheld by the communist party and the democratic socialism upheld by the social parties originated from the same historical source, and they were similar in policy. The transition was relatively easy, and the results were confusing.

It is widely accepted that both traditional socialism and democratic socialism originated from traditional European social democracy, which emerged before the European Revolution in 1848, and was later influenced by Marxism so deeply that it became basically synonymous with Marxist scientific socialism for a long period of time afterwards. At the end of the 19th century, with the spread of Bernstein's Revisionism among the international movements of workers, the traditional social democratic movement experienced an ideological split. The success of the Russian October Revolution and the establishment of the Bolshevik regime became the line of demarcation for the theory and the practice of traditional social democracy. From then on, the revolutionary Left-wing which was represented by Bolshevism or Leninism named itself the communist party, and led the world communist movement under the common banner of the Communist International. The Right-wing and the central factions of the original social democracy gradually converged, for they all opposed the October Revolution, Bolshevism or communism, and the dictatorship of the proletariat. They moved completely to social reformism, ever more distant from Marxism. During this period, they still called themselves socialist democrats in order to distinguish themselves from the "democracy" promoted by the bourgeoisie. By 1951, when the Socialist International was established, they tried to differentiate themselves from the socialism characterized by the Russian proletariat dictatorship, and changed their name to "democratic socialism" to mark their "democratic" nature.

Bolshevism or Leninism, which also originated from the traditional European social democracy, raised Marxism to a new level. Under its guidance, the Russians achieved victory in the October Revolution, establishing the first proletariat socialist regime in the world. Later, however, Stalin, brandishing the banner of Leninism, produced a series of theory for socialist construction, establishing socialism of the so-called Stalinist model. This model then spread to European countries from the USSR, and also to China and some other Asian countries. The new democratic revolution and the socialist revolution, and the massive reconstruction in China, were also carried out under the influence of the Communist International, the CPSU and the Stalinist Model. During this process, the Chinese Communists made many efforts to explore the possibility of combining Marxism-Leninism and China's realities, formulating the first sinicized Marxist theory – Mao Zedong Thought – but generally, their understanding of socialism at that time was still confined to some specific conclusions drawn from Marxist originators and Stalinism. The early Chinese construction was basically a copy of the Stalinist model, even in some areas much more enforced. After the 1960s when the USSR and eastern European countries tried to partially reform the model, China opposed any such reform, criticizing it as "revisionism." Especially during the period of the Cultural Revolution, Chinese socialism was transformed into an extreme version of the Stalinist model, leading to disastrous consequences in politics, economy and society. It was in such circumstances that the Chinese Communists represented by Deng Xiaoping, on the basis of deep reflection on past experiences and lessons, began to break through the confinement of Stalinist model, coming up with the thought of combining the universal principles of Marxism with China's prevailing reality and building "socialism with Chinese characteristics." After the drastic changes in the USSR and the east European countries, they took on the task of breaking through or negating the Stalinist model at its roots, and committed

---

The Great Proletarian Cultural Revolution, commonly known as the Cultural Revolution, was a social-political movement that took place in the People's Republic of China from 1966 through 1976. It was set into motion by Mao Zedong, Chairman of the Communist Party of China. Its stated goal was to enforce communism in the country by removing all vestiges of capitalism and traditional culture from Chinese society, and to seek the road of building socialism independently. During the Cultural Revolution, however, opportunists in the Party including Lin Biao, Jiang Qing and Kang Sheng fanned factional struggle among the masses. As a consequence, many people were framed and persecuted including a large number of cadres in the Party, the government and the army, leaders of democratic parties, well-known figures from all walks of life, and even ordinary people; institutions of the Party and government at all levels and people's congresses and conferences of people's political consultations at all levels were paralyzed; and even such institutions that safeguarded the social order such as public security, procuratorate and justice were in chaos. All this caused a great loss to China's economy. The loss of national income, calculated according to the added value of RMB 100 of investment in normal years, was estimated to be as much as RMB 500 billion.

themselves to a wholehearted push for reform and opening-up. In this way they blazed a brand-new trail for socialism in China. From this perspective, it is impossible for China to retrace its old steps.

Not to take the old road does not mean to take any other road, and the same source does not mean the final convergence. Socialism with Chinese characteristics, a negation of the Stalinist model, means following a new path, but it does not negate socialism or replace it with democratic socialism. The purpose of reform in China is to uphold and develop rather than abandon socialism. As is pointed out by Secretary General Xi Jinping, "Socialism with Chinese characteristics is no other 'ism' but socialism. The basic principles of scientific socialism cannot be discarded. Otherwise, it would not be true socialism." The CPC consistently holds that socialism with Chinese characteristics involves both adhering to the basic principles of scientific socialism and giving these principles distinct Chinese characteristics due to the constraints of the times and in accordance with the prevailing conditions in the country. Though socialism with Chinese characteristics and contemporary democratic socialism both belong to the progressive force of the Left-wing in the world, they nevertheless represent two distinct trains of thought. They are different in nature. For example, socialism with Chinese characteristics takes Marxist viewpoints and methods as its guiding principle, though it does not limit itself to any specific theory. Democratic socialism on the other hand is diverse in its guiding thought in addition to being multi-sourced in its ideology. Though socialism with Chinese characteristics adheres to in developing diverse forms of ownership, encouraging and supporting the development of private enterprise, China still considers its public sector as the dominant player and maintains its stance of ultimately eliminating private ownership. In contrast, contemporary democratic socialism takes the private sector as the dominant player, giving up the goal and the requirement of replacing capitalism. The most important difference is that socialism with Chinese characteristics features the leadership of the CPC and democratic centralism, but democratic socialism favors multi-party system and some form of absolute democracy. If the leadership of the CPC is discarded, the theories and policies advocated by socialists cannot be guaranteed, and any resulting form of socialism will no longer be a true version.

Nevertheless, to highlight the differences between socialism with Chinese characteristics and democratic socialism does not mean to ignore the merits that democratic socialism offers. For example, the practice and experience in establishing a social security system are worthy of study. As a matter of fact, the CPC has been doing what is supposed to do, because socialism with Chinese characteristics is an open system, and all civilized fruits of human beings would be taken as the nutritious food for bringing up socialism with Chinese characteristics. The CPC has no intention of belittling democratic socialism. The choice of path and system for the development of any country is based on its own prevailing conditions. Socialism with Chinese characteristics is rooted in the vast land of China, suitable to the realities of China. If the social system were changed to democratic socialism, incompatibility may result, but this does not mean it cannot suit other countries. It is the wrong path for China, but in other countries it may be the right one. As General Secretary Xi Jinping has expressed it: "If you want to know whether or not the shoes fit you, only your feet can provide the answer." Likewise, the feasibility of a system can only be sensed by the people of the country.

Why are the guiding thoughts of the CPC constantly adjusted?

Socialism with Chinese characteristics is essentially the localization of the socialist basic principles and the product of the combination of the basic theory of Marxism with China's prevailing conditions. It consists of Chinese characteristics applied to the socialist road in practice, the socialist system which has been proved effective through practice and the socialist theoretical system which is used to guide practice. Of numerous approaches, "wading across the river by feeling for the stones in the riverbed" has played an important role, and the theories formulated thereby are also indispensable. Lenin said: Once the theory appeals to the masses, it will become the material force, and no revolutionary theory, no revolutionary movement. But the theory here is not a rigid doctrine, and must be compatible with changing situations and new practical tasks. Otherwise, it will become an obstacle to development. Situation and tasks determine what guiding thoughts should be applied. If the guiding thoughts of the party are not adjusted constantly, the party will become rigid and outmoded, and is likely to commit dogmatic mistakes.

In a simple but not very accurate word, Mao Zedong Thought is the key to China's revolutionary problems; Deng Xiaoping Theory addresses issues of how to eradicate poverty and achieve prosperity. The Three Represents resolve the problem of how to build the Party in a situation of relative prosperity. The Scientific Outlook on Development deals with the issue of balanced and coordinated development. These changes in guiding thoughts reflect the fact that the CPC treats Marxism scientifically and properly addresses the dialectical relationship between adherence to ideology and the requirements of development, and also reflects the changes in targets, tasks, and requirements at the present stage of development, indicating that reform is being steadily strengthened.

A historic contribution of the 18th CPC National Congress was to confirm the Scientific Outlook on Development as the guiding thought and to integrate it in the Party Constitution, underlining that: "As we advance toward the future, thoroughly applying the Scientific Outlook on Development is of major immediate significance and far-reaching historical significance for upholding and developing socialism with Chinese characteristics. We must apply it throughout the course of modernization and to every aspect of Party building."

What is the Scientific Outlook on Development? In brief, it is a concept of balanced and sustainable development. More specifically, it is based on the following principles:

1) Always put people first. Material development is of course important, but the development of people is even more important. In the past, China was poor, and in order to eradicate poverty, China had to concentrate all its strength on promoting material wealth. During that phase people were largely regarded as the means to attain the objective. This could be justified for a certain period, but China today must attach more importance to the worth of people. It must always ensure that both the aim and the outcome of all the work of the Party and the state is to realize, safeguard and expand the fundamental interests of the overwhelming majority of the people.

2) Pursuing comprehensive and balanced development. As a developing country, China must take economic development as its central task, but it cannot neglect the interests of

its people. Other factors should also be taken into consideration, such as political, cultural and social progress to meet their various needs.

3) Pursuing sustainable development. This means that in the long run economic development must be driven more by scientific and technological progress and by a workforce of higher quality, not solely by labor and output, so as to build a resource-conserving and environmentally friendly society. Another aspect of sustainable development is that China shouldn't ignore other developing countries, but should combine the development of China with that of other such countries.

4) Maintain a broad outlook. This means giving comprehensive consideration to a broad range of issues in planning and decision-making. For instance, reflecting on whether reform will contribute to development or social stability if implemented; taking rural areas into consideration when city programs are designed, to encourage simultaneous development; taking opening-up into consideration when domestic development strategy is devised. It needs to be pointed out that the Scientific Outlook on Development not only reflects the innate law of development, but also reflects "the doctrine of the mean" of "going too far is as bad as not going far enough" in traditional Chinese philosophy; it is not only the "strong ideology guiding the whole work of the Party and nation," but also the guiding principle for individuals in their daily life and work.

It has been ten years since the Scientific Outlook on Development was proposed. There are two reasons to maintain this strategic thought. One is to adapt the CPC to the changing requirements of

On June 18, 2013, a pilot project on the trade of carbon emission rights started formal operations in Shenzhen, China.

In order to fulfil China's commitments to emission reduction at the Copenhagen Conference and to contribute to Shenzhen's development strategy of building a national low-carbon pilot project city, the Shenzhen United Assets and Equity Exchange led and initiated the establishment of the Shenzhen Climate Exchange. The exchange engages in the registration and trade of environmental rights and interests including emissions of greenhouse gases and pollutants, and emission reduction.

---

development. In the new stage of the 21st century characterized by industrialization, IT application, market orientation, and urbanization, there emerge new factors relating to the current stage, and the CPC faces a series of challenging contradictions and difficulties. For instance, development remains unbalanced, uncoordinated and unsustainable; the capacity for scientific and technological innovation is weak; constraints imposed by resources and the environment tighten; the industrial structure is unbalanced; the gap is widening between urban and rural areas in development and income. If

China does not make progress in changing its growth model, these difficulties and problems will not be solved effectively.

The other reason is to follow the trend of global development. After World War II, accelerating economic growth was the consensus of the international community, and the peoples of the world created an unprecedented wonder of economic growth. Subsequently, problems arose all over the world due to the neglect of development, social fairness, environmental protection, and energy and resource conservation. Some countries have paid a high price to address problems of resource and energy exhaustion and the serious deterioration of their environment; some countries have lost the momentum for growth due to their unbalanced economic structure and backwardness in social development; some countries have suffered from such questions as bipolarity, unemployment, corruption and political chaos.

The current situation of the world demonstrates that development should be comprehensive and coordinated, covering the economy, politics, culture and society, and it should also be sustainable, harmoniously coordinating the interests of people and nature. As the largest developing country in the world, China experiences the multiple pressures of accelerating economic growth and conserving the environment while trying to complete the tasks of industrialization and modernization. Therefore, China has to blaze a new scientific road with Chinese characteristics rather than retrace the road of some other countries.

However, we should keep in mind that scientific development is related to strengthening reform of the productive forces, the relations of production, the economic base, and the superstructure, and it is also related to adjusting ideology, system and patterns of social interests. It is not easy to achieve "scientific development." Therefore, in addition to raising consciousness, the most important thing is to have a firm grasp of the most salient features of the Scientific Outlook on Development expounded in the Report to the 18th CPC National Congress. These features are **freeing ourselves from outmoded ideas, seeking truth from facts, keeping abreast of the times, and being realistic and pragmatic**. How do we understand these features properly? In fact, they are something about the law of human practice and cognition, its whole process, a thinking method and also a mental state. If these features are completely clarified and grasped, the Scientific Outlook on Development will be better applied, and other things will also be done well.

"Freeing oneself from outmoded ideas" means consciously freeing the mind from the shackles of outdated notions, practices and systems; from erroneous and dogmatic interpretations of Marxism. If China had not eliminated the dogmatic doctrines of the planned economy and public ownership, it would not have developed the socialist market economy, nor encouraged or supported the development of private enterprise. Likewise, if China does not eradicate the obsessive focus on GDP, scientific development will also falter. This endeavor is crucial. As well as intelligence, it requires boldness, courage and even a spirit of self-sacrifice.

"Seeking truth from facts" means understanding practical realities. Thoughts and ideas should be evaluated by putting them into practice. They are extracted from practice and should be tested by practice. Through this process, we should identify sound ideas and correct erroneous thinking. The household-responsibility system, for example, emerged from the practice of farmers. One sound idea that contributed to China's rapid development was the concept of "wading across the

> **The Household-responsibility system** was a practice by which each family leased land and productive equipment from the collective. Its basic feature was that while the collective maintained some management of the collective-owned economy, it leased land or other productive materials to households. The household, in accordance with the contract, made its management decisions independently, and delivered to the collective a minimum quota of produce. The common practice was to allocate the land to households in proportion to the number of family members or the workforce and in accordance with the principle of combining responsibility, authority and interests. The household signed a contract with the collective.

river by feeling for the stones in the riverbed." This is an example of the process of practice and the process of seeking truth from facts.

"Keeping abreast of the times" means closely following current trends. The "times" refers not only to an era, but also to contemporary trends, fashions or styles. What is gained from practice may be right, but is not necessarily the most advanced approach. It may be advanced in a rural area, but a city might have something more advanced to offer. It may be advanced in China, but another country might have something more advanced to offer. Therefore mind and thought must both keep abreast of the "times." To keep abreast of the times, you must take the whole world into consideration and have an innovative spirit. It will be impossible to keep abreast of the times if you are self-absorbed.

"Being realistic and pragmatic" means standing on solid ground to avoid becoming impetuous, being too eager for quick success and being superficial. This is a general requirement.

In conclusion, these four aspects are an organic whole. They are the quartet of adhering to and developing socialism with Chinese characteristics. They represent the critical experience of the CPC in carrying forward the cause of socialism with Chinese characteristics, which, we believe, will also benefit other parties and other countries.

The Roadmap of the 18th
CPC National Congress
and The Chinese Dream

Chapter 2

Who Will Accomplish the Mission of the CPC?

To uphold and build socialism with Chinese characteristics, it is imperative to build a contingent of key cadres for governance who are firm in political conviction, competent and energetic, and exemplary in their personal conduct.

— Report to the 18th CPC National Congress

Mao Zedong said that once the political line was confirmed, cadres should play the decisive role in its implementation. The 18th CPC National Congress has committed to upholding and building socialism with Chinese characteristics. The Report to the 18th CPC National Congress specified that to attain the goals and accomplish the tasks involved, the CPC must "strengthen reform of the system for the management of cadres and personnel and build a contingent of competent key cadres for governance." As sailing the seas depends on the helmsman, and directing soldiers in battle depends on the commander, so there must be a contingent of competent key cadres for the CPC to accomplish its mission of governance successfully. There is a Chinese saying: "A poor soldier is a threat only to himself, but a poor general is a threat to the whole army."

Without a contingent of key cadres for governance, it is not possible to adhere to and develop socialism with Chinese characteristics. The core role of the competent key cadres is to provide principal leaders of the Party at all levels. Of course, competent cadres are not produced out of thin air. Without a good source of Party members, cadres can only be selected from the weak. Such cadres are not really competent. But even competent cadres require the support of competent leadership. Therefore, a variety of talents are necessary. Developing a good pool of Party members, selecting competent cadres, and cultivating high-level talent are all indispensable if the CPC is to accomplish its ruling mission successfully. Two sayings are currently popular. One is that "the Party supervises the performance of cadres" and the other is that "the Party exercises leadership over personnel management." These two sayings embody the responsibility of the CPC and they are also the guarantee whereby the CPC can accomplish its ruling mission. The 18th CPC National Congress has introduced many policies for building the Party and developing socialism with Chinese characteristics. These policies will play a significant role.

How does the CPC admit new Party members?

The former USSR leader Stalin used to try to inspire communist party members to struggle for the cause of the CPSU by saying "Communists are made of special material." The CPC used to quote his words, but this did not mean that the CPC Party members are special individuals. In the context, "special" actually means that a Party member must make greater efforts, offer a greater contribution, do more for the people, and "play an exemplary and vanguard role." On July 1, 2012, the day of the 91st anniversary of the CPC, 30-year-old Zhang Lili, a teacher who had saved her students from

---

Zhang Lili was a female teacher from a junior high school in Heilongjiang Province, China. On May 8, 2012, Zhang pushed aside two students who were about to be run over by a runaway car. She herself was struck by the car, and injured so badly that it left her paralyzed. Several days later, on recovering consciousness in hospital, she first asked if the children were safe. In response to the concerns of her family and her doctors about the fact that she was now paralyzed, she said these words to her father: "I still remember the scene of the accident. I feel lucky. If the car had run over my head, you would never have seen me again. I have saved my students, and my own life has been spared. In the future, I am sure I will be happy."

On July 1st, 2012, Zhang Lili took an oath during hospitalization and became a CPC member.

a car accident, took the oath to join the Party. She really was made of "special material" – at the moment of the accident, her first thoughts were not for her own safety or her own life, but for her students.

In contrast to many other political parties around the world, the CPC is neither a loose organization, nor one that can be joined simply on condition of agreeing to its political tenets. A person who wants to join the CPC must have some basic qualities and go through rigorous examinations. One of the qualities is that he/she must excel in work or study and be a generally acknowledged activist and accomplished individual. Party members not only live among the masses, but they are also trustworthy pioneers. Chapter

1 of the *Constitution of the CPC,* revised and passed during the 18th CPC National Congress, stipulates that any Chinese worker, farmer, member of the armed forces, intellectual, or other accomplished individual from any social stratum, who has reached the age of 18 and who accepts the Party's program and Constitution and is willing to join and work actively in one of the Party organizations, carry out the Party's resolutions, and pay membership dues regularly, may apply for membership of the Communist Party of China. It also stipulates that members of the Communist Party of China are the vanguard of the Chinese working class, imbued with communist consciousness; members of the Communist Party of China must serve the people wholeheartedly, dedicate their whole lives to the realization of communism, and be ready to make any personal sacrifice.

From the provisions of the *Constitution of CPC,* the following requirements should be met. Firstly, the application is voluntary. If a Chinese citizen wants to join the Party, he must apply for in writing to the Party organization of his or her working unit, department or community. Secondly, an applicant for Party membership must be an excellent, active and accomplished member of the community, and must be acknowledged as such by the community and by other Party members. Thirdly, an applicant for Party membership must go through a series of strict procedures, and the primary organizations of the Party must assume the responsibility of investigating, cultivating, and admitting Party members. Generally speaking, the following procedures are included: (1) personal application; (2) being cultivated by the Party organization (an applicant must be cultivated and observed for more than one year) and filling out the observation form; (3) filling out the application form and being recommended by two full Party members; (4) being examined by the Party branch and the decision being made by a general membership meeting of the Party branch and approved by the next higher Party organization; (5) being interviewed and approved by the higher Party organization; (6) taking an admission oath; (7) undergoing a probationary period (at least one year); (8) the Party organization observing the probationary member, and the admission proposal being formulated and delivered to the higher Party committee; (9) being investigated by the higher Party committee: those qualified will be granted full membership, and those unqualified will undergo an extended probationary period; (10) on being granted full membership: applying, being passed by a general membership meeting and delivering the application form to the higher Party organization for approval; (11) on being subject to an extended probationary period: the Party organization observes the applicant, and formulates the proposal which then will be delivered to the higher Party organization for examination: the qualified will be granted full Party membership; the unqualified will have the probationary membership annulled.

Not anyone can join the Party, and not only workers, peasants and intellectuals can join the Party. Suitable applicants from any other sectors can be admitted. In 2001, the CPC made the decision that "we should admit into the Party suitable applicants from other social strata who accept the Party's program and Constitution, work consciously for the realization of the Party's line and program, and meet the qualifications of Party membership following a prolonged period of testing." Since then, full membership has been granted to an increasing number of people from such new sectors as collective enterprises, foreign-funded enterprises, individually-owned businesses, agencies and freelancers as well as the traditional backbone of workers, peasants, intellectuals, military, and cadres.

In Zhongguancun, the first and renowned high-tech zone in Beijing, there are many people of great talent. In 2002, Haidian Science Park Working Committee, which was located in the core area of Zhongguancun, cultivated 65 activists, and 28 of them were granted full Party membership. In 2012, the numbers were 871 and 212 respectively, many times more than ten years earlier. A point worthy of attention is that 85% of these people have backgrounds in technology or management. The following graphs can help to provide a general understanding of the development of the CPC.

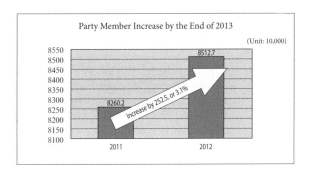

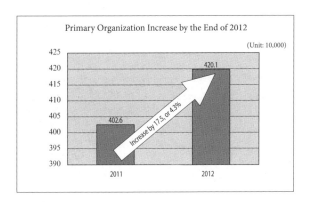

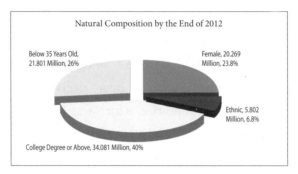

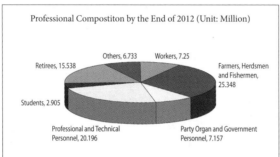

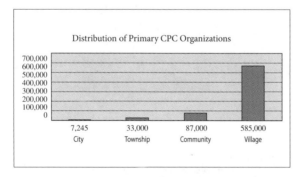

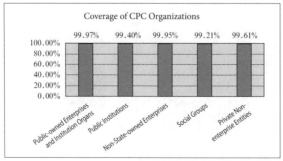

As distinct from ordinary citizens, every Party member enjoys certain rights and has certain duties to perform; they are the first to bear hardships and the last to enjoy comforts; they step forward and fight bravely in times of difficulty or danger; and they do not desert their post or consider themselves as ordinary citizens. As early as 150 years ago, Marx and Engels pointed out in the *Communist Manifesto*: "The proletarian movement is the self-conscious, independent movement of the immense majority, acting in the interests of the immense majority"; and communist party members "do not have any interests different from those of the whole proletariat class." Mao Zedong pointed out that "The CPC acts in the interests of the nation and the people and it doesn't pursue private ends." Deng Xiaoping said, "The motives and tasks of Party members can be briefly considered as serving the people wholeheartedly and having the people's interests at heart."

Party members operate under two most significant slogans: one is "Party members provide the lead" and the other is "Follow me." These slogans reflect the moral responsibility of Party members to be bold in taking the initiative. In recent years Party members, fearing no hardships, have bravely taken on the heaviest burdens, led by example, and played an exemplary and vanguard role in dealing with a series of major, challenging, and urgent problems such as the SARS outbreak, natural disasters caused by cold weather, flooding, and snowstorms, the massive earthquake in Wenchuan, the enormous service demands of the Olympic Games, and the impact of the global financial crisis, adding to the Party's influence and appeal.

The CPC has more members than any other political parties in the world, but the CPC does not solely pursue an increase in numbers. The 18th CPC National Congress underlined the need to refine the mechanism for recruiting and dismissing Party members so as to improve the quality of the membership. On January 28, 2013, the Political Bureau of CPC Central Committee held a meeting about new Party member admission, in which the following aspects were highlighted.

Firstly, criteria should be strictly followed, and political criteria should be prioritized. "Political criteria" refers to the principle of serving the people wholeheartedly and being loyal to and honest with the Party, matching words with deeds, and opposing double-dealing and scheming of any kind.

Secondly, democracy should be expanded in the recruitment process, and work procedures and discipline should be strict in order to enhance the quality of recruits. Favoritism and exploiting any dominant position are forbidden, and procedures cannot be circumvented.

Thirdly, effort should be put into recruiting Party members from the country's workers, farmers and intellectuals. In recent years, the coverage of the Party has been extending, but the proportion of workers, farmers and intellectuals is on the decrease, as is that of young workers, farmers and intellectuals. This trend, if allowed to continue, will cause the "aging" of the Party members, to the detriment of the future and capability of the CPC.

Fourthly, discipline should be strengthened to deal with unsuitable Party members. Those Party members who violate the Constitution or the disciplines of the CPC or who are not able to stand the test of all trials and tribulations must be dealt with fully and without exception. The Party branch will try to educate those Party members who lack revolutionary will, fail to fulfill the duties of a Party member, or fail to meet the criteria for membership, and require them to correct their mistakes within a prescribed time. If they remain incorrigible after education, they should be persuaded to withdraw from the Party. Their cases will be discussed and decided by the general membership meeting of the Party branch concerned and submitted to the next level of the Party organization for approval. If a Party member who is asked to withdraw refuses to do so, the case will be submitted to the general membership meeting of the Party branch concerned for discussion to decide on the removal of the said member's name from the Party rolls, after which the decision will be submitted to the next level of the Party organization for approval. A Party member who fails to take part in regular Party activities, pay membership dues, or do work assigned by the Party for six successive months without good reason is regarded as having given up membership. The general membership meeting of the Party branch concerned will decide on the removal of such a person's name from the Party rolls and report it to the next level of the Party organization for approval. In 2010, 119,000 Party members nationwide were disciplined by the Party, and 28,000 of them were dismissed.

Fifthly, the Party should improve the management of Party members, especially "floating Party members," who do not work or live in the place where their membership is registered and who cannot attend Party activities regularly. At present, mobility is increasing in Chinese society, and so is that of Party members. The Party should make every effort to organize and mobilize these Party members and to ensure that they play their role at crucial moments.

How does the CPC select and appoint cadres?

Many people are surprised at the capacity and creativity of the CPC. The CPC's ability to rally and lead the Chinese people on to great achievements derives from its ability to admit, cultivate and have a large pool of excellent cadres, as well as from its sound policies and the strength of "concentrating all forces on great undertakings." These cadres are the core force of the competent ruling Party members, and they are a key and indispensable factor for the CPC to accomplish its ruling mission.

Before the founding of the PRC in 1949, the main task of the Party was to rally and lead the people in the struggle for national independence and state liberation. Because of the difficulties of that time, the CPC mainly selected its cadres by way of appointment, democratic nomination, and election, with the former being prioritized. For some time after 1949, the CPC continued to follow a highly-centralized system of cadre management and selection, but it also investigated and institutionalized some new approaches to selecting cadres by combining selection with their tempering at the grass roots, with the help of retiring veteran cadres, with training, and with post exchanging.

In 1962, the Organization Department of the CPC Central Committee proposed a motion that cadres could not only be promoted but could also be demoted; could not only be retained but could also be dismissed. Since 1978, with the strengthening of reform and opening-up and the ongoing internal development of the Party, selection and appointment of cadres have become more and more democratic. This has broken the uniform mold of management and appointment, creating a situation where systems of selection, appointment, engagement and examination coexist. The system of selection is that Party cadres are elected directly through general election or indirectly by representatives; the system of appointment is that the Party cadres are appointed by the higher-level Party cadres; the system of engagement is that cadres are selected through contract; the system of examination is that cadres are selected through open competition and observation.

The Third Plenary Session of the 11th Central Committee of the CPC confirmed the "Four Mores" for selecting and appointing all ranks of cadres – more revolutionary, younger, more knowledgeable, and more professionally competent. The 18th CPC National Congress has underlined the "Three Shoulds" – the CPC should appoint cadres on their merits without regard to their origins; the CPC should select cadres on the basis of both their integrity and their professional competence, with priority given to the former; the CPC should promote cadres who are outstanding in performance and enjoy popular support. These different principles share two important points in common – moral integrity and talent – with priority being given to the former.

This is in conformity with China's ancient traditions and standards in identifying the most virtuous talent. The great Chinese philosopher Mencius once said, "It is at the core of politics to select the most virtuous... otherwise, the nation will be weakened." All dynasties in Chinese history attached great importance to selecting talent, highlighting "both moral integrity and ability, with moral integrity taking priority," as well as "searching for the virtuous with the determination of a thirsty man searching for water" and "choosing only the competent." Because the loyalty of a man to his country is determined by his virtue, an able man who is not virtuous may alter his stance at crucial moments, and even go over to the opposite side, causing serious damage to the cause. To the cadres of the CPC, being virtuous is primarily the same as being loyal to the people. In today's evolving circumstances many competent cadres have committed serious mistakes through a lack of moral integrity. For instance, Liu Zhijun, the former minister of the railway, made an enormous contribution to the step-change development of China's railways, but he was dismissed in accordance with the law because he violated discipline and the law.

Some Westerners think that there is a democratic deficiency in the CPC in that cadres in China are confirmed by the upper organizations or leaders, not by popular vote, and that the public has no authority to elect their intended cadres. This view does not hold water. As is mentioned above, there are many approaches for the CPC to select cadres, including competitive election. In fact, whatever approach is used, the most important thing is to single out the best person to take an important post. No system will work if it cannot promote the best talent to the most important posts, or if it prevents leaders from doing things effectively due to party interests.

Having investigated options over a long period, the CPC has come up with an effective system for electing talent, trying to select the best qualified and having those with both moral integrity and outstanding ability take its leadership posts. At all stages of its development the CPC has selected its cadres in accordance with the Party's central task of that stage, neither limiting itself to any particular form nor to any particular criterion. This system, including both "*xuan*" (voting) and "*ju*" (recommending) instead of a pure election, maintains the age-old tradition of "selecting officials on the basis of both their moral integrity and their professional competence" and this system also tallies with the prevailing conditions of the country and the Party. Canadian professor Daniel Bell has taken a considerable interest in this system, and evaluates it positively, saying, "Political meritocracy is the idea that a political system is designed with the aim of selecting political leaders with above-average ability to make morally-informed political judgments. That is, political meritocracy has two key components: (1) the political leaders have above average ability and virtue; and (2) the selection mechanism is designed to choose such leaders."

It should be acknowledged that the principle of selecting cadres on the basis of both their moral integrity and their professional competence, with priority given to the former, is neither perfect nor watertight. Evaluating moral integrity is a more subjective measure than evaluating competence. So it is critical to minimize such subjectivity in selecting cadres. To solve this problem, the CPC has already borrowed some effective and pragmatic measures from Western countries, and the 18th CPC National Congress proposes to strengthen reform of the system for the management of cadres and personnel. The relevant proposal covers three main points:

(1) Enhancing democracy in selecting cadres. The CPC should bring Party and government operations and personnel management under the control of an institutional checking process, and uphold the public right to be informed about, participate in, express views on, and oversee Party and government operations. The CPC should enhance democracy in the nomination process, improve the method for democratic recommendation and evaluation, and introduce scientific analysis of the results and their application, adding the will of the people to any voting procedure, which cannot alone determine the final result. The CPC should establish an open system to make public information about cadre selection.

(2) The CPC should fully and strictly implement the principle of selecting cadres in a democratic, open, competitive and merit-based manner, make the management of cadres more democratic, enhance democracy, improve procedures for selecting cadres through competition, increase public trust in the selection and appointment of cadres, and ensure that honest people are not disadvantaged and that the manipulative do not prosper. The CPC should continue to take improving the system of selecting cadres through competitive election as its central task for reforming the management of cadres and personnel, giving prominence to the specifics of post, competence and performance.

(3) The CPC should improve the competitive method for selecting cadres, and implement this method in recommending, observing, deliberating and voting. Since 2008, 328,000 cadres have been selected through competition nationwide. In 2011, 30.7% of the newly-promoted cadres of the middle rank were selected through competition in municipal, district and provincial institutions, and this rate reached 46% in China's state bodies. The CPC should improve the system for the management of cadres, conducting strict supervision over them, and strengthening training and selection of cadres as heads of Party and government bodies or for other key positions. The CPC should give special emphasis to cultivating, selecting, managing, and supervising a contingent of politicians who remain fully committed to the socialist road with Chinese characteristics, and who perform well in managing the Party and the state. The CPC should continue to search for effective approaches to transfer or remove cadres if they show that they are no longer fit for their posts, thereby establishing a mechanism of demotion. To resolve outstanding problems in selecting and appointing cadres, since

2008 the Organization Department of the CPC and 31 provinces, regions and municipalities have made available an exclusive complaint phone service with the number 12380, giving the people a degree of oversight over the work of selecting and appointing cadres, and have disciplined and punished some appointed cadres for improper conduct. In this process, the CPC has allowed the system to play its role. To date, there are 30 regulations on the system of cadre selection and appointment, including *Program on Strengthening Reform of the System for the Management of Cadres* and *Regulations on Selection and Appointment of Cadres of the CPC*.

How are the top CPC leaders elected?

On November 15, 2012, the 18th CPC Central Committee Political Bureau, composed of 25 members, was elected in the First Plenary Session of the 18th CPC Central Committee; Xi Jinping, Li Keqiang, Zhang Dejiang, Yu Zhengsheng, Liu Yunshan, Wang Qishan and Zhang Gaoli were elected members of the Standing Committee of the 18th CPC Central Committee Political Bureau; Xi Jinping was selected as the secretary general of the CPC Central Committee; the list of members of 18th CPC Central Committee Secretariat was approved; the list of members of the CPC Central Military Commission was confirmed; leading bodies which were elected in the First Plenary Session of the CPC Central Commission for Discipline Inspection were approved.

The changeover and succession of top state leaders are a major issue for every nation. Feudal dynasties adopted the order of succession, and capitalist nations adopted the general election. What kind of system in the change and succession of leaders should be applied for socialist countries ruled by communist parties? Lenin died before he addressed this question. After Stalin came onto the stage to power, he applied himself to dictatorship and personality cult, and no one dared to ask this question. This prevented the CPSU from formulating a standard, ordered and legal system for top leadership change and succession. By the 1980s, the political life of the CPSU had become known as "old-man politics." In November, 1982, the CPSU Secretary General Brezhnev died, and Andropov succeeded him. Fifteen months later, Andropov died and was succeeded by Chernenko. Only one year later, Chernenko died in March 1985.

The lifelong tenure of the CPSU top leaders was a serious shortcoming in the change of leaders, culminating in the obvious deterioration in the competency and quality of leadership after the death of Stalin, in that unqualified and sick men ruled the state. Because of the system of lifelong tenure, the CPSU had not sufficient time to choose, cultivate, test, and temper the successors to top leaders. As a consequence, people of low quality, or weakly-educated in theory, or lacking in leadership skills – even those whose only ability was in furthering themselves through manipulation – easily seized power at all levels of the party. Facing major turning points or social and political crisis, these individuals were feeble-minded, impotent, powerless, and confused, with the result that they provoked or even worsened the problems they faced.

As an important member of the international communist movement, the CPC paid close attention to drawing lessons from past failures. Confronted by the problems occasioned by the lifelong tenure of the CPSU and the CPC leadership, the CPC took the initiative of doing away with this system when reform and opening-up were introduced in China, and of devising a system of retirement for its cadres. China had never actively promoted lifelong tenure of its leaders, but the reality was that tenure had not been affected by age, health and term. In August 1980, the Political Bureau of the Party's Central Committee held an enlarged session, focusing on the question of reforming the leadership system of the CPC and the state. In this meeting, Deng Xiaoping made a speech entitled "On the Reform of the System of Party and State Leadership." He pointed out: "As far as the leadership and cadre systems of our Party and state are concerned, the major problems are bureaucracy, over-concentration of power, patriarchal methods, lifelong tenure in leading posts and privileges of various kinds.... Tenure for life in leading posts is linked both to feudal influences and to the continued absence of proper regulations in the Party providing for the retirement and dismissal of cadres." He also pointedly observed that: "Our problem is that we are in great need of a contingent of young and professional cadres. Without such cadres, the four modernizations cannot be realized."

In February 1982, the CPC Central Committee made the "Decision About Building a System of Retirement," the first in the history of the CPC to propose a system of retiring, resignation from a post, and taking a back seat. This system defined the maximum age for top leaders. In April the same year, the State Council circulated the notice of "Decisions on Retirement and Off-post Rest." The subsequent national congress clearly defined the number of terms of state leaders as a maximum of two. From the 12th CPC National Congress onwards, the *Constitution of CPC* stipulated that: "Leading Party cadres at all levels, whether elected through democratic procedure or appointed by a leading body, are not entitled to lifelong tenure, and they can be transferred from or relieved of their posts."

This stipulation was also applicable to the secretary general, but the *Constitution of CPC* did not define the number of terms. Nevertheless, since Deng Xiaoping retired, the lifelong tenure of the top leaders has in practice been abandoned. At the 16th CPC National Congress, with the exception of Hu Jintao, seven standing committee members of the Political Bureau with Jiang Zemin as the core all retired from the top leading posts. Their action created the precedent that Party leaders have only two terms of office, setting up not only a system of "retirement according to age" but also a system of "limited number of terms." At the 18th CPC National Congress, Hu Jintao proposed on his own initiative to retire from the posts of the CPC secretary general and the chairman of the military committee, marking another step forward in the system of changing top CPC leaders.

The system of changing top leaders in China certainly has its salient characteristics: In the West the system is aimed at changing both the leader and the Party at regular intervals; in China it is geared to changing the leader instead of the Party. A system cannot work well unless it is both flexible and sustainable. The Western system is flexible, but it is not sustainable in that sharp fluctuations cannot be avoided when the new administration is formed. The change of top power in China is carried out under conditions of one-party rule, nationwide selection, long-term cultivation, maximum age limit and change at prescribed intervals. Of these, the first three are inherited from the traditional political culture, the fourth one was created exclusively by the CPC, and the last one is borrowed from the West. This model synthesizes the strengths of both Eastern and Western political systems, while avoiding their shortcomings.

One-party rule makes possible the formulation of a long-term strategy for development. Through nationwide selection and long-term cultivation, the Party is better able to single out the most excellent, competent and experienced talent, at a moderate "production cost." Thus the Party can avoid becoming a party of limited ability whose only expertise lies in its selection. A maximum age limit and change at regular intervals can bring in new blood, limiting the risk of power finding its way into the hands of a political strongman or a person unwilling to leave power or post.

How are the CPC leaders and leading bodies elected? According to the *Constitution of the CPC*, the highest leading bodies of the Party are the national congress and the central committee elected by the Congress. The political bureau, the standing committee of the political bureau and the general secretary of the Central Committee of the Party are elected by the Central Committee in the

Ballot box in the conference hall of the 18th CPC National Congress.

On November 14, 2012, the 18th CPC National Congress of the Communist Party of China elected the new central committee and the new commission for discipline inspection.

How was the new central collective leadership elected?

According to the *Constitution of CPC,* the procedures of electing the 18th CPC Central Committee and the CPC Central Commission for Discipline Inspection (called the "two committees" in short) are as follows:

(1) Candidates for the "two committees" were identified by means of investigative groups. According to the plan of the Central Committee, from July 2011 till June 2012, 59 investigation groups were sent out to 31 institutions, municipalities, autonomous regions and provinces to identify candidates for the "two committees." These investigation groups distributed 29,000 opinion polling forms, solicited democratic recommendations among 42,800 people, and interviewed 27,500 people. Of these candidates, the overwhelming majority were on the top list in democratic recommendations from voting, majority of them won over 90% of the total votes for being qualified or better, most of them won 80% of the total affirmative votes in opinion polls. After a thorough process, 727 candidates passed through to the next stage of the process.

(2) The Political Bureau of the CPC listened to reports. The Standing Committee of the Political Bureau held 11 meetings to listen to the reports delivered by the investigation groups. Then a list of suggested candidates was put forward for electing the "two committees."

(3) The Standing Committee of the Political Bureau of the CPC, after a comprehensive study taking all factors into consideration, nominated a list of 532 preparing candidates. On October 22, 2012, the 17th Political Bureau of the CPC passed the list of preparing candidates, and agreed to submit the list to the 18th CPC National Congress for examination.

(4) After approval, the presidium of the 18th CPC National Congress passed this list of suggested candidates .

(5) The list was submitted to all representatives for full deliberation and discussion.

(6) During the meeting, every group of representatives held a competitive preliminary election. 224 candidates for the 18th Central Committee were nominated, and 205 of the candidates were elected. 190 alternate candidates for the Central Committee were nominated, and 171 of the candidates were finally elected. 141 candidates for the CPC Central Commission for Discipline Inspection were nominated, and 130 of the candidates were elected.

(7) The Presidium of the 18th CPC National Congress passed this list of candidates. On November 13, the third session of the Presidium of the 18th CPC National Congress passed the candidate list that had been produced through preliminary election.

> (8) On November 14, with Hu Jintao presiding, the 18th CPC National Congress held the formal election. More than 2,300 representatives and specially-invited representatives elected by secret ballot the 18th Central Committee of the CPC composed of 376 members and alternate members of the Central Committee, and the CPC Central Commission for Discipline Inspection composed of 130 members. The First Plenary Session of the 18th CPC National Congress elected the Political Bureau, including 25 committee members and seven standing committee members.

plenary session. The number of members and alternate members of the Central Committee is determined by the national congress. Vacancies on the Central Committee are filled by its alternate members in the order of the number of votes by which they were elected. The general secretary of the Central Committee must be a member of the standing committee of the political bureau. When the next national congress is in session the central leading bodies and leaders elected by each Central Committee continue to preside over the Party's day-to-day work until the new central leading bodies and leaders are elected by the next Central Committee.

What is the policy of personnel management that the CPC pursues?

There is a Chinese saying: "There are three hundred and sixty trades, and every trade has its master." Although he was educated only to junior high school level, Xu Zhenchao is an expert gantry crane operator. Twice in one year he broke the world record for loading and unloading container cargo, giving rise to the phrase: "the ten-hour shipload" (He had promised to complete loading and unloading in ten hours), and making "Zhenchao efficiency" famous among major international ports.

Talents like Xu Zhenchao are numerous in the various industrial sectors in China, so it is no exaggeration to say that China is a country of many talents. But this doesn't mean that there is a sufficiency of talent in China. On the contrary, China has great need of talent, especially advanced talent. On April 25, 2007, the *International Herald Tribune* published an article saying, "A shortage of world-class talent will be the biggest problem for China in the future." There are three aspects to the problem. Firstly, China does not have enough strategic scientists or experts who are leading figures at international level and can hold their own at international level. First-class experts are rarities. Secondly, China is short of high-level management. Thirdly, the present talent structure is unbalanced. There is a shortage of talent at the lower and higher levels, resulting in a bulge around the center. Since 2006, talk of acute shortages of advanced technicians can be heard from all corners of China. Of the ten jobs with a salary over RMB 5,000 per month in Beijing most in need of candidates, four were occupied by advanced technicians. According to a research conducted by the Ministry of Human Resources and Social Security, at present there are 70 million technicians in the country, but advanced technicians only account for 4% of the total. This proportion is much lower than that of advanced economies, where it is typically 30-40%.

The competition among countries in the world today is in essence a competition for talent. A country depends on talent for development; a party depends on talent to govern. For a party, a country or a nation, talent is the most precious resource. Although the CPC is the largest ruling party in the world, its 82 million Party members account for only one fifteenth of China's total population. Even fewer are cadres with qualities of leadership. Therefore, the CPC cannot depend on cadres or Party members alone to adhere to and develop socialism with Chinese characteristics. To accomplish its governing mission, the CPC must attract outstanding individuals from all sides for the cause of Party and country. Widening channels to attract talent is key to advancing the cause of the Party and the people.

Before the Third Plenary Session of the 11th Central Committee of the CPC was convened, Deng Xiaoping came to the conclusion that "respecting knowledge and talent" was of key importance. In 2000, Jiang Zemin proposed the scientific thesis that "talent is the primary resource." In 2002, the 16th CPC National Congress committed to respect work, knowledge, talent and creation. In the same year, the CPC Central Committee and the State Council circulated the *Essentials on China's 2002-2005 Talent Development Plan,* which put forward for the first time a commitment to "carrying out the talent strategy for rejuvenating China," a strategy which provided a grand plan for China's talent development, and clarified the guiding principles, goals and major policies for that period and for the future for building a contingent of talent in China.

On December 19, 2003, the CPC Central Committee and the State Council held China's first talent work meeting. After the meeting, the CPC Central Committee and the State Council circulated the *Decision on Continuing to Strengthen Work on Talent.* It was the first time in the history of the CPC as a governing party that the talent strategy had been raised to state level. It proposed that the basic task in the talent strategy for rejuvenating China was to build a talent contingent that was large in scale, balanced in structure, and high in quality, and to transform China from a big country with a large population to a strong country rich in human resources. As its fundamental goal, the Decision proposed a scientific outlook on talent, taking integrity, knowledge, competence and achievement as the standards to evaluate talent, and also proposed the "Four-Regardless" criteria for identifying talent: regardless of education background, regardless of profession, regardless of work record, and regardless of origin.

In March 2006, the talent strategy for rejuvenating China was listed in the 11th Five-year Plan as an independent chapter. In 2007, this strategy was incorporated in the Report to the 17th CPC National Congress and the *Constitution of CPC* as one of the three basic strategies for developing socialism with Chinese characteristics, further raising the status of this strategy in the overall strategy of the Party and the nation.

From 2008 to 2010, it took about two years for the Central Committee coordination group on talent to formulate the medium and long-term talent development plan, the *National Medium and Long-term Talent Development Plan (2010-2020)*, the first of its kind since the founding of the PRC. The Plan envisages that by 2020 China will have established a comparative advantage in talent, making China one of the talent-rich countries; the total number of individuals will have increased to 180 million; the proportion of GDP invested in human skills and resources will have reached 15%, and the talent contribution rate will have reached 35%.

In December 2003, the second forum on national talent work was opened, and this forum systematically organized and interpreted the scientific outlook on talent, expressing the theory in ten principles such as "Talent is the most vigorous advanced force of production," and "Investment in talent is the most profitable investment." The 18th CPC National Congress further proposes that the CPC should respect work, knowledge, talent and creation, accelerate the strategy of training competent personnel as a priority to build a large contingent of such personnel, and turn China from a country with a large labor force into one with a large pool of competent professionals; that the CPC should coordinate the training of all types of personnel, implement major projects for training and attracting high-caliber personnel, give more support to the training of innovative and entrepreneurial personnel, prioritize the training of people with practical skills, and encourage the flow of talent to the front-lines of research and production; that the CPC should fully develop and utilize human resources both at home and abroad, and actively attract high-caliber personnel from overseas and turn them to good use; that the CPC should accelerate reform of institutions and mechanisms for talent development, adopt innovative policies for this purpose, and establish a national system of honors, and that the CPC should form an internationally competitive personnel system that is capable of inspiring creativity and encouraging talent, and thus foster a dynamic environment in which everyone can fully tap their potential and put their talents to best use.

Since the start of the new century, the Central Committee, in accordance with the *National Medium- and Long-term Talent Development Plan (2006-2020)*, has formulated a series of policies and methods to attract top talent. Since 2010, the Central Committee has conceived and launched 12 major talent projects with the "National Plan for Special Support for Advanced Talent" at the top of the list. By the end of 2011, 307 talent projects had been carried out by cities, prefectures and provinces, and 2,380 projects had been launched by county-level cities. Today, China has more than 1,500 academicians of the Chinese Academy of Sciences and of the Chinese Academy of Engineering, 2,793 advanced experts introduced from abroad through the national "Thousand-talent Plan," 4,113 national talents selected through the "Million-talent Project," 5,205 national young and middle-aged experts who have made substantial contributions, about 10,000 advanced innovative talents and 158,000 experts who enjoy a special government allowance. Statistics indicate that since 2009, provinces, autonomous regions, municipalities directly under the Central Government, and municipal districts have introduced more than 20,000 talented individuals from abroad. The number of researchers per 10,000 workers has reached 33.6; the proportion of advanced technicians to all technicians is 25.6%; the proportion of professionals with college-education background to the working-age population is 12.5%; the proportion of investment in human resources to GDP has reached 12%; the proportion of talent resources to human resources has reached 11.1%; and the rate of talent contribution to economic growth is 26.6%.

To rally the experts at all levels round the Party, the CPC Central Committee set up the Party-committee-link-expert system. The Organization Department of the CPC Central Committee, on behalf of the Central Committee, has created a network of more than 4,400 advanced experts, and departments or committees concerned from 31 provinces, autonomous regions, municipalities directly under the Central Government, 15 sub-provincial cities, and ministries and state organs of the Central Government have built a network of more than 90,000 experts. The CPC Central Committee and the State Council have organized paid leave for experts in

Beidaihe resort every summer. Since 2003, 645 outstanding experts have been invited to Beidaihe. The organization departments of Party committees from provinces, autonomous regions and municipalities were successful in building networks of experts. In 2011, they organized 110 gatherings of experts, attended by 4,760 individuals. They also visited 4,659 experts themselves, and organized 13,800 medical examinations for experts. Enormous progress has been made in creating an environment where the country's pool of talent is growing fast, and is well provided for.

The Roadmap of the 18th CPC National Congress and The Chinese Dream

Chapter 3

What If Dissenting Voices Arise Inside the CPC?

Intra-Party democracy is the life of the Party. We should adhere to democratic centralism, improve institutions for intra-Party democracy, and promote people's democracy with intra-Party democracy.

— Report to the 18th CPC National Congress

As building socialism with Chinese characteristics is a cause without parallel in history, the CPC will have no experience to draw on, and will inevitably meet challenges or difficulties of various kinds. On the way, the CPC must maintain Party solidarity and unity as well as bolster confidence and select qualified cadres. However, because individuals have their distinctive stance, perspective, background, education and experiences, they often have different views on specific issues, and should not be forced into artificial unity of opinion. In the case of disagreement, what should the CPC do? The approaches adopted by the CPC can be summarized in three key words. The first is "democracy." The CPC allows its Party members to express their opinions and views freely and to draw fully on collective wisdom, and especially so concerning vital issues. The second is "centralism." The purpose of establishing democracy is to elicit opinions from the majority for decision making. The CPC is not an "idle-chatter" organization. It prevents its members from debating for the sake of debate, and prevents minority views from causing unhelpful disruption. The third is "discipline." Decisions made in accordance with opinions elicited from the majority might not be universally accepted. Dissenters are entitled to retain their opinions, but they must abide by resolutions passed by the Party organization. They are not allowed to go their own way, otherwise they will be disciplined.

The three key words above are the core of the Party's organizational principles and consultation rules. In fact, history teaches us that both democracy and centralism are indispensable in human relations, whether in the social life of a primitive society, or in the political life of a class-based society, or in modern political life in its various forms. All of these represent some form of democracy and centralism, or self-discipline and authority. If the CPC focused exclusively on democracy, it would not form an organizational force in achieving anything, or in playing any kind of leading role.

What is the organizational principle of the CPC?

In brief, democratic centralism is the organizational principle of the CPC. It is the basic organizational system and organizational principle of the CPC, formed by incorporating the prevailing realities of China into the early party building theory of the world proletariat. In the middle of the 19th century, when Marx and Engels established the Communist League and the First International, they strongly advocated "democracy" to counter flawed organizational principles, and the risks of conspiracy, autocracy and factionalism. They believed that "democracy" was suited to the nature and tasks of the proletariat party, while "centralism" led to conspiracy, autocracy and factionalism.

The democratic principle advocated by Marx and Engels was inherited by the Second International. In the late 19th and early 20th centuries, Lenin began to establish the Russian Bolshevik Party. In terms of the principle for building the party, he favored centralism, a choice he made in accordance with the prevailing situation in Russia and the international environment. At the time, as distinct from Western European countries, Russia was still a Tsarist autocracy with no space for democracy to sprout, and with no legal position for proletarian organizations, which might be dissolved any time. In such a harsh environment, the primary task of party-building was to strengthen the party's discipline and fight for its survival. In such a situation it was not feasible to copy the doctrines of Marx and Engels. Additionally, the Russian Social Democratic Labor Party of the period was rather slack in both ideology and organization. So Lenin, in the article *One Step Forward, Two Steps Back* of 1904, identified and analyzed in detail the importance of centralism in building the Party. Subsequently, with the transition of the revolutionary situation and the struggle emerging into the open, Lenin, spurred by the growing clamor for "democracy and cooperation" from figures both inside and outside the Party, began to rework his ideas about the organizational principle. Drawing on past experience and integrating elements of democracy, he gradually formed in his mind the scientific concept of the principle of "democratic centralism."

In December, 1905, during the First National Congress of the Russian Social Democratic Labor Party, Lenin used the phrase "democratic centralism" for the first time. During the Fourth National Congress of the Russian Social Democratic Labor Party held in April 1906, "democratic centralism" was written into the Party's constitution. Subsequently, "democratic centralism" was formalized as the basic organizational principle of proletarian parties. After the October Revolution, communist nations followed the Russian example in writing democratic centralism into their party constitutions. In the course of revolution and construction, the CPC gradually formulated the concept of "democratic centralism with Chinese characteristics." Generally speaking, this process involved five stages.

The first stage (1921-1935): The initial testing period

In 1920, the Second Congress of the Communist International passed *The Terms of Admission into the Communist International*, in which it was clarified that "any party affiliating to the Communist International should be set up in accordance with democratic centralism." From 1920 to 1926, core thoughts or principles such as "the minority is subordinate to the majority," "emphasizing centralism and unity" and "Party members are subordinate to the national congress and the executive committee" permeated the CPC's initial period of party building. On June 1, 1927, a meeting of the CPC Central Committee Political Bureau of the Fifth National Congress passed the revised *Constitution of the CPC*, clearly stipulating for the first time that "the guiding principle of the Party is democratic centralism."

The second stage (1935-1945): The development period

In 1937, Mao Zedong in his *Interview with the British Journalist James Bertram* elaborated the relationship between democracy and centralism: The two apparent opposites of democracy and centralization were united in a definite form, enabling the CPC to understand democratic centralism more deeply. In 1938, the Sixth Plenary Session of the Sixth Central Committee proposed the following four principles for upholding democratic centralism: Individual Party members are subordinate to the Party organization; the minority is subordinate to the majority; the lower Party organizations are subordinate to the higher Party organizations, and all the constituent organizations and members of the Party are subordinate to the National Congress and the Central Committee of the Party. This was a big step forward in fostering the guiding value of democratic centralism in social life.

The third stage (1945-1957): The improvement period

In 1945, the *Constitution of the CPC* as revised in the Seventh CPC National Congress integrated democracy and centralism for the first time, stipulating that "democratic centralism is a system that integrates centralism on the basis of democracy with democracy under centralized guidance." This indicated that after a period of constant development, the concept of democratic centralism was maturing. In 1954, *The Constitution of the People's Republic of China* confirmed the principle of democratic centralism, assigning guiding status to this principle in socialist construction. In 1956, the *Constitution of the CPC* revised in the Eighth CPC National Congress divided the principle of democratic centralism into principles of democracy and centralism, fully explaining the implications of democracy and centralism and their relationship.

The fourth stage (1957-1978): The period of frustration

The principle of democratic centralism encountered unprecedented frustration during the "Anti-Reckless Advance" movement in 1958, followed by the "Anti-Rightist Campaign," the 11th Plenary Session of the Eighth Central Committee, and the Cultural Revolution in 1966.

The fifth stage (1978-present): The period of restoration, development and enhancement

The Third Plenary Session of the 11th Central Committee held in 1978 made a commitment to "enhancing the democratic centralism of the CPC"; in 1979, Deng Xiaoping said, "Our democratic centralism is an integration of centralism on the basis of democracy with democracy under centralized guidance." In 1992, the *Constitu-*

tion of the CPC as revised in the 14th CPC National Congress specified democratic centralism as "an integration of centralism on the basis of democracy with democracy under centralized guidance," and listed six basic principles of democratic centralism, specifying that "Party organizations at all levels should increase transparency in Party affairs in accordance with regulations to keep Party members better informed of these affairs and to provide them with more opportunities to participate in them"; "the Party forbids all forms of personality cult" and "it is necessary to ensure that the activities of the Party leaders are subject to supervision by the Party and the people." Thus, democratic centralism was consolidated into a watertight and comprehensive system of theory and practice.

"Anti-Reckless Advance" movement and "Anti-Rightist Campaign":

In 1956, disagreement and debate arose over the issue of what economic strategy to adopt in the PRC. At that time, there were two opposing opinions. One was to speed up industrialization; the other was to develop in a balanced and sustainable way. The former criticized the reservations of the Rightists, while the latter defined itself as being anti-reckless advance. Influenced by the attitude of the CPC principal leader Mao Zedong, it was easy to arouse support for reckless advance in actual economic work, outmaneuvering the anti-reckless strategy of balanced and sustainable development. Under the influence of "Leftist" thought, the debate over economic development strategy escalated to the highest levels of politics. After the "Great Leap Forward" movement was launched, top CPC leaders such as Peng Dehuai, who supported the "Anti-Reckless Advance" movement and was skeptical about the "Great Leap Forward" movement, were criticized as "Rightists" in thought. This extended the political struggle of the "Anti-Rightist Campaign" through the whole Party. This struggle caused serious internal political damage to the Party at every level, from the Central Committee to the primary organizations. It influenced the economy by interrupting the process of correcting Leftist errors, prolonging the impact of these errors. As a result of the misguided "Great Leap Forward" movement and "Anti-Rightest Campaign," as well as natural disasters and the breach of faith of the USSR in repudiating its agreement with China, China's economy encountered serious problems from 1959 to 1961, and the state and the people suffered the consequences.

So how are we to understand democratic centralism? From extensive practice, the essence of democratic centralism lies in the unity of "dynamic and static." Taken as static, democracy and centralism are parallel. This easily results in their split as two unrelated parts which work independently. During the history of the international communist movement, we have frequently encountered the phenomenon of "first let go, and disorder will ensue; this then will be followed by tightening up." The former USSR is a typical example. The early crisis of the CPSU resulted from over-centralism, and later on it lost power mainly due to excessive decentralization and pluralism.

Therefore, we need to grasp democratic centralism from a dynamic perspective. Before the CPC governed China, its principal objective was to seize power. There was more centralism and less democracy. Democracy was just the means, while centralism was the end. In this sense, democratic centralism was "centralism of democracy." Because the opportunities for democracy were limited in those particular circumstances, it would be very hard to achieve revolutionary success without highly-centralized leadership. After the CPC took power, the conditions were much better to develop democracy. Democracy could be more extensive, more deep-rooted, more thorough, and more efficient. Of the lessons learned from the Cultural Revolution, Deng Xiaoping observed: We did not implement democratic centralism in actual practice. We gave too much emphasis to centralism, and not enough to democracy. Obviously, to give full play to democratic centralism under changing circumstances, the CPC must highlight that the emphasis and essence of democratic centralism now lie in democracy.

Deng's words cut to the heart of the democratic process. We can analyze his words as follows: The "democracy" involved in the process of implementing democratic centralism undoubtedly refers to democracy itself, but the "centralism" of the process is also related to democracy. Why? Because "centralism on the basis of democracy" is "centralism" based on the opinions of the majority, or "centralism of sound opinions"; while the "centralism" in "democracy under the guidance of centralism" involves providing further "instruction" on the basis of the opinion of the majority, that is, restricting and correcting the abnormal "democratic behavior" of the minority, or preventing the minority from changing the opinion of the majority. For this, the "centralism" in democratic centralism, in essence, reflects respect for the democratic rights of the majority. Therefore, it is democratic in nature and it should be so.

2,270 delegates were elected at the 18th National Congress of the CPC. They came from a broad range of backgrounds including economy, science and technology, national defense, politics and law, education, publicity, culture, health, sports and social management. This is concordant with the requirement that delegates should "come from all walks of life." "Centralism" contains the most extensive "democracy" and is realized scientifically in "democracy." This is the dynamic application of China's democratic centralism.

How were the delegates selected at the 18th CPC National Congress?

(1) Nomination. Nomination started from primary organizations, and all primary Party organizations and Party members were required to participate. Primary Party committees selected nominees and reported them to the upper Party committees in accordance with the opinions of the majority of Party branches and Party members. Party committees at the level of county (city) and municipality (prefecture) selected the best-qualified candidates from the nominees in accordance with the opinions of the majority of Party organizations. Nominees who passed to the next level were determined by the plenary session of the committee. Other units were to do likewise in accordance with the opinions of the majority of Party organizations or Party members: selecting nominees, convening the plenary session of the Party committee, and deciding on the nominees to be reported to the upper committees. The elective unit held the standing committee meeting of the Party committee (working committee meeting and Party organization meeting), and confirmed the list of initial candidates for examination according to the views of the majority.

(2) Examination. Subjects to be examined outnumbered those to be elected, and all subjects were informed in advance. Moral integrity was the primary criterion, followed by the views of the primary organization of the Party, the Party congress, Party members and non-Party members, and the opinions of the Party organization of the unit where the individual worked and the Party organs for discipline inspection.

(3) Confirming the list of initial candidates for delegates and making the list public. The selective unit held the standing committee meeting of the Party committee including the working committee meeting and the Party organization meeting to examine the list and made it public inside the unit in a proper way. It continued to elicit opinions from the Party organization, Party delegates and Party members. Before the list was confirmed, opinions from the Party organs for discipline inspection in the same unit were also elicited. As to the list put forward by financial institutions and enterprises, opinions were also taken as reference from such departments as administrative enforcement of law and supervision.

(4) Confirming the list of preliminary candidates. A plenary session of the Party committee was held including the working committee meeting and the Party organization meeting to confirm the preliminary candidates by ballot. As appropriate to the particular situation, the preliminary candidates could also be selected from the nominee list. Before the plenary session of the Party committee at the level of provinces, autonomous regions and municipalities, opinions were elicited from non-communist parties, associations of industry and commerce and non-party figures.

(5) Election. The Party congress or the Party delegate meeting (the enlarged meeting of the working committee) was held for a competitive election of delegates to the 18th CPC National Congress at a proportion rate higher than 15%.

(6) Examining qualifications. Before the 18th CPC National Congress was held, the qualifications of delegates were reviewed by the examination committee of the 18th CPC National Congress.

Chapter 3
What If Dissenting Voices Arise Inside the CPC?

Ma Gongzhi, a representative of the 18th CPC National Congress, is a movie projectionist in the countryside.

It has been proved by the experience of the CPC and all other international communist movements that by adhering to democratic centralism, the Party will maintain solidarity and unity, and will be powerful. Revolution and construction will succeed. If it violates democratic centralism, the Party will become loose or factionalized, its capacity will be weakened, and revolution and construction will encounter frustration or even failure. Throughout the long period of revolution and construction the CPC has remained powerful and strong, and maintained solidarity and unity. The most valuable contributions came from its adherence to democratic centralism in organization in addition to its firm faith. Deng Xiaoping described democratic centralism as "the most convenient system" and "the most appropriate system." It is the most appropriate because it upholds the majority principle which addresses problems in accordance with the interests, wishes, and requirements of the majority. It is the most convenient because it upholds the principle that the minority are subject to the majority in solving problems, discouraging delegates from debating only for debate's sake. Once a decision is made it must be implemented, with no person being allowed to go his or her individual way. Therefore, this principle is concise, flexible and efficient.

For this reason, Deng Xiaoping said: "Democratic centralism is our advantage, because it is conducive to uniting the people," and "the biggest advantage of socialist countries is that once a decision is made, it can be carried out immediately without being affected by other limitations…. This is our advantage; we must maintain this advantage, ensuring the advantage of socialism." At the same time, he warned the whole Party, that: "If democratic centralism is not well implemented, the Party may falter, the state may falter, and socialism itself may also falter." Democratic centralism is so important that the CPC has never stopped emphasizing its importance.

How does the CPC develop intra-Party democracy?

Deng Xiaoping observed that "democracy is the core of democratic centralism." The 16th CPC National Congress confirmed that intra-Party democracy is the life of the Party. The 18th CPC National Congress reiterated this point, emphasizing that the CPC should vigorously promote intra-Party democracy and enhance the Party's creative vitality. Intra-Party democracy is an important means to avoid conflict inside the Party by coordinating intra-Party interests. It is the core competitiveness of a Party. History and reality indicate that whether a party can win the extensive support of the people, whether it can maintain a ruling party, and whether it can ensure the security of the state, all depend to a substantial degree on the level of its intra-Party democracy. The CPC has realized that to implement democratic centralism it must actively promote intra-Party democracy, better protect the Party members' democratic rights, and ensure that Party members have the right to stay informed of, participate in, and oversee Party affairs. This is the best means to enhance the Party's creative vitality.

The nature of intra-Party democracy is to respect the principal position of Party members, to encourage Party members' initiative and enthusiasm, to sharpen their sense of responsibility towards the Party's cause, and to encourage Party members or Party delegates to express their opinions as fully as possible within the scope of the Party's constitution and to play an active leading role in the people's cause for the enhancement of the Party's discipline and unity. The report to the 17th CPC National Congress proposed to "respect the principal position of Party members" for the first time. In its wake, the Fourth Plenary Session of the 17th Central Committee was held in 2009, and the CPC leadership reiterated that: "The Party must uphold the principal position of Party members and better protect their democratic rights." The 18th CPC National Congress gave a clearer elucidation that: "We should uphold the principal position of Party members, better protect their democratic rights, and conduct criticism and self-criticism. We should foster comradely relations based on equality and democratic principles, a political atmosphere that encourages democratic discussion, and an institutional environment for democratic oversight. We should ensure that Party members have the right to stay informed of, participate in, and oversee Party affairs, as well as the right to vote."

Taizhou City in Zhejiang Province is a city on the east coast of China. On December 21, 2011, speaking to 364 Party members from the third constituency composed of Gujie community, Xinan community and Shangcheng community of Luqiao Distric in Taizhou City, Zhengmin, the committee secretary of Luqiao District, explained how to serve the people in concise language, and answered questions put forward by other Party members. To prepare for this electoral event, he had come to the constituency several weeks in advance, and visited Party members and non-Party members to hear their opinions and desires. After voting, Guan Meifang, an old Party member, said, "It is encouraging that the district committee secretary and ordinary Party members compete with each other and make promises in the presence of all."

In Luqiao District, any Party candidate from the district committee secretary and the governor to ordinary Party members can register for the election as equals and take part in the selection of the Party committee on the same footing. Since the end of 2004, Luqiao District of Taizhou City has held direct elections at the levels of district and township, introducing a competitive mechanism into the whole process of nominating and electing district Party delegates and introducing competitive debate between candidates into the direct election meetings. Statistics indicate that in the Party delegate election of Luqiao, 674 Party members registered for the election, and 373 candidates ultimately took part. Of these candidates, the proportion of cadres decreased while the numbers of grass-roots Party delegates with backgrounds in economy, culture, science and technology and agriculture increased. The result of this election was that some previous Party delegates who had no significant achievements in the preceding five years, or whose abilities were in doubt, were defeated by their opponents, and some did not even secure a nomination by the Party branch. Others who had played an exemplary role in proposing, advising, questioning, inquiring and linking Party members and the public, gained the support and praise of Party members and the public in return. Such direct elections have improved the intra-Party atmosphere, aroused the enthusiasm of Party members and heightened the sense of responsibility of the Party delegates. As a result, 97% of Party members in most districts have participated in election meetings. This partially reflects the determination of the CPC to push forward the reform of the intra-Party election system and expand intra-Party democracy.

In recent years, the CPC has conducted the following trials in expanding intra-Party democracy:

Firstly, a new step has been taken in improving the system of the CPC congress. This system provides an important guarantee of intra-Party democracy.

The CPC has increased the coverage and enhanced the quality of its delegates. The CPC has increased the proportion of grass roots delegates, especially workers and farmers. In the election of delegates to the 18th CPC National Congress, the proportion of candidates who worked in the forefront of production was 30.5%, an increase of 2.1 percentage over that of the 17th CPC National Congress; the proportion of workers increased by a large margin, with the number of worker delegates members increasing from 51 to 169 (including 26 immigrant farmer Party members) at the rate 7.4%.

The CPC has implemented and improved the system of Party congresses by adopting a tenure system for delegates. For a long time, delegates played their role only during the congress. Since the tenure system was introduced, the role of the delegates has changed from "once" to "often" in that the delegates begin to build links with non-Party members, respond to their wishes, conduct surveys, take part in decision-making, carry out democratic evaluation, and exercise supervision. The 16th National Congress of the CPC proposed that "We should explore ways to increase the role of delegates when Party congresses are not in session." The 17th CPC National Congress made the decision to "improve the system of Party congresses by adopting a tenure system for their delegates" and wrote this decision into the *Constitution of the CPC*. In the *Provisional Regulations of Tenure System for Delegates of the National Congress of the CPC and Local Congresses at All levels* circulated in 2008, the CPC made regulations specifying the rights, responsibilities, and working style of delegates of local congresses at all levels nationwide, providing guarantees that they would perform their duties, and making provisions to terminate their credentials. To date, 27 provinces, autonomous regions and municipalities have worked out methods to implement provisional regulations for the tenure system. The 18th CPC National Congress proposes to continue the implementation and improvement of the system of Party congresses by adopting a tenure system for their delegates.

The CPC maintains the tenure system corresponding to the Party congress. The tenure system corresponding to the Party congress means that after the congress has fulfilled its electoral responsibilities, the Party committee holds a session of delegates each year, which continues to exercise the authority of the congress. Party congress delegates continue to perform their duties, and there is no re-election. The Eighth National Congress of the CPC adopted the tenure system. At the time Deng Xiaoping said: "The biggest advantage of the tenure system of the Party congress is that the congress can be the Party's fully-effective top decision-making body and top supervisory body. The original system of holding sessions and re-electing delegates every few years cannot achieve this." At present, more than 300 counties and about 3,000 townships have tried out the system of annual sessions of the Party congress, and enhanced the capacity of the annual sessions. The 18th CPC National Congress proposed that the CPC will experiment with a system of annual sessions of the Party congress at town and township level, and proceed with trials of the tenure system of Party congresses with a fixed term in selected counties and county-level cities and districts.

The CPC has introduced the proposal-submitting system for delegates to Party congresses. This system was first proposed in the Report to the 18th CPC National Congress. It is significant for the following reasons. The Party congress has important decision-making powers. If a decision is made without referring to the views of primary Party organizations, Party members and ordinary people, mistakes are inevitable. As the new system is introduced, delegates to the Party congress can submit their opinions or suggestions about the Party's policies through an institutionalized channel, ensuring that decision-making is democratic and scientific.

Secondly, there has been new progress in the reform of the intra-Party electoral system.

The CPC has improved the means of nomination. Many places are trying different methods of delegate nomination, including self-recommendation, recommendation by the organization, recommendation by Party members, recommendations from the public, and recommendation by cadres. These methods can properly reflect the will of most Party members.

The CPC has improved the method of publicizing the identity of candidates. In the process of changing cadres at the level of townships and villages, some places have adopted new methods of publicizing candidates such as organizing speeches, question and answer sessions for Party members and the public, visiting the candidate, holding interview meetings, and publicizing their achievements. All these methods can help to encourage informed voting. Some places are even making use of multi-media, filming candidates and broadcasting information on them.

The CPC has increased the differential proportion of candidates. In the local Party committee elections for the 18th CPC National Congress, the differential proportion in 31 provinces, autonomous regions and municipalities reached 11.9% on average, an increase of 0.6% over the previous committees.

Thirdly, there has been further progress in intra-Party democracy at the community level.

The CPC has made great efforts to make Party work accessible to the public at community level. At present, public access to Party work has reached 80% in 29 provinces, autonomous regions and municipalities. In addition, the Party has added new means of access, such as building "Online Party Work Centers," holding press conferences and holding hearings for Party members and the public. All these have added momentum to the change in approach of Party organizations at all levels, and heightened the sense of integrity, honor and responsibility of Party members.

The CPC has gradually expanded the scope for public recommendation in elections for leading groups of primary Party organizations. Some primary Party organizations have integrated public recommendation by Party members and the public with recommendation by the upper Party organizations in elections for leading groups of primary Party organizations. At present, 186,000 primary Party organizations are piloting this idea. Of these, 565 townships began trials at the stage of leadership change during the 18th CPC National Congress.

The CPC has actively pushed forward the reform of democratic discussion in primary Party organizations. Some places are exploring various democratic means of discussion such as encounter meetings, political discussion days, and Party members'

In February 2013, a "township officials' administration symposium" was held in the Yunyang County in Chongqing. Secretaries of the CPC committees in 42 townships and towns came to the meeting and made commitments to their work priorities in 2013. Local radio and television covered the meeting in a live broadcast.

dialogue days. Many places have adopted intra-Party work hearing and inquiry systems, and the system of decision-making on the basis of democratic discussion, constantly improving the regulations and procedures of leading groups in primary Party organizations.

The CPC has multiplied the channels for intra-Party supervision in primary Party organizations. Many places give work reports or anti-corruption reports and listen to evaluations from Party members or delegates to Party congresses. Many city or county Party committees and primary Party organizations have opened up their Party work meetings by inviting Party members and non-Party members as nonvoting delegates to attend such meetings as Party congresses, plenary sessions of the Party committees, meetings of standing committees and other meetings of primary Party organizations. All places have made public all the information and put themselves under the supervision of Party members and the public in admitting and recommending Party members through newspaper, TV and website.

Of course, these methods are in the process of being tried out and tested, and there are evident deficiencies and improvements to be made. But we believe that with the constant improvement of intra-Party democratic theory and practice, intra-Party democracy with Chinese characteristics will gradually become scientific and institutionalized, and bear healthy fruits.

Why does the CPC constantly strengthen its discipline?

Developing intra-Party democracy doesn't mean letting people go their own ways and ignore discipline. On the contrary, the more democracy is developed inside the Party, the more discipline should be strengthened. The purpose of strengthening discipline is to get things right as often as possible. Once a decision is formulated, the Party must maintain discipline to keep the channels of implementation effective. In the past, the idea was "tighten discipline and the revolution will succeed"; today, this has evolved to "tighten discipline, and development will be enhanced by a united force." Therefore, the Report to the 18th CPC National Congress outlines that "The more complexities the Party faces and the more arduous the tasks it undertakes, the more imperative it is for the Party to strengthen its discipline and uphold centralized leadership."

Before 1949, China was a semi-colonial and semi-feudal nation, and it was also a nation dominated by the petty bourgeoisie. The united forces of capitalism and reactionary domestic groups were strong in their determination to encircle and strangle the revolution. This determined that the proletariat revolution against capitalism and feudalism would be long-lasting, complicated, and arduous. If there had not been iron discipline, the proletariat party could not have persevered in the struggle and defeated the enemy. The number of industrial workers was small, as this class had existed for only a short time. But its strengths lay in its natural association with peasants, small businessmen, craftsmen, and journeymen. Its weakness was that it tended to preserve or acquire sloppy habits. If there had been no iron discipline, the Party would never have united the overwhelming majority of the people. During the revolutionary period, the CPC formulated *Three Big Disciplines and Eight Attentions*, and required that every soldier and Party member was able to sing it out. It was this strict discipline that distinguished the new army led by the CPC from the old army led by the Kuomintang and brought final success to China's revolution. In the 1940s John Leighton Stuart, the American ambassador to China, testified to the qualities of the CPC members. He said that in sharp contrast to the Kuomintang, the CPC was corruption-proof, enabling its cadres to relate to the masses, and the discipline of the Party and the army was simple but practical, and well established. All these advantages were in evidence when the CPC army attacked Nanjing. The occupation was peaceful, with city residents almost undisturbed. Stuart was impressed, saying, "It is not a simple thing to behave themselves like this."

Nowadays, China is in a crucial phase of completing the construction of a moderately and comprehensively prosperous society in all respects, strengthening reform and opening-up , and accelerating the transformation of its economic development. Facing the complicated and capricious international environment, the demanding tasks of domestic reform, development and security, and a variety of difficulties and dangers, the CPC, a substantial ruling party with more than 82.6 million Party members, would be a loose agglomeration, would accomplish nothing,

---

"The Three Big Disciplines" refer to always acting under command; never taking from the masses even anything as trivial as a needle or a thread; and handing over anything captured in battle. **"The Eight Attentions"** comprised speaking courteously; exchanging fairly; returning what you have borrowed; compensating for what you have damaged; never beating or cursing anyone; not damaging crops; never taking liberties with women; and never ill-treating captives.

---

would be seriously weakened in its cohesiveness and capacity, and would lose its political strength, if there were not a general will and a strict discipline.

At present, there are about 100 binding regulations applying to Party members. One of them is the *Constitution of CPC*, which stipulates "Individual Party members are subordinate to the Party organization, the minority is subordinate to the majority, the lower Party organizations are subordinate to the higher Party organizations, and all the constituent organizations and members of the Party are subordinate to the National Congress and the Central Committee of the Party." Deng Xiaoping once said: "Party members must rigorously abide by these regulations. Otherwise there will be no solidity, and the CPC cannot act as the vanguard. The 'Four Subordinations' are important conditions for the Party to become integral, cohesive and capable."

The key to tightening Party discipline is to tighten political discipline, which in turn is most important and fundamental. The core of keeping the Party's political discipline is to uphold the leadership of the Party as well as its basic theory, lines, programs and requirements. All modern parties have the requirement of political discipline, for there will be no party without political discipline. Even in Western countries, all major parties exercise strict political disciplines over their party members, and require their principal officials to uphold their political proposition, stance and policies including their ideology. Observation tells us that Western parties are sharply divided when voting in parliament. Parliament members of a party come out all in support or all in opposition. What does this indicate? Undoubtedly, all parties exert political discipline on their party members. Party members who disengage themselves in politics or in action from the party will be punished in accordance with the discipline, and even eliminated from the party.

A party that lacks strict political discipline will inevitably disintegrate. Before the collapse of the USSR, the CPSU, under such slogans as "openness" and "democracy," abandoned the principle of democratic centralism, allowing party members to openly dispute decisions made by the party organization, and implementing the principle of autonomy at all levels of the party. Some CPSU members and even some leaders led the way in negating the history of the USSR, escalating the ideological chaos. This resulted in the final collapse of a powerful party which had survived for 90 years and ruled continuously for 70 years. People naturally reflected on this puzzle: When the CPSU had 200,000 members, it seized power; when it had 2,000,000 members, it defeated the Fascist invaders; but when it had 20,000,000 members, it collapsed. Why? One important reason was the relaxation of its political discipline.

In recent years when Westerners have talked about the reason for China's success, some have said that one of the secrets is "the capability of focusing all forces on major issues." The former British Prime Minister Tony Blair made the following comment: China's objective is very challenging. It is far from easy to reach such an objective. But China is a country of "word is action." In China, once the objective is made, it will keep its promise until the objective is fulfilled. But in our political culture, to establish an objective is to express a general will. If his view is correct, then China's success mainly resulted from the CPC's strict discipline and system, which have ensured efficient organization and coordination.

However, it should be recognized that there are Party members nowadays who regularly violate political disciplines; a small number of them openly disseminate or express dissenting views concerning the Party's basic theories, lines, programs and experience; some pay lip service to while covertly opposing the decisions and requirements of the Central Committee; some listen to gossip, make groundless accusations and concoct and distribute political lies, adversely influencing the public and disturbing the work of the Party and the state. All these run counter to the political discipline of the Party, for they damage the image and ruling status of the Party. For this reason, the Report to the 18th CPC National Congress underlined that, "All Party organizations and members must resolutely uphold the authority of the Central Committee and maintain a high degree of unity with it theoretically, politically and in action. We must faithfully implement the Party's theories, line, principles and policies and ensure that the decisions of the Central Committee are carried out effectively; and we will never allow anyone to take countermeasures against them or disregard them."

What are the intra-Party codes of the CPC?

According to the *Provisional Regulations on Intra-Party Code Formulation Procedures of the CPC*, the intra-Party code falls into seven categories: constitution, principle, regulation, rule, stipulation, measure and standard. We can take the intra-Party code system of the Party as a "massive tree": the constitution is its roots; principles and regulations are its trunks; rules, stipulations, measures and standards are its branches.

The Constitution, the fundamental intra-Party code, is the general code for maintaining, governing and supervising the Party. It is formulated, revised, and circulated by the National Congress. It has supreme authority and the strongest binding force. The constitution established by the Second National Congress was the first CPC constitution. The present constitution was passed at the 12th CPC National Congress in September, 1982, and was later revised by each of the following national congresses.

A Principle, next only to constitution in importance, lays down criteria for the political life, the organizational life and the conduct of all Party members. Currently there are two sets of principles: *Principles on Intra-Party Political Life* and *Principles on Honesty of the CPC Cadres in Performing Duties*.

Regulations are the code formulated by an organ of the Central Government to comprehensively define important relations or important tasks. Regulations are relatively stable, being extensive, principled and authoritative. Important regulations which have been previously formulated include *Provisional Regulations on Formulation Procedures of the Intra-Party Code of the CPC*, *Regulations on Safeguarding the Right of CPC Members*, and *Regulations on Punishment According to the Discipline of the CPC*.

Rules define the discussion procedures and working methods of the Party's leading bodies. They usually comprise discussion rules and work rules. Rules only apply inside the leading body, and do not apply to work or activities beyond.

Stipulations are the intra-Party code to adjust intra-Party policy issues or some kind of work. Compared with a regulation, a stipulation has a more limited scope; its measures and requirements are more concrete, and it is more flexible in that it can be revised as circumstances change, as was the case with *Provisional Stipulations in Ensuring Accountability of Party and Executive Cadres* and *Stipulations in Cadres Reporting Personal Issues*.

A Measure is an intra-Party code to specify the method and the procedure for implementing regulations, stipulations or some concrete tasks. They are procedural, specific and operational, such as *Measures for Circulating, Reading and Managing Documents by the Central Committee* and *Measures for Setting up an Inspector System for Cadres in Supervisory Work*.

A Standard is an intra-Party code which clarifies or reiterates regulations and stipulations in order to make them better understood, implemented and obeyed. Standards are supplementary to regulations and stipulations. They must not contradict regulations and stipulations, nor be used to establish new codes of practice.

For the CPC, to keep the Party's political discipline is primarily to abide by and maintain the *Constitution of CPC*. The Report to the 18th CPC National Congress states that Party organizations at all levels and all Party members and cadres, especially principal leading cadres, must willingly abide by the Party Constitution as well as its organizational principles and the guiding principles for its political activities; and no one is allowed to place themselves above the Party organization. Soon after the 18th CPC National Congress, Secretary General Xi Jinping made a speech on this, saying that, a person cannot draw a circle properly without compasses. The *Constitution of CPC*, that is, the fundamental code of the Party, represents the compasses for the whole Party. Every Party member, and especially every cadre, should firmly uphold the *Constitution of CPC*, making their words and behavior concordant with the constitution. In no circumstances should they change their political faith, stance and direction.

His words point to the crux of the problem inside the Party. Deng Xiaoping once opined: If China encounters any problem, the problem must stem from inside the Party. If a problem occurs inside the Party, it must arise from the relaxed political discipline and even the inner fragility of the Party. The CPSU collapsed for this reason, so did other strong and long-established parties elsewhere in the world. The CPC is a Marxist party based on revolutionary faith and iron discipline. Strict discipline is the Party's honorable tradition and exclusive strength. If such tradition and strength are lost, the Party will no longer exist. Herein lies the profound implication of strengthening the Party's discipline and upholding centralized leadership, which is underlined by the 18th CPC National Congress.

How does the CPC exercise its leadership?

The primary purpose of developing intra-Party democracy or strengthening the Party's discipline is to govern the country more effectively by strengthening and improving the way in which the Party exercises its leadership and governance. How does the CPC exercise its leadership in China? This is a question often asked by foreign friends.

In China, the CPC is the governing party, and its leadership must be maintained. But this does not mean that the Party is in charge of everything or manages everything. After much trial and exploration, the CPC took the view that the Party's leadership responsibilities mainly involve political leadership, ideological leadership, and organizational leadership – "assuming overall responsibility and coordinating manifold aspects." Political leadership means laying down general guidelines, bringing forward proposals for legislation, and turning the Party's propositions into the will of the state through people's congresses at all levels. Ideological leadership means mobilizing the Party and the people to actively and willingly implement the Party's propositions and state policies and law through publicity and education. Organizational leadership means setting up Party organizations in leading bodies, enterprises and social organizations at all levels to play their role as the leadership core and the coordination force so as to ensure the implementation of Party's propositions and state policies and law. Here we would like to analyze how the CPC exercises its leadership mainly from the perspectives of the formulation of general guidelines and the function of the Party organization.

As the governing party, the primary task of the CPC is to formulate general guidelines and put forward proposals for legislation. In response to the domestic and international situation, the Party should clarify the targets and the strategic plan for a defined historical period from a general perspective and in accordance with the interests of the people. For instance, at the Fifth Plenary Session of the 17th Central Committee held in October, 2010, the CPC proposed the "Twelfth Five-year Plan," which was approved as the state "Twelfth Five-year Plan" by the National Congress the following year.

The National Congress examines a proposal and then approves it. This is a legal procedure, which bridges the proposal and the state will. If the proposal is not approved it will be binding only on Party members but not on non-Party members. Therefore, the Report to the 18th CPC National Congress says: "The CPC should make good use of legal procedures to turn the Party's proposals into the will of the state." At present, governments at all levels from the state, provinces, municipalities and counties have their congresses whose

On September 16, 2011, the CPPCC Zhejiang provincial committee held a special hearing of democratic supervision on issues concerning the launch of the 12th Five-year Plan.

sessions are held once a year. Through these congresses the CPC, in accordance with legal procedures, turns its own will into the law and state policies which will be carried out by the government. The annual report on the work of the government and the government's programs are deliberated, discussed and ratified by the Party in advance. Taking the formulation of the Five-year Plan as an example: firstly, the CPC Central Committee puts forward a proposal for a Five-year Plan; secondly, the state council designs a program in accordance with the proposal of the Central Committee; thirdly, the program is discussed and revisions are proposed for discussion at the Chinese People's Political Consultative Conference; fourthly, it is examined and confirmed by secret ballot at the National People's Congress and then becomes the state development program.

Leading Party members' groups at all levels are responsible for the implementation of the policies of the Party. A leading Party members' group is established in the leading body of the central or local state organ, the people's organization, the economic or cultural institution or other non-Party organization. Its main tasks are: to ensure that the Party's line, principles and policies are implemented, to formulate measures for implementing decisions made by the Central Committee and its Party committee, which is set up under the agreement of the Central Committee, to discuss and decide on matters of major importance in its unit, to recommend, nominate, appoint and manage cadres within its jurisdiction, and in accordance with proper procedure, to guide the work of the Party organization of the unit and those directly under it, to provide leadership over ideological and political work and cultural and ethical progress, and to unite and organize the cadres and the rank and file inside and outside the Party to fulfill the tasks of the Party and the state.

Thus, leading Party members' groups apply the lines, principles and policies guiding the work of every department, district, group and sector by way of inducing, mobilizing, serving, coordinating and rallying. Premier Li Keqiang is the current secretary of the leading Party members' group in the State Council. Some departments are headed by non-communist party members in executive work, and the secretary of the leading Party members' group is assumed by a deputy who is at the same time a Party member. The CPC is the core force of leadership in government and state institutions at all levels, enabling these governments and institutions to work towards the goal set by the Party.

Of course, disagreements and differences of opinion may arise in the course of exercising leadership of the Party, due to the diversity of experience, education, perspectives and even interests. The key to this problem lies in the democratic centralism discussed above.

The Roadmap of the 18th CPC National Congress and The Chinese Dream

Chapter 4

Where Does the CPC's Advanced Nature Come From?

The whole Party must bear in mind that only by taking root among the people and delivering benefits to them can the Party remain invincible, and that only by being on guard against adversity in times of peace and forging boldly ahead can the Party remain in the forefront of the times.

— Report to the 18th CPC National Congress

The CPC is the core of leadership for the cause of socialism with Chinese characteristics. Its position as the governing party is specified in *The Constitution of the People's Republic of China*. This position is not proclaimed by the CPC itself, nor imposed by others but determined by history and the people. In Western countries, no party, whether in the British Revolution of 1689, the French Revolution of 1789 or the American War of Independence of 1775, could lead the state revolution and found a bourgeois republic. The founding of modern countries and the creation of basic political systems had no direct relationship with a party. Therefore, no party had any status as a "leadership party." But in China things were different. When the CPC was established, there were so many parties in China that we can describe that situation as a "forest of parties." There were in fact around 300 parties or party-like groups, all striving to play a key role in the revolutionary struggle against imperialism, feudalism and bureaucratic capitalism. The CPC succeeded in leading the Chinese people to victory in the Chinese revolution. This was because it had the right program, its Party members fought on faithfully in the face of all setbacks, and it did more a thorough job than other parties in allying itself closely with the workers and peasants and in serving the interests of the people. With the passage of time the Chinese people, together with the majority of 299 other parties, gradually accepted the leadership of the CPC. After the PRC was founded and modern socialist construction began under the leadership of the CPC, China's national strength was restored and standards of living improved. The position of the CPC as governing party became more and more secure. As many powerful parties elsewhere in the world have lost their position as ruling parties, a number of questions ensue: Can the CPC maintain its governing position in China? How long will it keep this position? How will the CPC maintain this position?

Once advanced, always advanced?

Foreigners, especially Westerners, often ask such questions as: What is the CPC's governing legitimacy? In other words, is the CPC's long-term government of China legitimate? When we address this question, in our view we must take into account differences in situation and history, and we must also take into account the fact that electoral success is only one of many channels through which to achieve and enhance legitimacy. In Western history, we can see that legitimacy has largely been based on election, through which power was passed, supervised and constrained. This type of legitimacy is more form-oriented and procedure-oriented. In contrast, pragmatism is more valued in China. Although it may be somewhat cynical to say, "The victorious is a hero; the defeated is a scurvy knave," it does reflect the attitude of the Chinese towards many things. Even if your words are fanciful and dramatic, the people will not support you if you cannot solve practical problems. Therefore, governing legitimacy in China is determined by whether you can seize political power by force, especially with the support of the people, and by whether you can benefit the people once you govern the country. If not, the people will topple you from your throne. This is the historical logic of China. Talk of legitimacy is meaningless unless it recognizes such factors.

The governing position of the CPC was the choice of the people during the violent Chinese social revolution. It was supported by the masses. Without such support, the CPC could not have won the war, or achieved its governing position. In the Huaihai Campaign, the people went to the front on their own initiative, providing manpower or material support that included more than five million peasant workers, 305 thousand stretchers, 880 thousand carts of various sizes and 206 thousand loads, 767 thousand head of cattle, 8,500 boats, and 480 thousand tons of grain. General Chen Yi, one of the commanders of this campaign, once said in poetic language, "The Huaihai Campaign was driven by the people with their carts."

After the CPC seized power, it united and led the Chinese people on to tremendous achievements in socialist construction and reform and opening-up, turning China into the world's second largest economy, and bringing steady improvements to people's standard of living and to public culture. Generally speaking, the people are satisfied with the CPC's performance in government, and continue to give their support. Since the end of the Cold War there has been considerable speculation about the fate of the CPC. As the USSR disintegrated, many thought that China would follow suit; as color revolutions occurred in Middle Asia, they thought China would follow the examples of Georgia, Ukraine and Kyrgyzstan; as West Asia and North Africa descended into chaos, they thought that China would be the next Tunisia, Egypt or Libya. But none of these predictions have come true. This shows that the CPC was on the right track not only when it led the people through the revolution, but also when it led the people into reform, opening-up, and the modernization of China. No minor disturbance can shake the governing position of the CPC. Therefore, to understand the CPC's governing legitimacy, we should not neglect Chinese tradition and reality, and we should not confine ourselves to a limited and conventional Western view of politics.

But the legitimacy of a ruling party cannot be permanent, nor can it be immutable. The foundation of the original legitimacy can be gradually undermined by inertia over the course of time. Any party which wants to secure its governing legitimacy must adjust its relations with the people and with changes in the world, the state and the Party, and must pass the test of the "people's consent." In the late 20th century, many prestigious parties which had ruled for extensive periods collapsed. The direct cause was that they neglected or even caused harm to the interests of the people. In this sense, the legitimacy of a governing party is not determined only by history nor by the nature of the party, but mainly by the faith, trust and consent of the people. If there is no such faith, trust and consent, the people's support will decrease and a legitimacy crisis will arise.

Clearly conscious of this point, the CPC does not rest on its past laurels or even its present record of merits, but stays vigilant against adversity in times of peace and conscious of possible danger ahead. It has repeatedly underlined that "The legitimacy of the Party cannot hold good for all time, nor is it immutable. The past cannot determine the present; the present cannot determine the future; that you owned legitimacy in the past doesn't mean you own it now; that you own it now does not mean you will own it in the future."

The Report to the 18th CPC National Congress pointed out, "The whole Party must bear in mind that only by taking root among the people and delivering benefits to them can the Party remain invincible, and that only by being on guard against adversity in times of peace and forging boldly ahead can the Party remain in the forefront of the times." It reiterated that under new conditions the Party is facing "Four Tests" and "Four Dangers," so: "We should steadily improve the Party's qualities of leadership and governance; and increase its ability to resist corruption, guard against degeneration, and ward off risks – this is a major issue the Party must solve in order to consolidate its position as the governing party and carry out its mission of governance."

The "**Four Tests**" are as follows. The first is the **test of exercising governance**. It is difficult to open a shop but more difficult to keep it open. Mao Zedong once said that the seizure of political power is only the first step of the long march, and the road ahead is longer and tougher. Although the CPC has more than 60 years of experience in government, it still faces many unprecedented situations, problems and challenges.

The second is the **test of carrying out reform and opening-up**. The further China develops, the more deep-rooted contradictions and problems it will encounter. These contradictions and problems, which cannot be avoided or diverted, must be solved through continuing to press forward with reform and opening-up.

The third is the **test of developing the market economy**. In the current conditions, the market economy is the best and most effective means and system for allocating resources in economic and social activities, and it is the optimum method to develop the forces of production, but at the same time it has defects such as short-sightedness, lack of spontaneity, and sluggishness. How to take advantage of its strengths while compensating for its weaknesses will be a major challenge for the CPC.

The fourth is the **test of the external environment**. Against a backdrop of the interaction between China and the world, the CPC faces the dual challenge of participating in international competition and cooperation by seizing opportunities for development on the one hand, and safeguarding its governance by resisting infiltration and damage by hostile Western forces on the other; trying simultaneously to assimilate the positives of other cultures and to reject any corrosive influences.

The **"Four Dangers"** first featured in a speech by Hu Jintao on the 90th anniversary of the CPC on July 1, 2011. The first is **the danger of lacking drive**. At present, the overwhelming majority of Party members have maintained fine Party traditions and vitality such as being enterprising, hardworking and pioneering, but there are indeed some Party members whose spirit has lost its vigor and whose faith has declined. Corrupt in thought, feeble of will, and withered in spirit, their behavior is arbitrary, weak, and lax.

The second is **the danger of incompetence**. The world is changing dramatically, the situation is developing rapidly, and the practice of socialism with Chinese characteristics is ongoing. New tasks, new situations and new problems confront the Party. Without their belief in serving the people, Party members would not seek benefits for the people whole-heartedly. Without the professional competence to serve the people, Party members would not be capable of acting on their beliefs.

The third is **the danger of losing touch with the people**. Once in power, peace, stability, and improving conditions could all lead to the kind of complacency that results in losing touch with the people. Whether the Party can maintain and develop its close ties with the people will play a decisive role in its future survival.

The fourth is **the danger of corruption**. Generally speaking, the main body of Party members is sound, but the fight against corruption – a protracted, complicated and arduous battle – cannot be neglected. This is the most inherent, imminent, terrible and mortal danger.

In fact, a governing party should be clear about its own strengths as well as soberly recognizing its shortcomings. Not until it is clear about both aspects can it move in the right direction. On June 28, 2012, Xi Jinping, in a speech during the national ceremony honoring the advanced and the outstanding, summarized the strengths of the CPC as **"Five Great Strengths."**

The first is **theoretical strength**. The CPC attaches high importance to the guiding role of the sinicized Marxist theory in practice.

The second is **political strength**. Lofty political ideals and unshakeable political faith, together with indomitable revolutionary will, have served as consistent and reliable sources of inspiration for Party members to overcome difficulties and achieve victory in seizing power, building new China and implementing reform.

The third is **organizational strength**. The CPC has always attached importance to organizational construction, with its branches established first in military companies and now in factories, construction sites and even office buildings. A scientific and coherent system has been set up including central and local organizations, and more than four million primary organizations, providing remarkable capacity for organization and mobilization.

The fourth is **system strength**. As discussed above, democratic centralism is a scientific and efficient system that can ensure that the Party formulates and implements sound lines and policies.

Chapter 4
Where Does the CPC's Advanced Nature Come From?

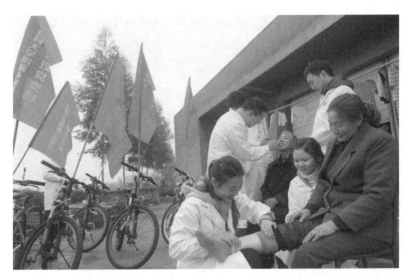

The CPC branch of the Yongchuan Hospital Affiliated to the Chongqing Medical University formed a CPC Member Gratuitous Treatment Mobile Team to provide free medical service in rural neighborhoods.

The fifth is **the strength of keeping close ties with the masses**. The CPC compares its association with the masses to the relation between fish and water or the connection between blood and flesh or the union between seeds and soil. This is the greatest strength of the CPC. This was highlighted at the 18th CPC National Congress: "The CPC must put people first, exercise governance for the people and always maintain close ties with them" and the CPC should "solve pressing problems of keen concern to the people, and raise its ability to do people-related work well under new conditions."

In general, the CPC is sober in the face of the problems and challenges presented by new situations, and it is also clear about its own strengths. On condition that the Party can press home its advantages, overcome its shortcomings, and improve its all-round ability, it will withstand any kind of test, maintain and develop its advanced nature, and strengthen its governing position.

What factors does the CPC depend on to maintain its advanced nature?

The most profound transformations experienced by the CPC over the past 90 years are that from a revolutionary party to a governing party, and that from a revolutionary approach to governance to a constructive approach to governance. The former was a transformation of position or status; the latter was a transformation of its method of governance. These transformations have proved challenging and costly. The theory of "carrying forward the revolution under the proletariat dictatorship" put forward during the Culture Revolution revealed that the CPC, the governing party, was still trapped in a revolutionary mindset, looking for enemies to confront. The slogan of "Boost production by conducting revolution" also demonstrated that the approach to developing the social forces of production still took the form of a political campaign. There was no shortage of excitement and enthusiasm, but it was unsustainable, because it was not in accord with the law of developing social forces of production. Not until reform and opening-up was introduced did the CPC truly appreciate that revolution and governance are polar opposites, that it is much more difficult to build a new world than to destroy an old one, and that the CPC lacked many of the accoutrements necessary for the realization of the Four Modernizations. So the CPC, on the one hand, shifted its working focus to economic construction – the core issue of governance. On the other hand, it began to explore the experience of governing. In this course, the CPC directed its principal efforts towards the following three aspects: firstly, the issue of representativeness; secondly, making decisions scientific and democratic (this was an issue of procedure); thirdly, developing its competence through learning.

Let us first address **"representativeness."** As is briefly mentioned above, it mainly refers to broadening and consolidating the social foundation of the Party. The more broad and solid the social foundation, the more extensive the consent and legitimacy will be and the more secure its governing position will be. At the present stage, with the strengthening of reform and opening-up, the development of the socialist market economy, and the diversification of the economic model, interests also tend to become diverse. The

On June 14, 2013, Zhang Kaisheng, who recently became a CPC member, drove his "CPC Member Pioneer" harvester to reap wheat in the city of Nanjing, Jiangsu.

original working class has changed in composition. Workers are no longer the "proletariat." In some enterprises, workers are no longer simply employees – since the stock system was adopted or since their company issued shares they have become stockholders; as the labor force moved to other sectors due to intensive farming in some well-developed rural areas, some farmers who had been tied to the land have become workers in modern enterprises; some 'workers' in a non-traditional sense (such as intellectuals) have gone into the contingent of the working class due to the scientific and technological revolution and modern management of enterprises.

The proportion of the classes in Chinese society has thereby altered. The number of workers in the traditional sense has dwindled, while jobs like white-collar workers, technicians, enterprise management personnel, cadres, teachers and freelancers are on the increase. Self-employed tradesmen and private enterprise owners have increased in huge numbers as they have evolved from a "supplementary" role in the socialist economy to an important component of the socialist market economy.

The CPC has advanced the important idea of the "Three Represents" with the "the Party must always represent the interests of the overwhelming majority of people" at their core, broadening further the governing legitimacy of the CPC. The reference to "overwhelming majority" tells us that all parties should be taken into consideration, not only the interests of workers, farmers, and intellectuals but also the interests of laborers, patriots and those who contribute to the unity of China. The expansion of the social base and the mass base is conducive to the Party playing its integrating role better in reform and opening-up and modernization.

Let us next consider the issue of "**procedure.**" Procedure is an important element of modern democracy. If you want to represent the people, you should ensure your decisions and your actions are sound. Otherwise, the people will not allow you to represent them. This calls for making decisions scientifically and democratically. Although this in itself does not necessarily guarantee that all decisions will be correct, it does at least serve to increase the ratio of sound decisions. The CPC has past experience of creating trouble for itself through poor decision-making, so it pays special attention to this issue. In China, major decisions are taken based on the following factors: the leadership of the Party, the overall interests of the state and the people's direct interests, the world and state situation, the circumstances of a particular period, in-depth research, experiences from different regions, the collective intelligence of the people, and legal procedure. This is a democratic, collective, scientific and legal process. Generally, the complete intra-Party decision-making procedure at the level of the Central Committee is as follows:

Conduct a survey at first to identify problems relating to China's development, and to seek opinions on further development from local governments, research institutions and wider society.

– Define areas of research on the basis of the survey, and ask relevant institutions to investigate these areas thoroughly, and submit their study reports.

– Form a group to draft documents for the Central Committee. After careful consideration of opinions from all sides, conduct further field research. Then draft outline documents and submit them to the Standing Committee of the Political Bureau for further discussion.

– The relevant group then holds further discussions, and revises the draft in accordance with suggestions made by the Standing Committee of the Political Bureau.

– As to major issues in drafting documents, the National Committee of the Chinese People's Political Consultative Conference (CPPCC) organizes the standing committee, other chosen committee members, and relevant experts, to conduct an in-depth study. They submit their opinions to the Central Committee for reference.

– Present the first draft of the document to Central Committee members, Party deputies, and cadres at the state and provincial level to elicit their opinions; at the same time leaders of the Central Committee listen to the opinions of the non-communist party leaders.

– Revise the document based on opinions from all sides, and then submit the revised version to the Standing Committee of the CPC Central Committee and the Political Bureau of the CPC Central Committee for discussion.

– Finally, hold the plenary sessions of the CPC Central Committee. Submit the revised document (submitted version) to the Central Committee members for examination and voting.

Finally, let us address **"competence."** The Party attaches great importance to developing its competence as a governing body. Without competence, a benevolent party may spoil its efforts. In 1949, when Mao Zedong left Xibaipo Village for Beijing, he described that transfer as "going to the capital for an examination." In fact, he was worried about whether the CPC could govern China well, so he warned the whole Party to maintain modesty, prudence, and hard-work. In May 2001, when on a tour of inspection in Anhui Province, Jiang Zemin said that cadres must uphold

How was the report to the 18th CPC National Congress drafted?

The Central Committee formed a group for drafting the Report to the 18th CPC National Congress with Xi Jinping as the group leader. Experts, scholars and leaders from departments of the Central Committee and different localities were invited to join the group, and they carried out work under the direct leadership of the Standing Committee of the Political Bureau of the CPC. Hu Jintao listened to the report several times and gave important advice. The Standing Committee repeatedly examined the report. In order to ensure a comprehensive report, the Central Committee circulated notices to elicit proposals concerning topics of the congress from departments of all regions. The Central Committee organized 46 units to investigate 15 major subjects, receiving 57 reports. The drafting group organized seven subgroups to conduct surveys in 12 provinces, regions and municipalities and asked various departments to submit their survey reports relating to their issues. Results of these surveys laid a solid foundation for drafting the report.

On July 23, 2012, Hu Jintao made a speech on major issues concerning the draft report to the 18th CPC National Congress in the seminar of principal leaders at state and provincial level. Participants at the seminar gave their opinions or suggestions on these major issues. After the draft was formed, opinions were elicited from all sides. The 17th Central Committee of the CPC, members of the CPC Central Commission for Discipline Inspection, deputies to the 17th and 18th CPC national congresses, leaders from the Party or political or military departments of the Central Committee, and people's groups and Party leaders from the Party committees of provinces, autonomous regions, municipalities and Party committees of large military units all attended the discussion. 4,511 people were invited to offer their opinions. General Secretary Hu Jintao himself held seven symposiums, directly eliciting opinions and suggestions from all sides. The drafting group also elicited opinions from some retired leaders. The Central Committee made a point of taking opinions from the central committee of non-communist parties, the leaders of the All-China Federation of Industry and Commerce, and non-party personages, and the overwhelming majority of their opinions were incorporated. On December 4, the Seventh Plenary Session of the 17th Central Committee passed the draft of the Report to the 18th CPC National Congress, and decided to submit it to the 18th CPC National Congress for examination.

the thought that to lead is to serve, and at the same time they must acquire the competence to achieve this goal. We must address the need for competence in stand and viewpoint as well as in working ability.

In September 2004, the Fourth Plenary Session of the 16th Central Committee of the CPC made a comprehensive plan to improve the art of leadership and strengthen the governing competence of the Party. The 17th CPC National Congress and the 18th CPC National Congress both proposed to strengthen the Party's governing competence, highlighting this as an issue that is absolutely fundamental to the Party's fate. Without competence, how does the Party preserve its advances? But how can the Party acquire such competence? The answer is to keep learning. Therefore, the 17th CPC National Congress determined to build a Marxist party and organizations committed to learning. The 18th CPC National Congress went even further, proposing to build the Party into an innovative, service-oriented and learning party. Of the three qualities, learning is most fundamental, as the improvement of service levels and the generation of innovative ideas all depend on learning as the last resort. In his speech at the 80th anniversary ceremony of the Party School of the CPC Central Committee, Xi Jinping said that the CPC members should always be learning and should rely on learning and practice to look to the future.

To facilitate learning, the Political Bureau of the CPC Central Committee established a collective learning system in 2002, which continues to operate. Over the past ten years, the Political Bureaus of the Central Committee of 16th and 17th CPC national congresses have carried out 80 collective learning activities, and invited 146 experts or scholars to deliver lectures. From November 2012 till March 2013, the Political Bureau of the Central Committee of the 18th CPC National Congress conducted five study exercises. Driven by the collective learning of the Political Bureau of the Central Committee, local departments have undertaken extensive learning activities in various forms, such as symposiums, collective learning classes, central group learning classes, and forums. The idea of collective, active, and lifelong learning is popular among Party members.

The National Development and Reform Commission held regular Youth Reading Forums to learn about the needs of youth through polls and cell phone messages, enabling youth to become the real masters of the forum. The rigorous selection of honored guests, topics and recommended books for each forum broadened their horizons and developed their competence. The central learning group of the Party committee of Shaanxi Province held 20 special learning activities, focusing on topics such as taking advantage of financial and capital markets, promoting the development of the private economy, developing producer services, etc.

The Organizational Department of the CPC Central Committee attached importance to training Party members at primary Party organizations as well as Party cadres, and held a series of modal training classes. Secretaries of primary Party organizations from 256 townships, villages

The CPC training institutions

There are six state-level training institutions: the Party School of the Central Committee of the CPC, the Chinese Academy of Governance, the China executive leadership academies at Pudong, Jinggangshan and Yan'an, and the China Business Executives Academy at Dalian. The first five mainly train senior and middle-ranking leadership cadres; the last one mainly trains senior chief managers of state-owned enterprises and financial institutions. All provinces and cities below have also established Party schools or administration colleges.

China Executive Leadership Academy in Pudong.

and communities went in several groups to Beijing to attend intensive modal training classes directly conducted by the Organizational Department of the Central Committee for strengthening social management. In addition, in joint efforts with relevant departments and committees of the Central Committee, the Organizational Department of the Central Committee held four model training classes for newly-appointed township secretaries, nine for college graduate village officials, and 16 for secretaries from primary Party organizations. Statistics indicate that over the past five years almost 175 million Party members have undergone training sessions, including 4.56 million rural secretaries, 13.83 million new members, 1.22 million village heads who were college graduates, and 44.81 million technical and business trainees.

Can the CPC check corruption?

After the 18th CPC National Congress put forward the subject of strengthening the Party's integrity, there were comments in the international community that the CPC was rife with serious corruption problems, and speculations that sooner or later the CPC would follow in the footsteps of the CPSU, which was renowned for serious corruption in its latter days. It can be acknowledged that CPSU corruption played a role in the disintegration of the USSR, but the CPC is different from the CPSU in that the degree of corruption is different, and attitudes towards corruption are also different.

We can illustrate this point with factual data:

The first set of data: From November 2007 to June 2012, China's disciplinary inspection and supervision agencies placed more than 640 cases on file, concluded more than 630,000 cases, and punished more than 660,000 people in accordance with Party or political discipline. Of these, 240,000 suspected criminals were transferred to the judiciary for further investigation and punishment. In other words, over a period of about five years, an average of 132,000 Party members were punished in accordance with Party discipline or state law each year.

The second set of data: By the end of 2007 and 2011, the number of Party members was 74.153 million and 82.602 million respectively. Even if we conduct our analysis on the basis of the 74.153 million Party members in 2007, we can see that 132,000 Party members who were sanctioned each year account for only 0.178% of the total number; 4,800 Party members convicted on criminal charges each year account for only 0.647 per one million.

The data above amply demonstrate that of the 82.6 million Party members of the biggest party in the world, those who violated regulations or laws are extremely small in number, and the Party as a whole is sound. It is because the Party preserves its integrity that its advances and capabilities can be maintained.

This analysis is not intended as any kind of whitewash. In fact, the CPC is very clear about intra-Party corruption. The Report to the 18th CPC National Congress made two clear statements of intent with regard to corruption. The first was: "Combating corruption and promoting political integrity, which is a major political issue of great concern to the people and is a clear-cut and long-term political commitment of the Party. If we fail to handle this issue well, it could prove fatal to the Party, and even cause the collapse of the Party and the fall of the state. We must thus make unremitting efforts to combat corruption, promote integrity and stay vigilant against degeneration." The second was: "We must maintain a tough position in cracking down on corruption at all times, conduct thorough investigations into major corruption cases and work hard to resolve problems of corruption that directly affect the people. All those who violate Party discipline and state laws, whoever they are and whatever power or official positions they have, must be brought to justice without mercy."

When the newly-elected Standing Committee of the Political Bureau of the Central Committee collectively met the press, Xi Jinping, the new secretary general of the Central Committee, stressed: "Under new conditions, our Party faces many severe challenges, and there are also many pressing problems within the Party that need to be resolved, particularly corruption, losing touch with the people, and excessive bureaucratism caused by some Party officials. We must make every effort to solve these problems. The whole Party must stay on full alert."

He also stressed: "To address these problems, we must first of all conduct ourselves honorably. Our responsibility is to work with all the comrades in the Party to uphold the principle that the Party should supervise its own conduct and run itself with strict discipline, effectively deal with major problems in the Party, improve our conduct, and maintain close ties with the people. By doing so, we will ensure that our Party will remain at the core of leadership in advancing the cause of socialism with Chinese characteristics." He has subsequently talked of corruption problems on several occasions. In his speech to the Second Plenary Session of the CPC Central Commission for Discipline Inspection, he said, "The building of a clean government and the anti-corruption war are major tasks for the Party. We must have the resolution to fight every corrupt case, punish every corrupt official, and constantly eradicate the soil which breeds corruption, so as to earn people's trust with actual results." The CPC is not only resolutely determined to combat corruption, but it has also formulated and introduced a package of important anti-corruption concepts and actions.

(1) Education. As thought precedes action, so corruption is preceded by temptation. This is the routine of all corruption cases. The Party is built on an ideological base, emphasizing loyalty and honesty. In combating corruption and forming a clean government, the Party first of all tries to strengthen relevant education. The 18th CPC National Congress has made the decision that educational activities should be carried out across the whole Party emphasizing the concepts of serving the people, being practical, and being honest, based on the general principle of "looking into the mirror,

straightening your clothes, taking a shower, and getting rid yourself of disease." The intention is mainly to remind Party members and cadres to harbor the interests of the people in their heart instead of thoughts of their own privilege.

(2) Openness. Many corruption cases result from opaque governance. In recent years, the CPC has made great efforts to make the exercise of power open, through measures ranging from publicizing administrative and Party operations to publicizing the expenditure of money on official receptions, vehicles and overseas trips and other "governing activities." The 18th CPC National Congress proposed to make the exercise of power more open and standardized, and increase the transparency of Party, government and judicial operations and official operations in other fields. The CPC is formulating a system that requires officials to disclose their assets and make them known amid increasing public outcry against corruption.

(3) Prevention and punishment. To combat corruption, China has set up the National Bureau of Corruption Prevention. In recent years, the CPC has begun to fight corruption in a comprehensive way, addressing both its symptoms and root causes, and combining punishment with prevention, with the emphasis on prevention.

(4) Supervision. The CPC welcomes supervision from other parties, groups and the public. The Report to the 18th CPC National Congress proposed that: "We should tighten intra-Party, democratic and legal supervision as well as supervision through public opinion to ensure that the people supervise the exercise of power and that power is exercised in a transparent manner." In recent years, for example, the online anti-corruption force has gained momentum, and has achieved positive results.

An internet anti-corruption case – the "Brother Watch" incident

Early in the morning of August 26, 2012, a serious car accident occurred in Yan'an City, Shaanxi Province, China, in which 36 people died and two were severely injured. Yang Dacai, a department-level official of the Bureau of Work Safety Supervision was seen smiling when he inspected the scene. This angered netizens so much that they used China's popular social networking websites to publicize his scandalous behavior, revealing that he had a suspiciously expensive watch collection. He was nicknamed by the netizens as "Brother Watch." Three days later, in a Sina micro-blog interview, Yang communicated with netizens about "smiling-gate" and "expensive watch-gate." Yang claimed that he had bought five watches over the past ten years with his own money. After the interview, however, netizens collected 11 photos of Yang wearing expensive watches of various grades. In the following days, Yang was found to have worn glasses and belts worth about RMB 130 thousand, and netizens mocked him, saying that he was "priceless all over." The day after the interview, the CPC Commission for Discipline Inspection of Shaanxi Province declared that an investigation had been launched into Yang's actions. If he had violated discipline or was corrupt, he would be punished accordingly. At the same time, a college student named Liu Yanfeng from Three Gorges University of Hubei Province sent an application form to the Financial Department of Shaanxi Province, asking for information on Yang's salary for the year 2011. About 20 days later, the CPC Commission for Discipline Inspection of Shaanxi Province publicized the result of the investigation, exposing his violations of discipline. He was dismissed from his posts as the committee member of the CPC Commission for Discipline Inspection of the 12th Provincial Party Congress and the Party organization secretary and director of the Bureau of Work Safety Supervision. In February, 2013, further investigation by the CPC Commission for Discipline Inspection of Shaanxi Province revealed that Yang was guilty of serious violations of discipline, and he was removed from the Party. Since he was also suspected of being involved in criminal activities, he was transferred to the judiciary for further investigation and punishment.

(5) System. China, an official-oriented country, places a high value on the operations of political power, featuring governance by able and virtuous people. Xi Jinping said: "We should rein power within the cage of regulations, and enhance restraint and supervision on the use of power. A disciplinary, prevention and guarantee mechanism should be set up to ensure that people do not dare to, are not able to, or cannot easily commit corruption." The Report to

the 18th CPC National Congress claimed, "To ensure proper exercise of power, it is important to put power, Party and government operations and personnel management under institutional checks and uphold people's right to be informed about, participate in, express views on, and oversee Party and government operations. We should make sure that decision-making, executive and oversight powers check each other and function in concert, and that government bodies exercise their powers in accordance with statutory mandate and procedures. We should improve the systems of inquiry, accountability, economic responsibility auditing, resignation and dismissal." In addition, the CPC is also considering drawing up an anti-corruption law.

(6) The Party should crack down on both high-ranking "tigers" and low-ranking "flies" by dealing with the illegal activities of top officials like Bo Xilai and Liu Zhijun on the one hand, and tackling malpractice and corruption cases which closely impact ordinary people on the other. In the battle against graft it was just as important to go after the "flies" as it was to tackle the "tigers," for if minor mistakes are let go, they may develop into major ones.

After the 18th CPC National Congress, Secretary General Xi Jinping and his colleagues in the Political Bureau of the Central Committee formulated the "Eight Requirements" to change their working style and keep close ties with the people. This was the solemn promise of the newly-elected Chinese leadership to "run itself with strict discipline." An online article on the first page of the Chinese website of Reuters said that the newly-elected Chinese leadership had used plain language to express their determination to build a clean and efficient government in response to people's aspiration. *The Wall Street Journal* carried an article saying: "The newly-elected

Details of the "Eight Requirements"

1) All members of the Political Bureau of the Central Committee should understand the real situation facing society through in-depth inspections at grassroots. Senior leaders should listen to the public and officials at grassroots levels, and address people's practical problems. This should be done especially in places where social problems are more acute, and inspection tours as a mere formality should be strictly prohibited.

2) The spending on officials' trips and inspections should be kept at the minimum necessary level, with no welcome banners, no red carpets, and no floral arrangements or grand receptions for officials' visits.

3) Political Bureau members should improve the conduct of meetings. They should strictly regulate the arrangements of national official meetings and major events and improve the efficiency of official conferences. Political Bureau members are not allowed to attend any kind of ribbon-cutting or cornerstone laying ceremonies, or other celebrations and seminars, without approval from the CPC Central Committee. Official meetings should be short, specific, and to the point, with no empty talk or rigmarole.

4) Political Bureau members should refine news-reporting and publications and make determined efforts to improve the style of writing. Redundant or undesirable documents should not be circulated.

5) Visits abroad should only be arranged when needed in terms of foreign affairs, with fewer accompanying members. Transportation vehicles should be chosen in accordance with the regulations, and on most occasions there is no need for a reception by overseas Chinese people, institutions and students at the airport.

6) Security work should be improved. There should be fewer traffic controls arranged for leaders' trips to avoid unnecessary inconvenience to the public. Work concerning news reporting should be improved. Whether or not conferences and activities regarding the work and activities of Political Bureau members should be reported is determined by the needs of the work, the news value and the social effect. The frequency, word content, and length of the news reports should be shortened.

7) The publication of articles should be strictly controlled. Except for those arranged by the Central Committee, no one should be allowed to publish books and speech collections, or to send congratulatory letters or telegrams, or to write inscriptions or sign autographs.

8) Political Bureau members should maintain a frugal lifestyle and strictly comply with regulations on housing and vehicles.

Chinese leadership is seeking to change the image of the CPC." *The Washington Post* described the requirements circulated by the CPC top leaders as "inspiring," and showed the determination of the CPC to serve and keep close ties with the people. Other media said that "the Eight Requirements would create a new atmosphere by tailoring the Party's working style from particulars." These reports reflect the international community's interest in and affirmation of the CPC's determination to run itself with strict discipline, and also show that the CPC has taken a new step on the road to improving the fight against corruption.

Of course, corruption is a difficult problem all over the world. For any ruling party, the fight against corruption is a long-term, complicated and arduous task. Measures taken to root out corruption vary between countries, and the impact is also different. The CPC is confident of containing corruption, but it is not easy to completely eradicate corruption. Therefore, in seeking to address this problem, the CPC is willing to communicate with other parties in other countries.

During the "Two Sessions" of the NPC and the CPPCC in March 2013, conference staff collected unused notepaper so that it could be used in the next meeting.

The Roadmap of the 18th CPC National Congress and The Chinese Dream

An examination of both the current international and domestic environments shows that China remains in an important period of strategic opportunities for its development, a period in which much can be achieved. We need to have a proper understanding of the changing nature and conditions of this period, profit from all opportunities, to respond with cool-headedness to challenges, and to take the initiative and build on our strengths to seize the day and attain the goal of creating a moderately prosperous society in all respects by 2020.

— Report to the 18th CPC National Congress

PART TWO

Where Will China Go After the 18th CPC National Congress?

Developing socialism with Chinese characteristics is a lengthy and arduous task of historic importance. China must be prepared to carry out a titanic struggle, clear one hurdle after another, and attain one goal after another. It is impossible to accomplish the whole task in one move. Promoting the cause of socialism with Chinese characteristics is the basic route for the CPC to lead the Chinese people towards rapid development. Thus the people can follow the direction more easily, knowing, rather than hoping or aspiring to know, what should be done today and tomorrow. This is the logic behind the strategic goals of the "Quadruple Growth" put forward when the policy of reform and opening-up was initially introduced, the "Three Steps" formulated at the 13th CPC National Congress, "building a moderately prosperous society in all respects" clarified at the 16th CPC National Congress, and the "Two Centenaries" elucidated at the 18th CPC National Congress. Furthermore, the Report to the 18th CPC National Congress restated the main task of achieving socialist modernization and rejuvenating the Chinese nation, and added the overall plan for promoting economic, political, cultural, social, and ecological progress in addition to concrete goals and policies for deepening reform and opening-up. In fact, goals, tasks, policies and channels have all been included in the report. If you still ask where China is going, we can give you an assertive answer that China will continue to follow the socialist road with Chinese characteristics, striving for its explicit goal. Would you like to go with China on the road?

"Quadruple Growth," "Three Steps" and "Two Centenaries"

The strategy of "Quadruple Growth" was first put forward by Deng Xiaoping, the core of the second generation of the CPC leadership collective. Accordingly, the 12th CPC National Congress formulated the programs, principles and policies for creating a new approach to all fields of socialist modernization and set the strategic goal and concrete steps to quadruple the total value of agricultural and industrial output over the 20 years from 1981 to the end of the 20th century.

In 1987, the 13th CPC National Congress advanced the overall strategic plan of the "Three Steps" for developing China's economy. The first step was to double the GNP of 1980 and ensure that the whole population had adequate food and clothing. This task had been largely fulfilled by the end of the 1980s. The second step was to double it again by the end of the 20th century, and this task had also been fulfilled by 1995. The third step was by the middle of the 21st century to reach the per capita GNP level of moderately developed countries and the people would live a relatively affluent life.

In 2012, the 18th CPC National Congress put forward the goal of "Two Centenaries": That is, "completing the building of a moderately prosperous society in all respects when the Communist Party of China celebrates its centenary" and "turning China into a modern socialist country that is prosperous, strong, democratic, culturally advanced and harmonious when the People's Republic of China marks its centennial."

The Roadmap of the 18th CPC National Congress and The Chinese Dream

Chapter 5

Will China's Economy Continue to Grow?

In contemporary China, the essence of adhering to development is pursuing development in a scientific way. Taking "the pursuit of development in a scientific way" as the underlying guideline and "accelerating the change of the growth model" as a major task is a strategic choice we have made for promoting China's overall development.

— Report to the 18th CPC National Congress

Over the past 30 years of reform and opening-up, China's economy has continued to grow rapidly. This is a major achievement. China's economy has risen from the sixth to the second place in the world. Its productive forces and economic, scientific and technological strength have increased considerably, living standards, individual incomes and social security have improved significantly, and the country's overall national strength and international competitiveness and influence have been substantially enhanced. The country has undergone historic changes. More significantly, while improving standards of living and welfare China has successfully avoided both the stagnation trap and the massive confrontation and disorder provoked by the social polarization which has afflicted many other developing countries.

Like other economies, China has also experienced ups and downs in its economic development. Especially during the periods of rapid economic and social change, problems of balance, coordination and sustainability have cropped up. For instance, the rate of investment to consumption may be lopsided, the industrial structure can be unbalanced, and the capacity for scientific and technological innovation may be weak. In addition, against the background of the slow recovery of the global economy, the external environment for China's economic growth does not give grounds for optimism either. Together these disadvantageous factors contribute to downward pressure on China's economic growth. In response, voices from China and from abroad have risen to predict that as China's economy loses momentum, China's economy will run the risk of a "hard landing" and "double-dip recession" in the short run, and will fall into the "middle income trap" in the long run, which might finally lead to economic stagnation.

As the world's second largest economy, China is seen as a good barometer of the global economy. Will China's economic growth slow down sharply after the 18th CPC National Congress? What measures will China adopt to prevent its economy from slackening? Is China able to reach the goal of "doubling its 2012 GDP and per capita income for both urban and rural residents" set at the 18th CPC National Congress? These questions concern not only China but also many "stakeholders" all over the world. In response, the CPC strongly argues that an examination of both international and domestic environments shows that China currently remains in an important phase of strategic opportunities for development and that it is possible for China to transform and upgrade its economy and to maintain its economic growth.

Why can China's economy maintain rapid long-term growth?

To this question, Chinese and foreign observers provide a variety of answers. The popular response points out that China has aroused public enthusiasm for production and boosted the efficiency of development by carrying out reform and opening-up, adopting the market economy, and defining property rights including private property rights. Of course, this sounds reasonable. But there are many developing countries which have adopted the market economy – why is only China able to achieve economic success? As to private property rights, many other developing countries have defined them more extensively, and they faced fewer restrictions when they began to build their market economy. Why is it so difficult for them to match China?

Another view is that China's economy is not exceptional among East Asian countries, and other than its economic scale, China is not fundamentally different from the four 'Asian Tigers' (a term used in reference to the highly-developed economies of Hong Kong, Singapore, South Korea, and Taiwan) during their fledgling period. But in world economic history, successful cases of large export-oriented economies are extremely rare. Therefore, we need to understand the real reason for China's rapid economic growth over the past 30-plus years. Only if we know the real reason, can we accurately forecast the trend of China's future economic development. The real reasons, we think, are as follows:

(1) The integration of independent action with participation in economic globalization. There is a consensus among many Chinese and foreigners that the role of opening-up in pushing forward China's economic development was not subordinate to that of reform. But China's opening-up is different from other countries' in that it has adhered to the following three points: firstly, full commitment to opening-up, with no interruption, no thoughts of giving up, no half-hearted measures, no hesitation in the face of problems encountered – even during the Asian financial crisis, for example; secondly, opening by steps, in order of priority and by degree; and thirdly, bringing key economic sectors under state control to protect state sovereignty and maximize national interests. These are the principal reasons why China has rapidly narrowed the gap with the advanced countries over the past 30 years. Many countries went further than China in the extent of their opening-up, but many of these have been reduced to little more than a stage on which international capital performs its maneuvers, because they set no limits, erected no defenses, and failed to ensure their capacity for independent action.

(2) Optimizing the allocation of resources through gradual marketization and limited privatization. In its marketization reform China did not inflict radical "shock therapy" on itself, or abandon its planned economy at a stroke. Instead, taking into consideration the reality and rational side of the planned economy, it adopted the twin-track method of freeing together with regulating, and took steps both to develop the market economy and to transform the planned economic system. China thereby avoided the confusion and economic disruption that arose in many other countries during their economic transition. The development of private property rights in China has also passed through several phases: the self-employed economy, the development of household private property, the operation of contracts, the joint stock limited company, and private capital economy. This has enabled society to pass through a process of understanding, adaptation and adjustment. What is of particular importance is that China's marketization and privatization have maintained a mixed economic form, that is, the coexistence of market mechanism and government intervention, the coexistence of private and public property rights, thus ensuring the macro-control and the stability and also ensuring state capital control over key fields of the economy. At the same time, through canceling the life tenure of officials and fighting corruption, China has succeeded in preventing officials from converting the state property into private or family capital, thus avoiding the proliferation of family business groups at state level, or collusion between officials and businessmen, and also bypassing the snares of conflict and turbulence in economic growth.

(3) Implementing the household land contract system featuring, both centralization and decentralization, which improved the living standards of farmers, avoided the annexation of land, and provided a steady source of low-cost labor for industrialization and urbanization. China, a backward agricultural country, built its planned economy on the basis of a dual economic structure separating cities from countryside. Through this structure, China implemented a most rigorous migration management and household registration system. China started its economic reform not by canceling or directly transforming its dual economic system, but by introducing the household contract responsibility system under the framework of the original collective economy in rural areas. China has thereby realized the most equal land use and income rights in history, quickly solving the problem of creating economic incentives in agricultural production in a developing country, and greatly improving the well-being of farmers, who still form the overwhelming majority of the country's population. What is more significant is that the household contract responsibility system emancipated the rural labor population which had been confined to the land by the original planned economy and the collective production mode. This triggered a chain of events. Having solved the problem of adequate food and clothing, farmers quickly transferred from exclusive grain production to industrial crops and livestock breeding. They then transferred to local non-agricultural sectors by setting up township enterprises. This was followed by the transfer of a large body of immigrant workers to cities and industries. The immigrant workers gradually became the main body of the Chinese working class, having a great impact on the original rigid employment system in state-owned enterprises and providing a steady supply of low-cost labor for industrialization and urbanization, thus greatly lowering this cost.

(4) Defining the scope of revenue and expenditure and encouraging local competition under the control of the Central Government. As China is a country which is vast in territory, large in population, and unbalanced in development, the relationship between the Central Government and local governments has been one of the core elements influencing China's economic and social development for centuries. China's reform and opening-up were inspired by the concept of benefiting the people by devolving power, that is, by changing the big pot of the unified planned economy into many small pots. From 1980 onwards, central and local governments have clarified their respective scope of revenue and expenditure, and signed contracts at different levels. Though there were some changes, the overall arrangement that central and local governments defined their respective scope of revenue and expenditure was retained. Because the Central Government monopolized the authority to circulate currency and bonds and the authority to issue debt, the only channel for local governments at all levels to attain development was by pooling all their resources to increase their revenues beyond the limits imposed by the Central Government. Against the background of taking economic construction as the core, governments at all levels became to some degree local corporations of limited responsibility, making overall plans and taking all factors into consideration to transfer and allocate local resources,

The 2012 monitoring and survey report on China's migrated workers indicated that the total population of migrated workers in China exceeds 260 million.

Chapter 5
Will China's Economy Continue to Grow?

creating advantageous conditions for the inflow of capital. Thus a unique system of local competition was formed, and this became one of the important drivers for China's economic growth.

Does China's economy still have potential to grow?

Objectively speaking, China's "economic miracle" from reform and opening-up is not cost free, and it cannot continue unconditionally. China has experienced considerable change since the global financial crisis – the initial factors that contributed to growth, and many other contributing conditions, began to change or disappear. Some drivers have declined, or even become an obstacle to further development.

Firstly, at the end of 1970s, because of the considerable disparity of development between China and the developed countries, China's opening surprisingly brought forth the later-development advantage and the comparative advantage, but nowadays these advantages begin to decline. The exchange of knowledge and information between China and the rest of the world has reached a high level. Dialogue and communication are still very important, but they have lost their initial impact. The science and technology gap has narrowed, but the potential threat of competition has made the impact of blockading technology and markets stronger. What was largely an inflow of capital has now become bilateral. The ratio of foreign trade to GDP had risen from below 10% to above 65% in the year 2006, surpassing America by a large margin, and there is limited room for further increases. The continuous growth in trade surplus has become a focus of economic conflict with other countries. It is impossible to increase or maintain a trade surplus forever. The export-oriented economy and the increase of foreign demand must inevitably change. The global financial crisis and the economic decline thus caused have only increased the urgency of adjustment. In general, the impact of opening-up on China has gradually evolved from a major advantage to a "double-edged sword." This is the reality that China must face.

Secondly, China has succeeded in carrying out gradual and growing market reform. It will become more and more difficult to extend reform in the future. At present, the degree of marketization of China's economy in the competitive sphere has reached a high level. Reform needs to continue in the relatively monopolized spheres of energy and resources, but reform in these spheres affects individual interests. Therefore, reform is no longer purely an economic issue, or simply a question of whether or not it is thorough. If not dealt with properly, reform may arouse public disagreement or lose public support. Reform in the fields of education, medical care and monopolistic public utilities is not only difficult, but sensitive too. As for reform in the system of ownership, China has retained elements of a strong state-owned economy. This has played an active role in maintaining economic stability, and avoiding polarization and social confrontation, but corruption and low efficiency are common. How to push forward the reform of the state-owned enterprises is and will be a major subject to which China must give deep and systematic consideration.

Thirdly, the household land contract system and the supply of low-cost labor on the basis of the dual economic structure have gradually turned from drivers of economic growth into obstacles. On the one hand, with progress in economy and technology, the concept of dividing the land into small pieces for contract management has become problematic, and the drain of young and middle-aged laborers from the countryside has reinforced a tendency towards land neglect and agricultural stagnation. On the other hand, the barrier of the dual economic system under which farmers are entitled to leave their home land, but are obliged to return, has deterred about 150 million non-agricultural farmers from involvement with the urbanization process. This has greatly reduced domestic demand in the process of industrialization and urbanization, and has led to an imbalance in the urban development and interest structure. To make things worse, before the urbanization of the overwhelming majority of farmers who naturally integrated into the city has yet to begin, the cost of urbanization has risen fast due to the high value of urban and suburban land and the influence of strong and vested interest groups. The potential for future development has been over-exploited and quickly consumed in advance.

Fourthly, the advantages and disadvantages of competition at local government level are still a matter of debate. The strong force of local government in pooling resources is a two-edged sword, as it has both the positive effect of creating a large-scale regional economy and the negative effect of creating executive allocations which distort the functioning of the market. Because of the power of local government investment, it is hard to avoid the temptation to approve investments pursued only for political advancement, leading to wasted GDP and officials seeking simply to feather their own nests. At the same time, such investment pushes out private capital. Because of the increase of domestic demand and the development of urbanization, the direction of the urbanization calls for local governments to transform from economic to service-providing governments, and from investment and land finance to public finance. The role of competition between local governments gradually decreases and this tendency is irreversible.

Finally, China has paid a heavy price for its extensive mode of economic growth, in resources, environment and health. It is imperative for China to transform this mode of economic growth and adjust its economic structure. But in many circumstances such a transformation means increases in cost, acting as a barrier to further growth.

Therefore, how to break through the bottleneck of development by finding and activating new economic growth triggers is far from a short-term issue. Over the next ten years, can China maintain the high-speed economic growth of the first decade of the 21st century? Will China enter a period of low to medium growth over the coming ten years? Assessment of this major issue should be the basis for making all strategic plans for development in economy, society, politics and other fields. In my view, though contradictions have accumulated in the process of China's rapid economic development, and difficulties similar to those of other developing countries have arisen, we still cannot draw the conclusion that economic growth has lost its momentum and that China will fall into the "middle income trap."

(1) China is still a relatively backward country trying to catch up with and surpass others. China's per capita GDP has never exceeded 5,000 US dollars, only about 7,000 US dollars even calculated according to purchasing power parity. This stage of development still puts China at the level of catch-up with other countries in science and technology, business methods and management. China should continue to learn about science and technology and management from developed Western countries. At this stage of development, China does not suffer from any limitations on progress in leading-edge science and technology and there is no lack of innovation. There is a big gap between catch-up countries and developed countries, but that gap represents potential.

(2) China's economy is a big-country economy. China has a large population of 1.3 billion and a vast market. Its economy is so enormous that its fundamental advantage lies in its domestic market potential. This potential is unlocked by the disparity between different regions. In China, there are not only big cities with per capita GDP surpassing 10,000 US dollars, like Beijing, Shanghai and Guangzhou, but also vast rural regions where per capita GDP is less than 1,000 US dollars. Because advanced cities and backward villages are in the same social management system, the gap between them constitutes the potential or the impetus for steady development of China's economy, a big-country economy.

(3) China has the advantage of capital accumulation for maintaining its rapid economic development. During their economic development, some countries in Latin America and Southeast Asia saw a tendency for consumption to rise and savings and investment to fall, leading to a steady decline in the speed and scale of capital accumulation, causing their economy to lose any basis for continuous growth. Since China entered the middle-income stage, it has maintained a high rate of saving and investment, and the scale of capital accumulation has been on the increase. Although relying too much on investment for economic growth may have some negative effects, a moderate increase in investment is still an important precondition for economic development because China is a developing country. If a proper and effective stimulation mechanism is formed and the investment structure is continuously optimized, China can continue to use its rapid capital accumulation as the impetus to promote its economic growth.

(4) China still holds the advantages of being a "late-developer" in the fields of political system reform and structural adjustment. Marketization reform produced great energy. It has been the major impetus for the past 30 years of economic growth. But in some other fields, there is still plenty of room for marketization reform. In particular, market elements such as labor force, capital, land, resources, and environment are over-regulated and seriously distorted. The price system cannot reflect the real degree of demand. Future reform of these market elements can lead and encourage structural adjustment and the transformation of the development mode through the adjustment of prices and the "return" of the market mechanism, so as to promote efficient resource allocation to encourage economic growth.

(5) Conditions in China are conducive to further development. On the one hand, China's "total wealth" after many years of accumulation has become considerable, as it not only has substantial foreign currency reserves, vastly improved facilities, and greater innovative competence in science and technology, but also has a more internationalized pool of first-class talent. Therefore, China has more scope for action in the future, and will be more confident. On the other hand, having gone through the challenge of the Asian financial crisis in 1997 and the global financial crisis in 2008, as well as the challenge of entering the WTO, China has increased its capacity to cope with major risks and problems, and has acquired much richer experience. All these represent a substantial body of wealth which will add impetus to China's economic growth.

In conclusion, China still has and will have potential and room for economic growth. An investment in China today is an investment in the future. Those who lose confidence now are making the wrong judgment.

How will China update its economy?

On the basis of a scientific assessment of the situation, the 18th CPC National Congress set itself the clear goal of completing the building of a moderately prosperous society in all respects and strengthening reform and opening-up in an all-around way, and also set itself the task of accelerating the improvement of the socialist market economy and the transformation of the growth mode. This shows that unity of development, reform and transformation is the new requirement as China enters a new stage of modernization. Firstly, the mode of development must be changed. The total value of China's economy has risen to the top echelons of the world, but China has paid high price for its economic growth. It is imperative for China to change its intensive growth model; there is no alternative. Secondly, there must be reform for this change to happen. Improper mechanisms are the biggest obstacle to the transformation of the growth model. China's great achievements in economic development over the past 30 years have depended on reform. Thirdly, reform is far from being complete. China has entered the crucial period of changing its mode, the transitional period for its development, and the critical period for its reform. At this stage, requirements and expectations for reform are on the increase, so are difficulties and complexities, but there is still room and potential. At a press conference held on March 17, 2013, Premier Li Keqiang presented the concept of "creating the updated version of China's economy" for the first time. This concept is actually the genuine requirement and a metaphorical expression of the above goals and tasks. The following eight major relations must be dealt with properly in creating an updated version of China's economy.

(1) The relation between speed and performance: "We should accelerate the creation of a new growth model and ensure that development is based on improved quality and performance." The practice of 30-plus years of high-speed development proves that taking economic construction as the central task is essential for rejuvenating China. Development is the key to solving the country's problems. So it is necessary to maintain a certain pace of economic growth. But it should be clarified that the development that China pursues is one that consists of speed, quality and performance, instead of only speed. The development should be shifted from pursuing speed to pursuing quality and performance. Quality and performance should be reflected by an increase of the interests of enterprises and also by increases in payment for labor, individual incomes, and financial revenues. At the present stage, the key to improving the quality and performance of development is to improve the efficiency of production. At present, the efficiency of production in China is still low. It is obviously much lower than that in advanced countries, lower even than the world average. There is, therefore, great potential to exploit.

(2) The relation between domestic demand and foreign demand: "We should firmly maintain the strategic focus of boosting domestic demand." Boosting domestic demand is the most important structural adjustment. Since 2008, China has depended on its domestic demand to diminish the impact of the global financial crisis. Faced with the prospect that the world economy may slow down in the long run, China will continue to depend on domestic demand to maintain sustainable development. International experience shows that this is the only way for big countries to develop. As the largest new market in the world, China has great potential for domestic demand. Actively boosting domestic demand can not only facilitate China's own development, but can also benefit the adjustment and development of the world economy.

(3) The relation between investment and consumption: "We should make efforts to unleash the potential of individual consumption." The imbalance between investment and consumption is a long-standing difficulty which hampers the development of China. Insufficient domestic demand is reflected to a large degree by insufficient consumption. In recent years, China's consumption growth has been lower than investment growth. The consumption rate is generally on the decrease, but because consumption demand is the final demand, a low long-term consumption rate is harmful to the virtuous cycle and the sustainable development of the economy. Therefore, China will address boosting domestic demand as the fulcrum of building a long-term mechanism for strengthening consumption, optimizing its consumption environment and cultivating consumption hot spots. At the same time, investment should not be neglected for its immediate effect on promoting economic growth, and the further development of industrialization and urbanization should also be supported by balanced investment. In the future, China will continue to optimize its investment structure, improve its investment performance, and seek more junctions between investment and consumption for the purpose of increasing investment, boosting consumption, and benefiting the public.

(4) The relation between innovation and imitation: "We should accelerate the strategy of innovation-driven development." When the policy of reform and opening-up was introduced China was at a low scientific and technological level. Since then, much of its production and technology have been at a stage of imitation, with few independent intellectual property rights. There have also been cases where foreign intellectual property rights have been violated. Though China is the largest manufacturing country in the world, its products are not technology-oriented and value-added, and its core competitiveness is not strong. In terms of this issue, China has enhanced the protection of intellectual property rights on the one hand, and adhered to the road of independent innovation with Chinese characteristics on the other hand. The 18th CPC National Congress made a point of stressing the importance of scientific innovation as the core of overall state development, saying: "We should increase our capacity for making original innovation and integrated innovation and for making further innovation on the basis of absorbing advances in overseas science and technology, and place greater emphasis on making innovation through collaboration."

(5) The relation between the artificial economy and the real economy: "We should focus on developing the real economy as a firm foundation of the economy." The sound and moderate development of the artificial economy, especially the modern financial sector, is conducive to providing sufficient and timely financial support to the real economy and sharing operational risks. It is also conducive to optimizing the allocation of social resources and

In December 2012, over 200 projects from more than 60 universities and colleges participated in the First Jiangsu Provincial Exchange Meeting on College Student Scientific and Technological Innovation and Entrepreneurship Achievements. These achievements covered 11 industries including equipment manufacturing, energy conservation and environment protection, and biological technology.

provides further alternatives to the necessary disintegration and re-integration of the market entities. But the artificial economy is self-centered. It has a tendency to over-expand, raising the possibility of distorting the real economy which might cover up the genuine problems such as over-heating in the real economy, resulting in a bubble economy. The global financial crisis warns us that the artificial economy should be developed but not be over-developed. Without the foundation and support of the real economy, the development of the artificial economy could be catastrophic. The Report to the 18th CPC National Congress argues that "we should adopt policies and measures to better facilitate the development of the real economy, and we should deepen reform of the financial system and improve the modern financial system so that it will better contribute to macroeconomic stability and support the development of the real economy." This is both a conclusion drawn from China's experience in dealing with global financial crisis, and a commitment to action based on the lessons learned.

(6) The relation between public ownership and private ownership: "We should remain steadfastly committed to two points." Issues of ownership from the debate over "socialist" or "capitalist" to "public" or "private" troubled China's economic development for a considerable period after the policy of the reform and opening-up was introduced. On this question, the 18th CPC National Congress offers the answer that: "We should remain fully committed to enhancing the vitality of the state-owned sector of the economy, and at the same time we must steadfastly encourage, support and guide the development of the non-public sector." But in reality what is the relation between them? Is there such a phenomenon as "the state sector is advancing and the non-public sector is retreating," on which there have been considerable debates? There are three aspects worth our attention. Firstly, they are different in status. China's basic position is that the public-owned economy is the main body, alongside which other forms of ownership are encouraged to develop simultaneously. It is justifiable that the public-owned economy maintains the dominant position, but being dominant does not mean maintaining a higher ratio. In fact, from 2003 to 2011, the proportion of state-owned enterprises and state-holding industrial enterprises to the total in China decreased from 17.47% to 5.24% in number, from 55.99% to 41.68% in asset ownership, and from 40.53% to 27.19% in core business revenues. Secondly, they are equal in legal position. There is no discrimination. The Report to the 18th CPC National Congress argues that: "We should ensure that economic entities under all forms of ownership have equal access to factors of production in accordance with the law, compete on the same level in the market, and are protected by the law as equals." Thirdly, China wants neither the tradition that "the state sector is advancing and the non-public sector is retreating," nor the market fundamentalism that "the state is retreating and the non-public sector is advancing." China's need is that "state and non-public sectors are both advancing" on the basis of optimizing the economic structure and following market regulations. China should extend the reform of state-owned enterprises and constantly enhance the vitality, controlling strength, and influence of the state-owned economy, as well as creating a healthy environment for the development of the privately-owned economy. China should not attend to one and lose sight of the other, nor should it favor this and disfavor that.

(7) **The relation between the city and the countryside: "We should integrate urban and rural development."** For many years, China has followed a dual social structure for rural and urban areas. This structure has made a significant contribution to China's economic development, but lately many problems have begun to surface. One major issue is that immigrant workers find it difficult to merge into the city where they work or live because they don't have

city residence identities and benefits. At the same time, the rural areas that supply immigrant workers find it hard to develop their local economy because of the shortage of labor and the decentralization of the land. To solve this problem completely, China must integrate urban and rural development. On the one hand, China must press forward with "people-oriented urbanization," accelerating the reform of the household registration system, registering rural migrant workers as permanent urban residents in an orderly way, and endeavoring to ensure that all permanent urban residents have access to basic urban public services. On the other hand, China will support agricultural modernization, promoting harmonized development of rural and urban areas. For this reason, the Report to the 18th CPC National Congress proposed such major measures as: "We should give more to farmers, take less from them and lift restrictions over their economic activities"; "we should give high priority to rural areas in developing infrastructure and social programs in the country; "we should develop large-scale agricultural operations in diverse forms; "we should establish a new system for intensive agricultural operations that are specialized, well-organized and commercialized"; "we should ensure equal exchange of factors of production between urban and rural areas, and balance allocation of public resources between them." Future progress can be confidently expected in the integration of urban and rural development.

(8) The relation between government and market: "We should deepen structural economic reform." The Report to the 18th CPC National Congress stressed that: "The underlying issue we face in structural economic reform is how to strike a balance between the role of the government and that of the market, and we should follow more closely the rules of the market and play a better role as the government." This is an important conclusion, drawn from past practice. Experience has taught us that to develop its economy well, China must bring into play the basic function of market in allocating resources, and avoid any excess in control, management, and interference. But China should not give free rein to the market either, or have blind faith in market strength. The major task of macro-regulation and macro-management of the government is to keep the total economic volume balanced, restrain inflation, optimize the macro structure, safeguard social fairness and justice, create a healthy environment and positive conditions for transforming the economic development mode, and maintain sound and rapid economic development. At the same time, the government should actively improve and regulate the market entry system, build a modern market system where operations are unified and competition is orderly, safeguard the order of the market, and guarantee the basic function of the market in allocating resources.

However, if the scope and degree of government intervention surpasses the limit required to compensate for "market blindness" and maintain the normal operation of the market mechanism, or if the government does not intervene wisely, or makes mistakes, the government will not be able to correct the market, but on the contrary it will restrain the normal operation of the market mechanism. The market economy is the most efficient and vigorous mechanism of economic operation and means of resource allocation that has yet been found, but it also has the functional deficiencies of regulating automatically after the event, encouraging monopolization, neglecting common interests, and triggering polarization. Crucially, it cannot overcome these deficiencies on its own initiative. Therefore the market economy that is completely free of government intervention and regulation will see its deficiencies overshadow its strengths. The key to developing a socialist market economy is to seek the optimum meeting point between government intervention and market function in order to ensure that the government is present when required, but avoids excessive interference and other misconduct when it intervenes to adjust the economy and compensate for the blind operation of the market. This is the major theoretical and practical issue that must be dealt with effectively in the process of building and improving China's socialist market economy.

The Roadmap of the 18th CPC National Congress and The Chinese Dream

Chapter 6

Where Will China Go in Reforming Its Political Structure?

The reform of the political structure is an important part of China's overall reform. We must continue to make both active and prudent efforts to carry out the reform of the political structure, and make people's democracy more extensive, fuller in scope and sounder in practice.

— Report to the 18th CPC National Congress

China was subjected to feudal autocracy for more than two thousand years, but the people waged numerous struggles for democracy and freedom. Especially in modern times when Western influences spread to the East, concepts of freedom, democracy and republic took root more deeply in people's minds, and China's struggle for freedom and democracy also became an important part of the world wave of democratization. Since the PRC was founded in 1949, and especially since China began reform and opening up in 1978, the CPC has attached great importance to democratic political construction, steadily pressed ahead with its reform of the political structure, and made notable progress.

However, there are still people who argue that China's democracy is not complete. They criticize China as an autocratic country and consider the CPC as an obstacle to political reform. The reason is that they have taken a dogmatic view of democracy, holding that only Western-style democracy is real and all other styles are illegitimate. In fact, there is no universally adaptable mode or pattern for democracy. There are only concrete or tangible forms such as American-style democracy, German-style democracy and Indian-style democracy. For China, there is only "Chinese-style democracy." To evaluate China's democracy by the American, German or Indian standard would be as foolish as a man cutting short his feet to fit his shoes, in that the shoes will remain unchanged but the feet will be hurt.

If you ask where China will go in reforming its political structure, we can give you the definitive answer that China will become more democratic. The Report to the 18th CPC National Congress stressed: "People's democracy is the life of socialism and an inspiring banner that has always been held high by our Party. We must continue to make both active and prudent efforts to carry out reform of the political structure, and make people's democracy more extensive, broader in scope, and sounder in practice." But such democracy is based on the Chinese people's understanding. It is not "Western-style."

What is "Chinese-style democracy"?

In China, the more precise wording of "Chinese-style democracy" or "democratic politics with Chinese characteristics" is "the socialist path of political development with Chinese characteristics." The Report to the 17th CPC National Congress detailed for the first time: "We must integrate the leadership of the Party, the position of the people as masters of the country, and the rule of law. We must uphold and improve the system of people's congresses, the system of multiparty cooperation and political consultation under the leadership of the CPC, the system of regional ethnic autonomy, and the system of self-governance at the primary level of society. All this will promote continuous self-improvement and development of the socialist political system."

The Report to the 18th CPC National Congress stressed: "We must ensure the integration of the leadership of the Party, the position of the people as masters of the country, and law-based governance. To guarantee the fundamental position of the people as masters of the country and to reach the goal of enhancing the vitality of the Party and country and keeping the people fully motivated, we should expand socialist democracy, accelerate the building of a socialist country based on the rule of law, and promote socialist political progress." "Chinese-style democracy" means that "we must ensure the unity of the leadership of the Party, the position of the people as masters of the country, and law-based governance." These three principles – "one core and two guarantees" – are united under the prime purpose of serving the people and also united under the major goal of development at the primary stage. Of the three, the position of the people as masters of the country is the essence of socialist politics; law-based governance is its legal guarantee; adherence to the leadership of the Party is its political guarantee.

Democracy has always been connected with law. Without the guarantee of law, democracy may ring hollow. But there remain the questions of who makes the law and whom it will serve. If the Chinese people reject the leadership of the Party, democracy may become the democracy of the rich or the minority. With the double guarantee, the position of the people as masters of the country can genuinely be secured instead of becoming merely a formality. In China, the fundamental political system that embodies the position of the people as masters of the country is the system of the people's congress; the basic political system is the system of regional ethnic autonomy and the system of self-governance at the primary level of society; the political system that embodies law-based governance is the socialist law system with Chinese characteristics, the core of which is *The Constitution of the People's Republic of China*; the basic political system that embodies the leadership of the Party is the system of multiparty cooperation and political consultation under the leadership of the CPC.

The reason why Chinese-style democracy emphasizes adherence to the leadership of the Party, some scholars think, is because a stable political authority has been required in Chinese political culture for a long time. This authority is the pivot and the guarantee for Chinese society to function. It is hard to see how the Chinese people, who have been influenced by traditional Chinese culture for thousands of years, can become accustomed to frequent changes in the ruling party and the government. Such change, from their point of view, brings uncertainty not only into politics, but also into their work and their daily life.

The establishment of the leadership and the governance of the CPC are related to this tradition. That is to say, the salient features of Chinese-style democracy are that China attaches importance to both the form and the performance of the democracy and that China both develops democracy and avoids being shackled by it. This is the most distinctive characteristic of Chinese-style democracy, and this is also the key to understanding China's political path of development. This means looking at Chinese-style democracy from the perspective of system. If we look at it from the perspective of procedure and operation, the most distinctive aspect is "consultative democracy" as an adjunct to traditional "voting democracy." But consultative democracy is closely associated with the system of multiparty cooperation and political consultation under the leadership of the CPC. We will come to this later.

Why does China not adopt the multi-party system?

The political party system is an important component of modern democratic politics, and can divide into the single-party, the two-party and the multi-party system. It is not formed by imagination. In any given country its formation is influenced by the form of state, the socioeconomic base, and the balance of forces such as class and walk of life, and it is also influenced by the traditions of that country and the prevailing international environment. The diversity of the party system demonstrates the diversity of human civilization. A system will be viable and effective if it is concordant with national conditions, character, and historical conditions, and if it is conducive to the stability of the political situation, the people's happiness and the improvement of the forces of production.

The political party system China has adopted is multi-party cooperation and political consultation under the leadership of the CPC. It is different from the Western two-party or multi-party system, and also different from the single-party system implemented in some other countries. It has three important characteristics: the leadership of the CPC, multiparty cooperation, and political consultation. This system, formed through the long-term practice of revolution, construction, and reform, fits China's national conditions and traditional culture. It is a historical necessity that is realistic and rational.

Some foreign friends ask why other parties should accept the leadership of the CPC? Will China adopt the Western multi-party system at some point in the future?

To answer this question, we must understand Chinese history and the background against which this system was formed. At the beginning of modern era, China's semi-colonial and semi-feudal nature caused enormous damage to its politics, economy, and culture. Therefore, the two major historical tasks of the Chinese people were to overcome the three major obstacles of imperialism, feudalism, and bureaucrat-capitalism, and to attain national independence and prosperity. In the course of the Chinese revolution, the "multi-party situation" featured twice. In the early 20th century, the 1911 Revolution led by Sun Yat-sen and championed by the national bourgeoisie was successful. At that time, all social classes offered their support and organized their parties, bringing about a multi-party situation where "assemblies and associations met at frequent intervals, and nearly a hundred parties sprang up like mushrooms after the rain." Sun Yat-sen and other leaders of the Chinese Revolutionary Alliance also emulated the West in pressing for parliamentary democracy and multi-party competition, but their efforts ended in failure.

As Sun had to acknowledge: "The Chinese social tradition which has prevailed for thousands of years is extraordinarily different from that of Europe and America. Since the social nature is different, the politics that are used to manage the society should not be the same. We should not slavishly copy Europe and America." Later on, he began to rethink the future and the strategy of the Chinese revolution, realizing that it was impossible to change Chinese society solely through the strength of the Kuomintang. So he put forward the Three New Principles of the People (alliance with Russia, alliance with the CPC, and giving support to peasants and workers) and began to cooperate with the CPC. But because the right-wing of the Kuomintang betrayed the revolution, the Great Revolution in China ended in failure. Thus began the 22 years of single-party governance by the Kuomintang. When the Anti-Japanese War ended in 1945, the Kuomintang and the CPC held the Chongqing Negotiations, bringing about a system of "multi-party politics" for a second time. They negotiated for 40 days. Ultimately Chiang Kai-shek, the leader of the Kuomintang, said to the CPC: "There cannot be two suns in China's heaven." His words backed the CPC into a corner, and Mao Zedong had to respond: "Then let the people of China make the final decision. One will be retained and the other removed." As a result, the Chinese people retained the CPC.

The system of multiparty cooperation under the leadership of the CPC originated from the Constitutional-Democratic Movement through which the Chinese people mobilized to end the Kuomintang administration during the Anti-Japanese War. In the latter period of the Anti-Japanese War, in order to defeat the Japanese invaders, the CPC proposed an end to the one-party autocracy of the Kuomintang, and the formation of a joint government. This received a positive response and support from all other parties and from the general public. Following victory in the Anti-Japanese War, the CPC made a genuine effort to establish a joint government, but their overtures were rejected by the Kuomintang. The Kuomintang maintained their autocratic rule, resulting in the democratic parties abandoning the "middle line." Thus was created the general situation where the CPC and the democratic parties cooperated with each other and fought together against the Kuomintang reactionaries. On April 21, 1949, the CPC held the Chinese People's Political Consultative Conference (CPPCC) and passed the Common Program, marking the formulation of the system of multiparty cooperation and political consultation under the leadership of the CPC.

After 60 years of country-building and social development, the system of multiparty cooperation and political consultation under the leadership of the CPC as a political system has provided China and its people with an important guarantee for the development of the state and the happiness of the people.

Firstly, this system has contributed significantly to the political stability of China. As was pointed out by Deng Xiaoping: "The question of overriding importance is stability. Without stability, nothing can be done successfully, and what we have achieved will be lost." On the one hand, this system has ensured that there is a supreme modern political authority, promoting modernization and social stability. On the other, it has rallied various forces into the current political system during a period of social transition, and completed and refined the position of the people as masters of the country by providing them with lawful, smooth and institutionalized channels to express and safeguard their interests.

Secondly, it has brought about social integration. With the transition of Chinese society, there has come complexity in the social structure. Social interests and ideas have multiplied, and the relationship between the party and the state or the society has undergone dramatic change. How the CPC achieves the integration of the largest society in the world will have immense significance for both the CPC and the international community. Relying on its strong organizational network, its capacity to allocate social resources, and its aptitude for ideological leadership, the CPC together with democratic parties is engaged in the ideological integration, interest coordination and political identification of various social classes. Finally, it has promoted democratic supervision. That the CPC and democratic parties supervise each other is conducive to enhancing the function of inner-system supervision, thereby avoiding many potential drawbacks. On the one hand, because the democratic parties represent the particular interests and reasonable aspirations of various interested parties, they are able to implement the policies of the CPC in all aspects. On the other hand, because they are able to call on the support and opinions of various classes to supervise the work of the Party and the government, decisions can be made scientifically and democratically.

It should be noted that the two-party and multi-party system had played a positive role in opposing feudal autocracy, but they could not necessarily ensure political democracy, social stability and clean governance. The shortcomings of distributional coalitions characteristic of the two-party or multi-party system are becoming more and more obvious in modern political life. On the one hand, major parties proceed from their own interests to make policies and devise systems. On the other, with social differentiation and diversification, major parties make more broad-based and vaguer policies based on the need to gain the support of the people in election. Additionally, it is ever harder to keep policies consistent, and politics is becoming more money-oriented – precisely the dilemma of the Western system during the global financial crisis. There is a risk of serious damage to the interests of the state and the people if a party transplants a Western political system while neglecting its national conditions. Typical of this is the political disorder prevalent in some of the African countries which implemented the multi-party system under the influence of Western countries after the World War II, and the economic damage and the social instability in some coun-

Emblem of the Chinese People's Political Consultation Conference.

Its symbols include a red star standing for the leadership of proletariat, gear and wheat ears standing for the worker-peasant alliance as the foundation, four red flags standing for the grand coalition of the working class, the peasantry, the urban petty bourgeoisie and the national bourgeoisie, and "1949" standing for the year in which the Chinese People's Political Consultation Conference was born.

---

tries which transplanted the political system of other countries in the 21st century.

Some may take the view that the fact that multi-party system was not feasible in China 100 years ago does not mean it is still not feasible today; the fact that the hopes of the two-party system in China faded after the Anti-Japanese War does not mean it is still not viable today. To this question, Zhou Tienong, the former chairman of the Revolutionary Committee of the Chinese Kuomintang, gave a very interesting answer: "In practice, the current political system has guaranteed political stability and 30 years of economic prosperity in

China. This is a known quantity, but change to another party system will be an unknown quantity. Of course, there are some problems with the known quantity, but in general it is positive and acceptable. Since the known quantity is positive and acceptable, why would we take the risk of picking an unknown quantity to replace it?"

It is for reasons such as those that the Report to the 18th CPC National Congress reiterated: "We should adhere to and improve the system of multiparty cooperation and political consultation under the leadership of the Communist Party of China. Guided by the principles of long-term coexistence, mutual supervision of the various parties, treating each other with all sincerity, and sharing weal and woe, we should strengthen unity and cooperation with the democratic parties and with public figures without party affiliation, and pursue the common goal with unity in thought and action."

Why does China not apply the separation of powers?

In terms of party system, Chinese-style democracy is characterized by the system of multiparty cooperation and political consultation under the leadership of the CPC; in terms of the organizational form for state power or the form of government, it is characterized by the system of National People's Congress built on the basis of democratic centralism. Article 2 of *The Constitution of the People's Republic of China* stipulates: "All power in the People's Republic of China belongs to the people. The National People's Congress and the local people's congresses at various levels are the organs through which the people exercise state power. The people administer state affairs and manage economic, cultural and social affairs through various channels and in various ways in accordance with the law." In other words, the system of the National People's Congress is a form of government in which legislature and administration are combined, instead of a form in which powers are separated into three branches for checks and balances.

Why does China not apply the Western-style system of power separations?

Firstly, the system of the National People's Congress is the choice of the Chinese people in social development, and it is an important outcome of the long-term struggle of all the Chinese people led by the CPC. At the end of the 19th century and the beginning of the 20th century, there were many forms of political system available to China. After the Sino-Japanese War in 1895, with the Qing Dynasty in severe crisis, reformists represented by Kang Youwei (1858-1927) and Liang Qichao (1873-1929) in Qing government tried to turn the feudal autocracy into a constitutional monarchy by reforming culture, politics and education, drafting a constitution and establishing a parliament. The movement proved to be short-lived, ending in a coup d'état ("The Coup of 1898") by powerful conservative opponents led by Empress Dowager Cixi (1835-1908). Thus the Qing government missed the opportunity for reform.

Prior to the 1911 Revolution, Cixi wanted to establish a constitutional monarchy while the revolutionary parties strove to overthrow the autocratic monarchy and establish a republic. After the 1911 Revolution succeeded, the Kuomintang imposed the military administration and then the Instruction administration, but later on Chiang Kai-shek, the leader of the Kuomintang central committee and the top military commander, placed himself above state power and implemented an autocracy. After the Anti-Japanese War, the Kuomintang government convened the "National Congress" and drafted the so-called "constitution" in order to buy time for its preparations for civil war. But the "constitution" was never implemented. When the civil war broke out, Chiang Kai-shek abandoned the National Congress and the constitution. Thus the bourgeois republic also failed in China.

What kind of system in China can absolutely guarantee the position of the people as masters of the country? The responsibility for answering and solving this historical subject fell onto the shoulders of the CPC. Represented by Mao Zedong, they carried out a long-term program to create a new type of people's political power and build its organizational structure by drawing experience from the Paris Commune and the October Revolution according to Marxist state theory. As early as in the periods of the First and the Second Chinese Revolutionary Civil Wars, the CPC created the On-strike Workers' Congress, the Peasants' Association and the Soviet of Worker, Soldier and Peasant Representatives. During the periods of the Anti-Japanese War and the Liberation War, the CPC established the consultative council for people from various classes and the people's conference for all ethnic groups and all walks of life. On the eve of the founding of the People's Republic of China (PRC), the CPC undertook an in-depth review of the development of China's democratic politics and the practice of building a new democratic government in modern times. It highlighted that the government to be established once the new democratic revolution had succeeded would be none other than a people's democratic dictatorship led by the working class and based on the alliance of workers and peasants; the form of government concordant with this form of state would be none other than the National Congress on the basis of democratic centralism.

Secondly, the system of separation of powers does not fit China's national conditions and traditions. What are China's conditions and traditions? Analyzed from the perspective of culture, the Chinese people tend to value collectivism rather than individualism and stress cooperation and unity rather than competition and separation. This is the underlying reason why China has adopted neither the multi-party system, nor the separation of powers. The concept of separation of powers has been devised according to the theory that "power breeds corruption; absolute power breeds absolute corruption." Therefore, there must be a system that separates powers for checks and balances. Such a system refers to a form of government according to which a constitutional government has three separate branches of government: the Legislature, the Executive, and the Judiciary. Each of the three branches will have defined powers to check the powers of the other branches, and the branches of the government are kept distinct in order to prevent abuse of power. Countries with presidential systems have fully implemented this system and the federal government of the United States has done most fully. The head of government in countries with parliamentary systems, comes from the majority in parliament; he/she also holds the legislative power. Therefore, executive power and legislative power are not completely separated. But under these two systems, the judiciary branch keeps independent of the executive and the legislature, so it can administer checks or balances. This system has played a positive role in checking government power and guaranteeing the freedom and the right of citizens. In the process of separating power and creating checks between the branches, conflicts and frictions can easily occur, and this can result in stalemate in government operation. America's "fiscal cliff" is a typical example. If such circumstances were to arise in China, the people would not accept it, because this would mean that they had lost a common authority and a stable living environment.

In the structure of the state prescribed by the constitution, the highest organ of state power is the National People's Congress with the standing committee as its permanent body. It not only has legislative power but also administers checks on the government, the court and the procuratorate. It exercises the function and power of electing the administrative, judicial and procuratorial organs of the state, which are responsible for it and report to it. As is said in the Report to the 18th CPC National Congress: "The CPC, China's leading and governing party, should improve the mechanism for deputies to maintain contact with the people through establishing deputy liaison offices in people's congresses...," and it should "improve the age mix of the members of the standing committees and special committees of people's congresses and widening the areas of their expertise.... This will serve to support and ensure the exercise of state power by the people through people's congresses."

Additionally, the CPC exercises effective leadership of the state power organs and smooth governance inside and outside state power organizations by setting up Party organizations and Party committees in such state organs as congresses, governments, courts and procuratorates and by selecting Party members to occupy leading positions. The relationships between the people's congress, the court and the procuratorate are not those of separating powers and checking the power of the other but a relationship of power organ and administration organ. Chinese culture values the concept that "words must be followed by action, and the result must be achieved." The Chinese people want positive policies to be carried out immediately, and they hate endless debate with no following action. Obviously, a form of government that combines legislature and administration tallies with the people's requirement that words and actions should be consistent.

Thirdly, while China has not adopted a system of separation of powers, it still attaches high importance to the issue of checking and balancing power. During the autocratic period in China, the Confucian scholar official class envisaged and operated an indirect check on the emperor's power through advice and remonstration provided by top officials, and thus a system of imperial censors was set up. The emperor also established his own supervisory system to check the executive power of officials. Through setting up separate branches of supervision and execution, the emperor attempted to fulfill his purpose of controlling the executive power of officials. At one point during the Tang dynasty (618-907), *zhi gao quan* (the decree-issuing power), *feng bo quan* (the decree-examining power) and the executive power were separated in three different branches to allow them to check and balance each other. But reviewing China's history of more than 2,000 years of autocracy, we can see that power tended to concentrate in the hands of the emperor or his institutions.

In the course of the bourgeois democratic revolution, Sun Yat-sen, having accepted the theory of separation of powers and having taken into consideration the prevailing conditions of China, put forward the idea of the Constitution of Five Powers, proposing that the five powers of legislature, execution, judicature, supervision and

In March 2013, deputies to the First Session of the 12th National People's Congress heard the work reports of the president of the Supreme People's Court and the procurator general of the Supreme People's Procuratorate and the explanations of the state councilor and the secretary general of the State Council on plans for reform of the organs of the State Council and the transformation of their functions.

examination should be exercised by five independent branches to allow them to check and balance each other, but the concept was never put into practice.

For a period after the founding of the PRC in 1949, the CPC followed a twisting road in building and improving the leadership system of the Party and state with the principle of democratic centralism as its basis. From 1949 to mid-1950s, the democratic atmosphere in the Party and state life had been lively. After 1957, however, Mao Zedong made the error of extending class struggle when he took different opinions inside and outside the Party as the new development of class struggle. The democratic atmosphere and the principle of democratic centralism were ruined. Thus emerged the centralized leadership system, in which power was centralized in the hands of Party leaders at all levels, especially the top Party leader, and was immune from supervision and checks. It was this immunity from any supervision or check that led Mao to abuse his power and launch the Cultural Revolution, bringing ten years of tragedy and disorder to China.

After 1978, China brought an end to the Cultural Revolution and chose a new path of reform and opening-up. The CPC had come to the understanding that highly-centralized power with no supervision and checks would easily lead to the abuse of power and corruption of the first leader in command. Since then, the CPC has constantly explored mechanisms for separating and checking powers, including separating Party and government, allocating separate powers of personnel, finance and property, and most importantly, enabling the powers of decision-making, administration and supervision to check each other. The reports to the 16th and the 17th CPC National Congresses clearly pointed out: "We must establish a sound structure of power and a mechanism for its operation in which decision-making, enforcement and oversight powers check each other and function in coordination." The Report to the 18th CPC National Congress also stressed: "We should make sure that decision-making, executive, and oversight powers check each other and function in concert and that government bodies exercise their powers in accordance with statutory mandate and procedures."

This has provided policy support to the reform of the political structure in separating powers for checks and balances, and opened ample space for the innovation of the political system. In the future, the policy-making power of the Party committee and the executive power of the government will be guaranteed. At the same time strengthening the supervisory power of congresses and consultative conferences towards the Party committee and government will become a viable means of ensuring that powers of decision-making, execution and supervision check and coordinate each other. Thus China will not walk the old Western path of separating power into three branches for checks and balances, but establish a new principle, with its own characteristics, whereby the powers of decision-making, execution, and supervision are separated for the purposes of checks and balances.

Is law-based governance compatible with the Party's leadership?

China is a country with an age-old tradition of rule by leaders, and the CPC was founded in a situation where there was no democratic form. But the CPC had been exploring the question of how to lead and govern the country for many years. Before seizing power, the CPC had established in the revolutionary base areas the democratic government of workers and peasants, the Anti-Japanese democratic government and the people's democratic government, forming a centralized administrative structure and its corresponding mode of action under the leadership of the CPC. After taking power in 1949, the CPC converted from a political party that had led the revolution to a governing party which held power and led the reconstruction. For the following 17 years, the CPC gradually developed the concept of "putting all under the direct guidance of the Party," and firmly upheld the theory that "policies and strategies are the life of the Party."

In actual practice, the CPC governed the country mainly through the policies of the Party. The CPC not only acted as the core of leadership, but also directly commanded state power organs as the core of public power. Nevertheless, there was still no lack of attention to the idea of governance by law. From the early years of the PRC to the middle and later years of 1950s, Mao Zedong attached great importance to the development of the legal system. He pointed out that the CPC should guarantee the leadership of the Party through the law as well as through its own "lines, policies and principles." In 1954, the first *Constitution of People's Republic of China* stipulated, "All staff of the state organs must be faithful to the democratic system, abide by the constitution and other laws, and serve the people whole-heartedly." It also stipulated, "All citizens of the People's Republic of China are equal before the law." However, as "leftist" thought began to dominate the Party, the development of the fledgling legal system was suffocated.

After China began reform and opening up in 1978, some intellectuals began to argue in favor of the "rule of law" or "law-based governance." This attracted the attention of the CPC leadership. Deng Xiaoping observed that a bad system may prevent a man from doing good deeds and even cause him to do something bad. He also said: "We should see to it that there are laws to abide by, that laws already enacted are observed and enforced to the letter, and that violators are brought to justice." These words have become the core of the socialist legal system. Under the guidance of this principle, in 1982, the 12th CPC National Congress proposed: "We should promote a highly-developed socialist legal system." It also proposed that: "We must integrate socialist democratic development with the development of the socialist legal system, institutionalizing and legalizing the socialist democratic system." The *Constitution of CPC* revised in this congress stipulated: "The Party must conduct its activities within the framework of the Constitution and laws of the country. It must see to it that the legislative, judicial and administrative organs of the state and the economic, cultural and people's organizations work with initiative and independent responsibility and in unison."

By the end of 1982, the National People's Congress passed the current constitution, which is the PRC's fourth. Having affirmed the leading position of the CPC, this constitution stipulated: "The Constitution has the highest legal position. All state organs, the armed forces, all political parties and public organizations and all enterprises and undertakings must abide by the Constitution and the law. All acts in violation of the Constitution and the law must be investigated. No organization or individual may enjoy the privilege of being above the Constitution and the law." At the end of the 1990s, the concept of rule of law officially entered government documents and gradually became the long-term goal for China's political development. In 1997, the Report to the 15th CPC National Congress clearly set itself for the first time the goal of "building a socialist country governed by law." In 1999, at the Second Session of the Ninth National People's Congress, it was written into the Constitution that: "The People's Republic of China practices governing the country in accordance with law and building a socialist country of law." In 2004, at the Fourth Plenary Session of the 16th Central Committee, it was pointed out that "law-based governance is the Party's basic means of governance under new historical conditions." In 2007, the Report to the 17th CPC National Congress again pointed out that: "We need to carry out government administration in accordance with law, and promote the spirit of the rule of law. This is a strategic task that fits the new situation of building a moderately prosperous society in all respects and facilitates promoting law-based governance."

In 2010, the socialist legal system with Chinese characteristics was set up, featuring 230 laws, 690 administrative regulations, and 8,600 local regulations. Since then, the rule of law has taken deep root in the hearts of the Chinese people, and law-based governance has become the basic principle in construction, realizing social fairness and justice, and promoting all-round and sustainable development. The Report to the 18th CPC National Congress stressed that: "The rule of law is the basic mechanism for running the country. We should promote comprehensive law-based governance of the country. We should give greater scope to the important role the rule of law plays in the country's governance and in social management. We should ensure that leading officials are guided by law in both thinking and action in their effort to strengthen reform, promote development, solve problems, and maintain stability." The CPC as the governing party also acts under the constitution and law which is enacted by China's state power organ, the National Congress. How then, many foreign friends wonder, does the CPC exercise its leadership? As has previously been explained, the leadership of the CPC is shown through turning the propositions of the Party into the state law or the state will.

Most legislative organs of other countries are parliaments. In the earliest days of parliamentary government, there was parliament before there was party. It was the parliamentary culture that gave birth to the party. Individual parties exercised their will under the procedure: competing to gain seats through election, forming political groups, putting forward proposals in the interest of the party, and realizing the stance and strategies of the party in important legislative activities. But the governing position of the CPC was determined by history and the people and confirmed by the

Constitution. The relationship between the political parties in the state legislative organ - the National People's Congress - is that between governing party and parties participating in the management of state affairs. The CPC as the governing party holds the leading position, and the other eight parties participate in state affairs; both sides take the socialist direction. This is different from the confrontational mode of Western parties. A little knowledge of the different positions between the governing party and the participating party is a precondition to understanding the contemporary party relationship in China's legislative organ. As distinct from the parliamentary political groups through which Western parties exercise control over legislature, deputies to the National People's Congress are not elected through party competition, but through district-based election. They come from various parties and should be first of all responsible for the people who vote for them. None of the parties in the National People's Congress establish political party groups (The "Party organization" of the CPC established by the Standing Committee of the National People's Congress is different from the Western political group in Western parliament.). Deputies to the National People's Congress from the various parties are equal in status with deputies with no party affiliation, and they attend the Congress not as members of any party but as local deputies who play their role by participating in legislative activities. A little knowledge of the election and position of deputies to the National People's Congress is the second precondition to understanding the contemporary party relationship in China's legislative organ.

With these two preconditions, we can understand why the CPC is different from Western parties in leading and participating in legislative work. The CPC leads legislative work mainly through making major policies, putting forward legislative proposals, recommending key officials, publicizing ideological principles, and giving play to the role of Party organizations and Party members. Thus the propositions of the Party can be turned through legal procedures into the state will and into norms of society as a whole.

The overall legislative plan and key legislative issues of the National People's Congress and its Standing Committee for a defined period are determined according to the arrangements and the proposals of the Central Committee of the CPC. For instance, in 1992, the 14th CPC National Congress established the goal of building a socialist market economy; in 1993 when the Constitution was amended, such important aspects as "developing the socialist market economy" and "enhancing economic legislation and improving macro-economic regulation" were written into the Constitution. In 2002, the 16th CPC National Congress proposed as its goals for the first two decades of the 21st century to build a moderately prosperous society of a higher standard, and to strengthen legislation and improve its quality. Then the Tenth National People's Congress and its Standing Committee, which had tenure from 2003 to 2008, provided the legislative outline with the goal of creating a socialist legal system with Chinese characteristics and with the emphasis on improving the quality of legislation. This fully illustrates that the CPC can influence the formulation of legislative policies and programs, making it possible that the Party's proposals can enter the legislative procedures and become the state will.

Western parties enact statutes mainly through their members exerting their influence on parliament; CPC members should also be in a certain proportion to the deputies to the National People's Congress. Reviewing the composition of the past National People's

Congresses, we can see that on average CPC members account for more than half of the total deputies. As speakers in Western parliaments generally come from the party or the party alliance which has won a majority of seats, key leaders of the Standing Committee of the National People's Congress and the standing committee of congresses at various levels are also recommended by the CPC, with the list submitted to the plenary session of the congress for confirmation. Taking the National People's Congress and its Standing Committee as an example, the list which is directly recommended by the CPC Central Committee includes the chairman, the vice-chairmen, the secretary-general, the vice-secretary-generals, members and the director and the vice-directors of special committees. Of course, a reasonable representation among the vice-chairmen, the vice-secretary-generals and the vice-directors also come from non-communist party deputies or from deputies with no party affiliation. For example, six of the thirteen vice-chairmen of the 12th National People's Congress were from non-communist parties.

Is elective democracy the only legitimate form?

Democracy is the rule of the people or the rule of the majority. In the Chinese context, democracy is called "the position of the people as masters of the state." These are actually the same in meaning. But the way to realize democracy varies from one country to another. If we conduct a research into the variants of democracy around the world, we can find there are three forms. The first one is elective democracy, which is the model that is most often discussed between Western politicians or scholars and China. Its characteristics are that resolutions and laws are enacted, or the person and the party are elected to govern the state through a vote, on the principle that the minority are subject to the will of the majority, and government is executed in accordance with the interests of the majority of voters. The second is negotiation democracy, which is prevalent in international politics and the political structures of many countries. Its characteristic is to share out benefits through negotiation in order to satisfy all sides. The third is consultative democracy. Its characteristic is to reach consensus or to establish the common point or the common interests, in order to make policies applicable to all, through extensive discussion or dialogue on the basis of equal participation in making policies.

The theory of consultative democracy was produced in Western politics in the 1990s as a response to the defects of the free democracy theory and as a compensation for the deficiencies of the majority-determination principle and elective democracy. In elective democracy, which is based on the theory of free democracy, the majority of less prosperous citizens enjoy equality in terms of their vote, but they do not have equal participation in policy-making. This form of democracy also seems to lack the power to resolve deep and extensive moral conflicts in a diversified society. As a democratic policy-making system or a rational policy-making form, consultative democracy enables every citizen to participate equally in making public policies, and to express their opinions and listen freely to others' views.

At present, most Western countries practice elective democracy. But in China the two important forms of Chinese socialist democracy are that the people exercise their power by voting in elections, and that all people achieve consensus about questions of common concern by holding full consultation before important policies are formulated. That is to say, in terms of form, Chinese-style democracy is not a simple elective democracy, but the integration between election and consultation in that both hand (voting) and mouth (consultation) are used, with the latter preceding the former. The socialist democratic political system with Chinese characteristics is one that guarantees the position of the people as masters of the state through "election plus consultation." Improving this democratic political system through a range of measures is an important element of reforming China's political structure. We can see that China's democracy began with the Chinese People's Political Consultative Conference (CPPCC) held in 1949. The CPC, having achieved overwhelming victory in the Liberation War, did not seek to dominate the state power alone, but adopted the form of political consultation on state affairs with other parties and with public figures without any party affiliation, and together they formulated the "Common Program." On the basis of the "Common Program," the central people's government of the PRC was established through election. The ruling position of the CPC was therefore established on the basis of the integration of consultative democracy and elective democracy. Later, under the leadership of Mao Zedong and following an extensive nationwide discussion, the CPC drafted the constitution and held the National People's Congress in accordance with the constitution. This is a form of democracy with Chinese cultural traits.

There are many forms and channels for China's consultative democracy. The Report to the 18th CPC National Congress proposed to promote "extensive, multi-level, and institutionalized development of socialist consultative democracy." The major organ that holds democratic consultation is the Chinese People's Political Consultative Conference (CPPCC). The CPPCC is different from the National People's Congress, and from bodies such as the senate of a Western parliament, and the administrative organs like government and other kinds of social group. It is the Chinese people's united front organization composed of the CPC, the other eight parties, the social groups, deputies from all walks of life and ethnic groups, compatriots from Taiwan, Hong Kong, and Macao, returned overseas Chinese and some specially-invited individuals. It is an important institution for multi-party cooperation and political consultation under the leadership of the CPC. Obviously the CPPCC is a form of consultative democracy, and not all Chinese citizens can participate, but there is direct and equal opportunity for participation by representative citizens or by broadly representative citizen groups. Therefore, this is a form of consultative democracy with Chinese characteristics appropriate to the fact that China is the most populous country.

At present, the CPC, proceeding from the prevailing national conditions, is trying to improve the democratic political structure with Chinese characteristics by seamlessly integrating elective democracy and consultative democracy. First of all, the CPC will continue to develop elective democracy: (1) improving direct electoral processes within citizen self-governing organizations; (2) expanding multi-candidate election and improving the mechanisms for candidate nomination in those local governments or institutions where indirect election is practiced; (3) gradually expanding direct election to leading bodies of primary-level Party organizations.

At the same time, the CPC is committed to improving the mechanisms of consultative democracy:

(1) adhering to and improving the system of multiparty cooperation and political consultation under the leadership of the CPC, making the CPPCC serve as a major channel for conducting consultative democracy, and focusing on the themes of unity and democracy in order to improve systems of political consultation, democratic oversight, and participation in the deliberation and administration of state affairs, and to deliver improved results in coordinating relations, pooling strengths, and making proposals in the overall interests of the country;

(2) making political consultation a part of the policy-making process, conducting consultations before policy decisions are made and during the process of decision-making, and making democratic consultation more effective;

(3) conducting intensive consultation on the handling of proposals affecting special issues with those who work on these issues, with representatives from all sectors of society, and with relevant government authorities;

(4) carrying out active and basic democratic consultation. The CPC will progressively improve the system of democratic symposium and hearings currently held at all levels of government, giving full play to the role of people's groups in democratic consultation.

Whether the issue is elective democracy or consultative democracy, there are problems to be studied, and both forms need to be improved in practice. But this improvement is a process, and should not be carried out in haste. More than 2,000 years ago, the ancient Chinese sage Lao Zi pointed out in his *Dao De Jing* (*Classic of Way and Virtue*), "Ruling a large kingdom is indeed like cooking small fish." He meant that a cook must have good skills and do the cooking slowly, and a country can be ruled well only if it is done cogently, carefully, and properly. His words express a high abstraction of the acute intelligence of Chinese political civilization developed over thousands of years. Reviewing the past three decades of reform and opening-up, we notice that the reform of China's political structure has advanced steadily.

In the following list, we can see the steps of China's democratic political development and the values pursued in reforming its political structure. We should not consider so-called democratization as the exclusive means of reforming the political structure, nor should copying the Western political system be seen as the exclusive road to such reform. The correct approach is that we should proceed from China's prevailing national conditions and cultural traditions to push forward active and steady reform, neither acting in haste nor stubbornly adhering to past practice. The general direction should be to follow the strategic plan formulated by the 18th National Congress of the CPC: "We should place greater emphasis on improving the way the Party exercises leadership and governance. We should attach greater importance to improving the system of democracy. We should give greater scope to the important role the rule of law plays in the country's governance and in social management. We must ensure the unity of the leadership of the Party, the position of the people as masters of the country and law-based governance."

Democracy: When China began reform and opening-up, Deng Xiaoping, in *Adhering to the Four Cardinal Principles*, proposed: "Without democracy, there will be no socialism and there will be no socialist modernization." In 2002, the Report to the 16th CPC National Congress proposed, "We should extend socialist democracy"; in 2004, "Democratic governance" was advanced; in

2007, the Report to the 17th CPC National Congress asserted: "People's democracy is the lifeblood of socialism."

Rule of law: When China began reform and opening-up, the concept of "legal system" was used. In 1997, the 15th CPC National Congress determined to take "governing the country by law and building a socialist country ruled by law" as the basic strategy for governing the country, and this was written into the Constitution when it was revised in 1999. In 2004, the State Council circulated the *Outlines of Pushing Forward the Law-based Governance in an All-round Way*.

Clean government: Since China began reform and opening-up, curbing corruption has been a priority. Since 1992, even more attention has been paid to the problem of corruption. In 1999, the report on the work of government proposed to build a clean government. The year 2008 saw the circulation of the *Working Plan for Building and Promoting the System for Punishing and Preventing Corruption from 2008 to 2012*.

Transparency: In 1998, the system of publicizing village affairs and managing villages democratically began in rural areas nationwide. In 2008, *Regulations on Publicizing Government Information* was introduced.

Participation: In 2000, the Fifth Plenary Session of the 15th Central Committee passed the *Suggestions of the CPC Central Committee for Making the Tenth Five-year Plan for Economic and Social Development*, proposing for the first time to "expand the political participation of citizens in order and lead the people to manage their own affairs in accordance with the law." In 2007, the 17th CPC National Congress proposed: "We must ensure that all power of the state belongs to the people, expand orderly participation of the public in political affairs at each level and in every field, and mobilize and organize the people as extensively as possible to manage state and social affairs as well as economic and cultural programs in accordance with the law."

Service: In 1994, the construction committee of Yantai City, Shandong Province, took the initiative of implementing the service responsibility system. From 1992 onwards, strengthening the service-providing function of government has gained strength. This goal was emphasized in the report of the central government in 2005.

Responsibility: From 2003 onwards, responsible government has been a priority. On September 4, 2006, Premier Wen Jiabao spoke of strengthening the institutions of government to improve innovation and encourage responsibility. In 2005, at the summit meeting to celebrate the 60th anniversary of the United Nations, Hu Jintao said that China would become a responsible country in developing a harmonious world.

Cooperation: In 2004, in *Decisions on Increasing the Governing Capacity of the CPC,* the Fourth Plenary Session of the 16th Central Committee of the CPC put forward the principle that "the Party commands the overall situation and coordinates the efforts of all quarters." This principle is regarded as the first expression of the "cooperation" theory, which was later developed through such actions as "developing consultative politics," "constructing communities" and "participating in international cooperation."

Harmony: In 2002, the 16th National Congress of the CPC advanced the proposal that the goal behind building a moderately prosperous society was "a more harmonious society." In 2006, the Sixth Plenary Session of the 16th National Congress of the CPC passed the *Decisions on Major Issues of Building a Socialist Harmonious Society*, placing harmony side by side with prosperity, democracy, and civilization as the goals of building a modern country.

System building: When China began reform and opening-up, Deng Xiaoping pointed out the difference between the functions of a good system and a bad one; in 2002, the Report to the 16th CPC National Congress put forward relevant "procedures"; the 17th CPC National Congress advanced the proposition that: "We must maintain the features and advantages of the socialist political system and define institutions, standards and procedures for socialist democracy"; the 18th CPC National Congress proposed: "We should place high importance on systemic building."

How do the Chinese people participate in and deliberate on state affairs?

With the rapid development of China's economy, the material living standards and the educational level of the people are rising steadily, as is their enthusiasm for participating in and deliberating on state affairs. How to satisfy a growing public need for political participation has long been a major subject for CPC reflection and study. In recent years, China has conducted extensive research into this topic, and has achieved positive results.

Firstly, China has extended the coverage of deputies to people's congresses. According to the Constitution, the electoral law of people's congresses and the deputy law of people's congresses, all citizens of the People's Republic of China who have reached the age of 18 have the right to vote and stand for election, regardless of ethnic group, race, sex, occupation, family background, religious belief, education, property status, or length of residence, except persons deprived of political rights in accordance with the law.

But in practice, from 1953, when the first election law was enacted, to 1995, the population/deputy ratio between rural and urban areas was 8:1. In 1995, the Standing Committee of the National People's Congress revised the election law, improving the ratio to 4:1. In March 2010, the Third Session of the 11th Central Committee improved the ratio to 1:1. That is, urban and rural deputies to people's congresses are now elected on the basis of the same population ratio. This undoubtedly enables the rural citizens who once accounted for 80% of the total Chinese population and nowadays 49% to enjoy more equal and more extensive rights to participate in state affairs. The Report to the 18th CPC National Congress proposed: "The proportion of primary-level deputies to people's congresses, particularly those elected from among workers, farmers and intellectuals on the front lines of various fields should be raised, while that of deputies chosen from the ranks of leading Party and government officials should be reduced." Of the deputies to the 12th National People's Congress, 401 are front-line workers and farmers, accounting for 13%, an increase of five percentage points compared with that of the 11th National People's Congress; 610 are professionals, accounting for 20%, an increase of just over one percentage point; 699 are women, accounting for 23%, an increase of two percentage points; 1,042 are Party cadres, accounting for 35%, a decrease of seven percentage points.

Secondly, a legal framework has been established for the people to participate in legislation and policy-making. In 2000, the National People's Congress passed the *Legislation Law*, stipulating that there must be public participation in the process of legislation. In the wake, provinces, municipalities, and autonomous regions adopted similar local laws and regulations, stipulating that public opinion should be openly elicited in drafting official documents, and that public participation is a necessary procedure in shaping important policies. Moreover, before major administrative policies being made, in-depth research should be conducted, experts should be organized for consultation and approval, and extensive opinion from all sides should be sought and given full consideration. Information such as which opinions have been taken, and the reasons why, should be fed back or publicized in a proper form. The hearing system in major administrative policy-making should be improved, and its scope should be expanded, to guarantee the listening process in making administrative policies. Hearings should be organized on administrative policy-making or any other policy-making concerning major public interests or the immediate interests of the people in accordance with the relevant laws, regulations and stipulations. To ensure the implementation of the stipulation that the public should participate, some local governments even include the solicitation of public opinion in their system of government performance evaluation. For instance, in 2011 Sichuan Province established the *Evaluation Criteria of Administration by Law for the Provincial, Municipal and County Governments, Sichuan Province*. The second and third articles of the Criteria stipulate that the solicitation of public opinion should account for 9% in government performance evaluation.

Thirdly, increased public participation has been encouraged in electing and appointing cadres. In 1997, China enacted the *Organic Law of Village Committees*, which stipulates that the village committee, the management body of village affairs, should be elected by the villagers. At the same time, the competitive election in which all candidates are nominated by villagers was introduced. Of 700,000 villages in China, about 60% have adopted this new form of election. Following pilot operations over seven years, China issued the *Regulations on the Work of Selecting and Appointing Leading Party and Government Cadres* in 2002, which stipulates that there must be a procedure of democratic evaluation in electing and appointing leading Party and government, that is, the people's opinion should be taken into consideration. In this process of evaluation, those who cannot achieve the required degree of support cannot be selected as candidates for leading posts.

Fourthly, the channels through which the people participate in legislation and policy-making have been constantly enriched. There are five main channels through which the public participate in legislation and major policy-making: (1) participating in hearing meetings; (2) putting forward suggestions through letters, e-mails and internet BBS; (3) attending forums held by legislative and decision-making organs; (4) selecting legislative programs and policy-making plans through Internet voting; (5) participating in drafting laws.

In 1999, Jiangsu Province for the first time sought open opinions from the public on its draft regulations. In the same year, the Standing Committee of the People's Congress of Jiangsu Province publicized the *Draft Management Regulation on the Labor Force Market of Jiangsu Province*, and sought open opinions from the public. By the end of 2007, that committee had issued 12 draft regulations on labor contracts, collection of social insurance fees, wage payment, the protection of rural land contracts and management rights, prevention and handling of accidents among primary and middle school students, voluntary service, promotion of small

In May 2013, Beijing Municipality held a hearing on adjusting taxi fares. Twenty-five representatives attended the hearing, which include representatives of consumers, enterprises and drivers and those from governmental departments and social organizations.

and medium enterprises, production safety, road traffic safety, city appearance and environmental sanitation management, prevention and cure of ambient noise pollution, and prevention of crimes involving abuse of privilege. Since 2008, public opinion has been sought for all draft laws and regulations.

At state level, in 2008, the Standing Committee of the National People's Congress passed seven laws and examined 17 draft laws, and the State Council issued 30 administrative regulations. Of these, 11 draft laws were publicized, and opinions from the public were elicited through various channels. More than 7,000 opinions were received in the process of examining the draft of the *Law of the People's Republic of China on Protecting Against and Mitigating*

Earthquake Disasters (2008 Revision). Among these, opinions recommending an increase in state activities encouraging and leading volunteers to participate in the relevant activities, and recommending the emergency publication and education of relevant knowledge and emergency drills in government organs, social groups, enterprises and public institutions, have been absorbed into the enactment of the law. In the process of examining the *Food Safety Law (Draft)*, 11,300 opinions were received. Among these, opinions concerning streamlining the system of food security supervision, multi-level management of food sales, food recall, and the management of dietary supplements, were carefully studied, and corresponding articles of the law were revised.

Facts prove that public participation in legislation and major policy-making has produced positive effects. In March 2003, Sun Zhigang, a youth from Hubei Province died in suspicious circumstances in a Guangzhou penitentiary hospital. In April 25, the *South Metropolitan Daily* reported this event, which immediately provoked considerable discussion on the Internet and attracted the attention of central and local governments. On May 12, all 18 culprits from six provinces were arrested, prosecuted and sentenced. On June 4, Guangzhou government announced that 23 officials were removed from their posts or given a demerit because they shared some responsibility for Sun's death. Pressed by the media and some legal scholars, the State Council ended the two-decade-old system of internment and deportation on June 20 and at the same time promulgated the *Measures for Internment and Deportation of Urban Vagrants and Beggars*. In less than three months, an old law was annulled and a new one was enacted. This demonstrated the enormous force of the people in participating in state affairs.

The Roadmap of the 18th
CPC National Congress
and The Chinese Dream

Chapter 7

How Should Its People Build China into a Cultural Power?

To comprehensively complete the building of a prosperous society and achieve the great renewal of the Chinese nation, we must create a new surge in promoting socialist culture and bring about its great development and enrichment, improve China's cultural soft power, and bring into play the role of culture in guiding social trends, educating the people, serving society, and boosting development.

— Report to the 18th CPC National Congress

China is a country with a profound wealth of resources and deposits of tradition and culture. However, because there has been a modern tendency to regard traditional culture as an important contributory factor to China's backwardness, traditional culture had found itself being neglected or discarded. It is undeniable that the CPC made a major mistake in this area. But, from the start of reform and opening-up, and particularly since the beginning of the new century, as the status and role of culture have become more and more prominent in terms of international profile and image, the CPC has attached increasing importance to culture. In 2002, it was proposed at the 16th CPC National Congress that, in order to comprehensively build a prosperous society, we must vigorously develop socialist culture and promote the progress and prosperity of socialist culture. In 2007, the 17th CPC National Congress raised cultural construction to an unprecedentedly important position. It proposed to strengthen the construction of China's cultural soft power and promote the healthy development of Chinese culture. In October 2011, the Sixth Plenary Session of the 17th CPC Central Committee was devoted to discussing culture. It deliberated and adopted the *Decision of the CPC Central Committee on Several Important Issues on Deepening the Reform of Cultural System and Promoting the Grand Development and Prosperity of Socialist Culture* and set the strategic goal of building socialist cultural power. In November 2012, it emphasized once again the need to work practically and steadily to create socialist cultural power. This emphasis on culture attracted extensive attention both in China and abroad. Outside the CPC there was a general interest in why China was dedicating so much attention to culture, and what a culturally powerful China would mean to the world.

What kind of a cultural power does China want to become?

When the international community hears China speak of becoming a cultural power, some instinctively picture a situation in which Chinese culture fills every corner of the world, and they connect this image with the "China Threat" theory. In fact, the word "powerful" here should be interpreted in contrast to "weak." The reason that the CPC proposes building a socialist cultural power is mainly because of the consideration that, although China is a country of ancient civilization and a wealth of cultural resources, these were not being adequately presented, and its rich cultural heritage was not being fully utilized. If timely measures to address the problem were not taken, it might even be possible that at some point in the future, China's cultural resources would disappear. Culture is the blood line of a nation and the soul of its people. Without the positive guidance of culture, without the exceptional wealth of the moral world of the people, and without the moral power of the whole nation being utilized to its fullest extent, a country cannot stand out among the many nations in the world.

At present, the world is experiencing a period of major developments, major changes, and major adjustments. Processes of communication, convergence, and conflict between various ideologies and cultures are becoming increasingly frequent. The status and role of culture are increasingly prominent in the international arena. The task of ensuring the health of a nation's culture becomes more difficult and arduous. Strengthening China's cultural soft power and the international influence of Chinese culture is of growing importance. A prosperous and flourishing Chinese culture must be an essential element of realizing socialist modernization. However, the practical situation is that Chinese culture struggles to adapt to the developments and changes taking place in other important areas of life in China. Weak links and imperfections become apparent. It is urgent that these problems be addressed through deepening reform. The CPC has proposed building a cultural power, for both practical reasons and for the purpose of strengthening China's self-confidence, self-awareness and self-improvement . This can be seen from the CPC's approach to and structuring of its objectives in building a cultural power.

At the Sixth Plenary Session of the 17th CPC Central Committee, six objectives were proposed on cultural reform and development by 2020.

Namely, advance the construction of core socialist values and further advocate fine ethics and customs. There is a remarkable improvement in the cultural qualities of the general public. There is a greater wealth of cultural products adapted to the needs of the people. Works of great quality and masterpieces emerge steadily, and cultural initiatives prosper. A comprehensive system of public culture is emerging, and the culture industry is becoming a pillar industry. Its overall strength and international image are enhanced. Diverse forms of ownership, public and private, coexist in harmony. Management and output of cultural products are vigorous and efficient. Culture is opening up, and on the basis of the national culture, which plays the dominant role, foreign cultures are introduced and absorbed, and Chinese culture is promoted to the world. Schools of high-quality cultural talent guarantee the future prosperity and development of culture.

Chapter 7
How Should Its People Build China into a Cultural Power?

> **At the 18th CPC National Congress, four aspects of cultural development were emphasized**
>
> Strengthening core socialist values, comprehensively improving the ethical quality of the public, enriching the moral and cultural life of the people, and enhancing the overall strength and competitiveness of culture.

When expressed in popular language, these are: First, people should have ideals, convictions, and morality. They should not always put money before everything, indulge themselves in material pleasures, and neglect all spiritual pursuits. Second, people of talent should constantly produce and distribute works of quality. At present, there are many cultural products, but there are also some bad ones among the good. If this situation does not change, it will cause damage to people's values. Third, public culture must be improved, and action must be taken to redress the imbalance in cultural development between the city and the countryside and between different regions. Fourth, the contribution of the cultural industry to the overall economy must increase. In the USA, the cultural industry currently accounts for 25% of total GDP. In Japan, this figure is 20%. In China, it is only 2.5%. Fifth, Chinese cultural products must be internationally competitive. According to the blue paper *Annual Report on China's Cultural Soft Power Research 2010*, the USA holds 43% of the world's culture market, the EU holds 34%, and China holds less than 4%. Sixth, high-quality cultural talents must be cultivated. Seventh, in order to guarantee that culture serves the people, the government should take the lead in building a public cultural service in which publicly-owned enterprises are the main development agent.

These objectives and measures represent no threat at all towards others. The development of cultural power should be seen as an initiative designed to achieve a steady improvement in people's ideals, convictions and moral condition which mirrors their improving economic prospects, to gradually strengthen public cultural undertakings, and to gradually strengthen the position of Chinese culture stronger relative to US and European culture.

Will an emphasis on core values affect cultural diversity?

The relationship between cultural diversity and core values is an issue that every country needs to address in building cultural power. A culturally powerful country must be a country that adheres to and promotes cultural diversity, and also a country that adheres to and promotes its core values. If a country only develops a mono-culture, there will be no real cultural prosperity. If there are many kinds of culture in a country but it does not have core values, then it will be like a person who does not have a soul, and its prospects will be limited. Therefore it was proposed in the Report to the 18th CPC National Congress that in order to build a socialist cultural power, China should adhere to the guideline of "letting a hundred flowers bloom and a hundred schools of thought contend" and to the direction of "serving the people and serving socialism." The first half of the proposition refers to promoting cultural diversity and the second half to adhering to core values.

According to the guideline of "letting a hundred flowers bloom and a hundred schools of thought contend," the key in building a socialist cultural power is "strengthening the creative dynamism of the entire nation and letting all sources of cultural creation fully exert their functions." The expressions of "the entire nation" and "all" are used in an emphatic manner in the Report to the 18th CPC National Congress. For a country that consists of 56 ethnic groups, this means strengthening the creative dynamism of both the Han majority and the ethnic minorities. Outsiders need not worry that China might overlook the development of minority ethnic culture. It is clear that 5,000 years of experience has made the Han culture the foundation of traditional Chinese culture. However, from the time when the First Qin Emperor unified China in 221 B.C., the majority of the Chinese central regimes operated a policy of "rule according to local customs" with regard to minority ethnic groups. Under the premise of realizing political unification, they would retain the existing social systems and cultural practices of minority ethnic groups. In the process of the generational transfer and growth of the Han culture in China, the cultures of minority nationalities in various parts of China have always been important components and have always provided nourishment to the Han culture. Early in the period of the Han and Tang dynasties, the regions of the Central Plains attached great importance to absorbing the splendid cultures of the western regions. After Zhang Qian's diplomatic mission to the western regions, people in the Han Dynasty drew the image of the ostrich, which came from the western regions, onto the walls of their palaces to show their appreciation of the cultures of the western regions. Soon after the grape was introduced from the western regions, carvings of grapes appeared in the emperor's mausoleum. These examples demonstrate that China had already formed an attitude of tolerance, absorption and integration towards the cultures of minority ethnic groups, rather than one of exclusion.

Modern Chinese society attaches great importance to the protection and inheritance of the cultures of minority ethnic groups and their integration with the culture of the Han ethnic group. It is stipulated in the *Constitution of the People's Republic of China* that the state should help minority ethnic groups to accelerate the development of cultural undertakings based on their characteristics and needs. Through various policies and measures, the Chinese government respects and protects the cultures of minority ethnic groups, supports the bequest, development and innovation of the cultures of minority ethnic groups, and encourages the ethnic groups to strengthen cultural communication and to develop the prosperity of their own cultural undertakings.

In recent years, the Chinese government has further strengthened its protective measures. In 2002, the State Council made the *Decision on Strengthening Reform and Accelerating Education Related to Minority Ethnic Groups* and subsequently took comprehensive and appropriate actions. In 2005, it was specifically emphasized in the *Compendium on the 11th Five-year Plan on the Development of the Educational Undertakings of the State* that people should give preference to regions of minority ethnic groups in the resources and funds provided to public education. It was noted in *Several Opinions of the State Council on Further Promoting the Prosperity and Development of the Cultural Undertakings of Minority Ethnic Groups* in 2009 that by 2020, there would be relatively complete cultural infrastructure in regions of minority ethnic groups and a basic public cultural service system that covers minority ethnic groups and regions of minority ethnic groups. It was further proposed in this document that the government should provide funds to regions of minority ethnic groups to implement a series of cultural projects and programs, par-

> At present, there are 55 minority ethnic groups in China, speaking over 80 languages. With the exception of the Hui and Manchu ethnic groups, all the ethnic groups have their own ethnic languages. At important national political occasions in China like the CPC National Congress and the National People's Congress, translation and interpretation services are provided in seven minority ethnic languages: Mongolian, Tibetan, Uygur, Kazak, Korean, Yi and Zhuang. There are 154 radio and television broadcasters using minority ethnic languages in the autonomous administrative areas of the minority ethnic groups. China's central and local radio stations broadcast in 21 minority ethnic languages. Each of the 55 minority ethnic groups has its own colleges for its students. The number of college students per ten thousand population in a dozen of the minority ethnic groups, including the Uygur, Hui, Korean, and Naxi ethnic groups, has already exceeded the average national standard. China has established a national group and general office to plan the collation and publishing of ancient books of the minority ethnic groups and carried out collection, sorting, and protection of these works. The list of national intangible cultural heritage published by the State Council includes all 55 minority ethnic groups. Thirty-five of the 55 minority ethnic groups in China have researched and collated their own medical literature. As a result, ethnic minority medicine has been developed and applied extensively.

ticularly those that might produce cultural and artistic works of excellence that could highlight the features of minority ethnic groups. It should also provide funds to the general population among the minority ethnic groups to create and produce more and better cultural products adapted to the demands of their consumers. The Chinese government will provide support in the form of policy, human resources, and funds, in the areas of language, education, cultural heritage protection, ethnic customs and traditions, and protect the environment for such projects and programs.

Of course, cultural diversity does not only refer to respecting and developing the cultures of minority ethnic groups. It also covers many other aspects, such as borrowing and absorbing from other cultures. But cultural diversity does not mean mindless accumulation of worthless paraphernalia. There must be purpose to the

A class in Lhasa Elementary School in Tibet, photographed by Paul Keene from the UK.

Both Chinese and Tibetan are teaching languages in all the elementary schools in rural and husbandry areas, and in some of the towns in Tibet. Main courses are taught in Tibetan.

process. Otherwise there is a risk that one country might abuse its cultural influence to interfere with another for malicious purposes. That is to say, the cultural diversity of a country must be established on the basis of an established philosophy and set of values. Only in this way can people ensure that the culture of this country progresses rather than regresses.

When reviewing the historical development of human society, clear evidence can be seen of a dominant ideology in any country or region at any time, which includes values, ethical codes, ideals and convictions. Such ideology reflects the interests of the dominant elite of that society. This group adheres to, carries forward, and exploits their culture to oppose or influence other non-mainstream ideologies, values and beliefs and thereby maintain their established interests. The dominant ideology in a society is generally a guiding thought that is unitary rather than diversified. It is not only the subjective demand of the development of human society but also the objective reflection of social development that people adhere to a singular guiding thought in a society.

In China, the dominant guiding thought is the system of socialist core values. The Report to the 18th CPC National Congress expounded on the core elements in this values system from the three perspectives of state, society and citizen. "We should promote prosperity, democracy, civility, and harmony, uphold freedom, equality, justice and the rule of law, and advocate patriotism, dedication, integrity, and friendship so as to cultivate and respect core socialist values." This is the specific embodiment of the idea that culture "serves the people and socialism." It is also the specific interpretation of the national spirit, the spirit of the time, patriotism, collectivism, and socialism in modern China.

Can cultural freedom and cultural responsibility be unified?

Freedom is a beautiful word. It is a goal of life pursued by many. The bourgeoisie take "liberty, equality and charity" as their ideals and values. Hungarian poet Petőfi Sándor wrote a well-known poem: "Life is dear; love is dearer. Both can be given up for freedom." Communists love freedom and many revolutionary martyrs have died in its pursuit. It is stipulated in China's Constitution that the Chinese citizens enjoy freedom of speech, of press, and of religious belief. In order to realize the grand development and prosperity of the socialist culture, people must liberate and develop cultural activity and "carry forward democracy in academic study and art." But freedom is not anarchy, and is far removed from doing as one pleases. Freedom is connected to self-discipline, rule of law and responsibility. Jean Jacques Rousseau said, "Man is born free and everywhere he is in chains." So if culture fails to clearly realize its responsibility and follow core values, it will lose any sense of discipline, and like a boat with no crew will sooner or later end up on the rocks. The East and the West share the same idea on this issue. But while the West takes the individual as the starting point and lays its stress on freedom, the East takes the collective as the starting point and lays more stress on responsibility. In the end, they will reach the same goal by different means.

Some foreign friends are concerned about whether China has any genuine cultural freedom, arguing that China does not have the freedom in the press, in religion, or on the Internet. In fact, many of their concerns are based on misunderstandings. On the issue of religion, it is stipulated in China's Constitution that citizens have the freedom of religious belief. But the Constitution stresses two aspects. On the one hand, it says, "No state organ, public organization or individual may compel citizens to believe in, or not to believe in, any religion." On the other hand, it says, "The state protects normal religious activities. No one may make use of religion to engage in activities that disrupt public order, impair the health of citizens or interfere with the educational system of the state." The former means that freedom of religious belief also includes the freedom of not believing in any religion. The latter stipulates the social responsibilities that religious believers must respect. If people want to uphold core values, both are indispensable.

In recent years, the Communist Party of China and the Chinese government have done much work in safeguarding religious belief and guaranteeing the freedom of religious belief. For example, the Chinese Islamic Association has since 1985 taken the responsibility of organizing the hajj pilgrimages of Chinese Muslims going to Saudi Arabia at their own expense. Since 2007, it has organized travel for over ten thousand people each year. At present, there are over 1,700 facilities in Tibet for Buddhist activities and for over 46,000 monks and nuns to live in. There are over 24,300 mosques and 29,000 clerical staff in Xinjiang. In 2004, China promulgated the *Regulations on Religious Affairs*. The regulations are intended to guarantee the citizens' freedom of religious belief, maintain religious and social harmony, and regulate the management of religious matters. In the area of judicial guarantee, China has also made specific regulations punishing infringements of the right to freedom of religious belief.

Representatives of the international community, particularly people of vision in the West, are gradually coming to an understanding of Chinese policy on the freedom of religious belief, and offering

In June 2013, believers stood before the Id Kah Mosque, the largest Muslim mosque in Xinjiang, in the city of Kashgar in the Xinjiang Uygur Autonomous Region.

their support. In September 2009, Xinjiang independence protagonist Rabiye Qadir misrepresented the religious policy of the Chinese government at the European Parliament Subcommittee of Human Rights. Nirj Deva, parliament member from the UK and chairman of the EU-China Friendship Group of the European Parliament, refuted Rabiye's claims. He pointed out that if these were true and the Chinese government was oppressing Uygur people, depriving them of their freedom of religious belief, and trying to destroy their language and culture, how then could Rabiye, as a Uygur, became a millionaire and be elected as a member of China's CPPCC National Committee? How could she give birth to 11 children? How could she make a speech in fluent Uygur denouncing China at the European Parliament? Rabiye had no answer. In June 12-20, 2009, Patrick Fluckiger, news director of *L'Alsace* in France, traveled to Tibet for a one-week visit. After returning to France, he published a series of articles titled *A Province That the Chinese People Dream of, From Tradition to Modernity*, and *A Popular Slogan: Build Up Family Fortunes and Enrich Oneself*. He recounted his experiences in these articles on Tibet, and described what he saw and heard there. In particular, he was positive about the current conditions on freedom of religious belief. On December 18, 2008, the *Straits Times* in Singapore published a commentary saying that the number of Christians was growing rapidly in China. Many Christians have more freedom to carry out their religious activities. All of this indicates that the Chinese government is giving the people more freedom in religion.

There are always different voices and understandings in the international community on the issue of freedom of religious belief. There are often disputes even within certain countries on how much freedom of religious belief the government of a country should and can allow. One typical example is an act proposed by Marianne Thieme, political leader of the Party for the Animals in the Netherlands. It requires that all animals must be stunned before slaughter. The act brought Islamic and Jewish religious leaders together to defend their religious freedom, because their dogma forbids eating animals that are unconscious when slaughtered. Thieme put forward the view that "religious freedom stops where human or animal suffering begins." The Dutch parliament gave religious leaders one year to prove that the slaughter method prescribed in their religious canon would not cause more suffering to animals than the stun-and-slaughter method. If they could not prove it, the stun-and-slaughter provision would take effect. Peter Singer, professor of Bioethics at Princeton University and a laureate professor at the University of Melbourne, observed that there should be proper limits to religious freedom. The world should prevent the concept of religious freedom from being abused.

In the area of the freedom of the press, China lays stress on both freedom and responsibility. It is specifically stipulated in Article 35 of the *Constitution of the People's Republic of China* that citizens have freedom of speech and of the press. Citizens have the right to criticize and make suggestions regarding any state organ or functionary. China protects freedom of speech in accordance with the law. In the past decade, the Chinese media has gone through many changes. As China has moved towards a market economy, many newspapers and periodicals have become more market-oriented. They have tried to increase the readability of their publications so as to increase circulation and expand profits.

China Central Television has a very popular program called "Topics in Focus." The reason for the popularity of this program is that they conduct various types of in-depth survey and reporting, including introducing the dark side of the society to the audience, such as corruption and other social issues. Many provincial television stations have followed suit and are producing similar survey programs. This indicates that the Chinese media are making progress in guaranteeing the rights of the citizens to know, to participate, to express, and to supervise. In 2011, China published a total of 369,523 books, 9,849 periodicals, 1,928 newspapers, 9,931 audio products, 9,477 video products, and 11,154 digital publications. It has 2,607 broadcasting facilities including 197 radio stations, 213 television stations, 2,153 radio and television stations, and 44 education television stations. Without a good policy and social environment, it would be impossible for such positive progress to be made in China's press and publication industry.

However, China opposes the freedom of press that produces unscrupulous information that has not been proved accurate and cannot stand the test of fact. It requires that the news media establish a high degree of social responsibility and promote the truthful, accurate, comprehensive and objective communication of news information. In the view of the CPC, the media has a responsibility to guide social opinion. It has an increasingly profound impact on various aspects of people's thought, work and life. If the view of the media becomes biased to the extent that they cannot report events and phenomena truthfully, accurately, comprehensively and objectively, they can very easily influence the social order and cause social turbulence. In China, there have indeed been instances where media reports that were not accurate and objective caused the distortion of facts and resulted in negative influences. In such cases, the Chinese government requires that the news media become clearly aware of their responsibility and refrain from spreading false information. Chinese laws stipulate that news media cannot be operated free of restraint by private entities. The main consideration for this stipulation is because they might not be able to meet their social responsibilities.

Some Western governments and media regularly criticize China for interfering in the freedom of the press. However, there is plenty of information to show that they are practicing double standards. At present, a very small number of media giants in the West, relying on their own prodigious financial resources, provide news to a much broader range of other media around the world which have to purchase their international news from the giants due to their own limited financial resources. Thus these media become the speakers or amplifiers of these Western media. Over 90% of the international news disseminated around the world is provided by Western media. Of this, news from Associated Press, Reuters and Agence France Presse accounts for four fifths. As a result, the world's attention is directed by Western media giants towards the places that it chooses. The voices of the media from the extensive community of developing countries are overlooked, suppressed, or drowned out. The freedom of the press is not absolute even in the West. On major issues the press submits completely to government and serves its interests. In the book *News That Matters: Television and American Opinion*, the authors Shanto Iyengar and Donald R. Kinder pointed out that there was a distinctive feature of being a stenographer of the government and mainstream ideology when US television news presented society and politics in the USA. It is specifically pointed out in the book *Black List*, co-authored by 15 American reporters, that the USA's freedom of press is in danger.

The next issue is freedom on the Internet. In recent years, the Internet and other new media have seen rapid development in China. By the end of 2012, the number of Chinese web users had reached 564 million and Internet penetration was 42.1%. The growth rate of mobile phone networks in China comfortably surpassed traditional networks. The number of mobile phone web users was 420 million, showing an annual growth of 18.1% and accounting for 74.5% of the total of web users. The emergence of the Internet facilitates public participation in and supervision of democracy.

Wang Meng, a famous Chinese writer, once said: "In China, it is often web users who first reveal and attack wrongdoers and wrongdoings. State leaders have started to use the web to interact with web users directly, which is a good thing." But what is worthy of attention is that the emergence of the Internet and other new media also has negative influences. Some messages on the web, particularly untruthful information published on microblogs and mobile phone SMS messages, spread quickly and without verification and supervision. These messages may cause confusion to public opinion or even affect social stability.

For example, the riots that occurred in London, UK, in August 2011 had much to do with the lack of supervision over new media, and the rapid spread of rumors. A 25-year-old young man named Jamie Counsel created a webpage on Facebook entitled "Bring the Riots to Cardiff" and encouraged people to start riots in the center of that city. He claimed that it was just a joke and "a windup for all those who were posting messages saying how terrible the rioters were." But he was then arrested by the police on charges of "encouraging disorder" and sentenced to 20 months imprisonment. Later, the UK government held meetings with representatives of some social media websites. They discussed the question of social media being used to incite crime during the riots and looked at means of supervising and controlling the Internet in the future.

The riots in the UK taught a common lesson to all countries: Just as in wider society, there can be no absolute freedom of the Internet. The Internet needs management. At present, the Chinese government is gradually enhancing supervision of the Internet in accordance with the basic principles of "utilizing positively, developing scientifically, managing in accordance with the law, and guaranteeing security." In recent years, China has promulgated a series of laws and regulations related to the management of the Internet, principally the *Decision of the Standing Committee of the National People's Congress on Maintaining Internet Security*, the *Decision of the Standing Committee of the National People's Congress on Strengthening the Protection of Internet Information*, the *Measures on the Ad-*

ministration of Internet Information Service, and the *Measures on the Administration of the Protection of the Security in the International Network Interconnection of Computer Information Network*. These laws and regulations prescribe the responsibilities and obligations of stakeholders such as Internet service providers, government administrative departments, and Internet users. It was further proposed in the Report to the 18th CPC National Congress that there is a need to both "strengthen and improve the construction of web content" and "strengthen web social management and promote the orderly and regulated operation of the Internet in accordance with the law."

Will China engage in "exporting its culture"?

No culture can develop without communication and interaction with other cultures and without borrowing from and absorbing other cultures. Therefore, the Report to the 18th CPC National Congress proposed to "expand opening up to the outside world in the area of culture and actively absorb positive foreign cultural achievements." However, engaging in foreign cultural exchange is totally different from exporting a culture. The former is an objective process that cannot be stopped under the background of economic globalization. The latter is a strategic choice that involves bluntly occupying the culture market. The international community can rest assured that China has no such strategy.

Viewed from the perspective of history, although China has a profound and extensive culture dating back 5,000 years, the Chinese have seldom ventured spontaneously outside their country to spread its culture. The reason is that China adheres to a philosophy on cultural values and cultural soft power that: "The peach and the plum do not speak, yet a path is worn beneath them." A man of true worth attracts admiration; it has no need to promote itself through word or deed. Over China's history of foreign exchange, spreading culture has never been the main intention, but a "by-product." During the Tang Dynasty, Xuan Zang travelled west to India in search of Buddhist scriptures. Zheng He's seven maritime expeditions to the western seas were intended to display the "bounties bestowed by the Heavenly Dynasty." The main reason that Chinese culture spread to Japan, Korea and Vietnam was that people from these countries came of their own accord to study in China. The reason that Chinese culture had an influence on the Renaissance in the West, particularly on the Enlightenment Movement in Europe, was because Western missionaries played the role of a bridge. It was they who brought the then advanced Chinese culture back to Europe.

However, in the modern era the Opium War drove China into decline. This breached not only the pride of the Chinese nation, but also their confidence in Chinese culture. At a moment of existential crisis, China reflected on its cultural weaknesses and started to learn from the West and tried to catch up with Western society. After the founding of new China, the world entered a period of global Cold War. Cultural exchange between countries became trapped in this war of ideological confrontation. China's cultural exchanges were restricted to the former Soviet Union, Eastern European countries that shared a similar ideology, and the extensive community of developing countries. China also experienced the ten-year catastrophe of the Cultural Revolution. During this period there was an obsession with "left-wing" thought, and traditional culture suffered unprecedented damage. China's cultural development stagnated, and foreign cultural exchange simply ceased.

After the beginning of reform and opening-up, the phenomenon of "Chinese culture going abroad" appeared first in non-governmental communication. In 1988, the Chinese film *Red Sorghum* won the Golden Bear award in the Berlin International Film Festival. This was the first time since the founding of new China that a Chinese cultural product had won an international award. This encouraged more Chinese people to promote their cultural products and through them to represent their thoughts and ideas to the globe. Later, Chinese scholars began to propose the view that China should strengthen its "cultural soft power." They called for promoting cultural products rich in modern Chinese characteristics on the international stage, and gradually expanding Chinese influence in the world. These scholars expounded their views at influential assemblies like the CPPCC conference, advocating the idea of "culture going abroad." In 2011, the Sixth Plenary Session of the 17th CPC National Committee adopted the *Decision of the CPC Central Committee on Several Important Issues on Deepening Cultural System Reform and Promoting the Grand Development and Prosperity of Socialist Culture*. Ultimately a decision was taken that "culture going abroad" would be promoted and implemented as a national strategy.

Why should China implement the strategy of "culture going global"? Firstly, there have been historical changes in the relationship between China and the rest of the world. China has become increasingly integrated. China's future and destiny are closely connected to the future and destiny of the world. However, there is a disconnect between the international influence of Chinese culture and the world's desire to learn about it. China needs to respond properly to the attention and concerns of the outside world. It should introduce

Mo Yan, author of *Red Sorghum* and laureate of the Nobel Prize for Literature in 2012.

more of its language and culture to the world and let the world better understand the situation in modern China, including its current condition, values, development road and domestic and foreign policies.

Secondly, "culture going global" represents a need for China to restore its confidence in its culture. Through the initiative of "culture going global," China can establish communication and cooperation with other countries, and through this the Chinese people are able to find where their cultural strengths and shortcomings are, thus increasing their cultural confidence.

Thirdly, "culture going global" is also part of the strategy in the adjustment of the economic structure to face the challenges of the post-financial crisis. Since the international financial crisis, China's export-oriented economic model has been challenged, and its economic structure must adjust in response. As a new economic form, the cultural industry has more advantages in environmental protection, energy conservation, independent innovation, social and economic transformation and upgrading. At present, more than 20 provinces, municipalities and autonomous regions have proposed the goal of building a strong cultural province or municipality.

Fourthly, as a responsible big country, China has a duty to allow the essence of traditional Chinese culture – with its belief that "harmony is precious" – to circulate abroad during this era of globalization, and to make its contribution to eliminating cultural conflict and constructing a harmonious world.

However, this increase in China's foreign cultural communication has provoked discussion and concern in the West. Some question the true purpose of China's "culture going global" and worry that China might thereby try to export the "China model" in the name of "culture going global." Such thinking mainly comes from a failure to understand the current development philosophy and policy of the Communist Party of China and the Chinese government.

Firstly, China has no incentive to export the China model. For many years China has adhered to the position that "each country has the right to take its own path and do its own things well in accordance with its own national conditions and reality." The Report to the 18th CPC National Congress takes "diversification of development models" as key pillar of China's foreign relations strategy. The basic starting point for the CPC in promoting its "diversification of development model" is that multiple models can compete in development and complement each other, each with its own strengths in a situation of economic globalization. Such a situation is not only a source of power that brings vigor to economic development, but also a fundamental guarantee of long-term international peace and general prosperity. In the eyes of the Communist Party of China, if a country does not have the right to choose its own development road and social system, it will not be given respect as an equal member of the international community. In such a situation it will be impossible to construct a just and reasonable new international order.

Secondly, China does not have the ability to export the China model to the outside world. For several centuries, Western culture has held a dominant position on the international cultural stage and held international right of speech. In contrast, China's cultural values have been in a position of structural weakness. So let we ask, how can a country in such a position export its model to the globe?! The proposition is implausible. Besides, Western cultural products in the form of media such as books, magazines, films and television programs, have far greater traction on the Chinese public than that of China's products on the Western public.

Thirdly, China is willing to exchange its development experience with other countries. In this unaccustomed situation of global economic recession, China's rise and rejuvenation has undoubtedly attracted attention. If other countries are interested in China's development model and wish to learn or borrow from China, China is of course happy to exchange experiences with them. China believes that communication and convergence between different civilizations can help to promote the common development and progress of human society. In 2011, Hervé Machenaud, executive vice president of Electricite de France, pointed out that "the world needs China to examine its own ideology, politics and social model, and China needs the world to refine its model." As an ancient Chinese saying goes, "The stones from another hill might be used to polish jade." The Chinese people believe that China's road, theory and system can be helpful to other countries. As long as the matter is approached objectively, learning and borrowing from each other is always better than exploring alone. Being prepared before it rains is always better than looking for umbrellas after the rain has started.

The Roadmap of the 18th CPC National Congress and The Chinese Dream

Chapter 8

Can China Really Build a Harmonious Society?

Strengthening social development is an important guarantee for maintaining social harmony and stability. People must speed up improving and completing the basic public service system, strengthening and making innovations in social management, and boosting the building of a harmonious socialist society in order to uphold the fundamental interests of the most extensive majority of the people.

— Report to the 18th CPC National Congress

Every society has its conflicts and issues. The Communist Party of China foresaw a new China in which everyone lived in equality and happiness precisely because it had seen the social issues and sharp conflicts of the old China under the rule of the Kuomintang. But does this mean there were no longer any conflicts or issues in new China? For a long time after the founding of new China the CPC truly believed this. But the truth was different. The conflicts and issues present in socialist China were just as prevalent as in the past. The only difference is that most of them were internal social contradictions rather than conflict between enemies. In particular, as China promoted reform and opening-up and implemented a market economy, diversification of views and interests exacerbated conflicts and issues. It was in response to this situation that the CPC proposed the idea of building a harmonious socialist society. In principle this is a sound ideal, but can it really be achieved? What is the path to such a society? In response to such questions, it is emphasized in the Report to the 18th CPC National Congress that "guaranteeing and improving the people's livelihood should have a higher priority. China must strengthen and innovate in social management and correctly address the relations between reform, development and stability. It should unite all the forces that can be united and strengthen the factors supporting harmony to the maximum. It should enhance creative dynamism in society. It should ensure that the people live and work in peace and contentment, that society runs in peace and order, and that the country enjoys lasting peace and stability."

What kind of changes have occurred in Chinese society?

It is sometimes said that the CPC was forced to proposed the building of a harmonious society because social unrest was extensive in China. There is a case to be made for such a view. After all, issues must arise before the solutions to them can be found. But it is not completely true. The inherent meaning of harmony is the unification of diversity. Harmony is the accord of several different tones. It refers more to the balanced coexistence between different interests and requirements. People cannot highlight only one aspect and overlook the other. In fact, the main reason that the CPC has proposed the building of a harmonious society is that new changes are emerging in society, and there is the new tendency towards disequilibrium.

The first change is to social structures. New social classes and interest groups are developing and maturing. It is becoming more difficult to coordinate the interests between different social strata. Before reform and opening-up, the social structure in China was relatively simple. People called it "two classes and one stratum," referring to the working class, the peasantry, and the stratum of intellectuals. The stratum of intellectuals belonged to the working class. So the entire social structure, in essence, comprised two major classes. Under the socialist system, these two classes have no substantive conflict of interest; they are similar, and their interests converge. It is relatively easier to coordinate and manage such a society. Then, with the advent of reform and opening-up, new social strata and interest groups emerged such as entrepreneurs and technical personnel in private high-tech enterprises, management and technical personnel employed by foreign-funded enterprises, self-employed entrepreneurs, owners of private enterprises, employees in referral institutions, and the self-employed. Politically speaking, these are all "builders of socialism with Chinese characteristics." Although the conflicts of interest between them are not radical, they do exist in various forms.

For example, the interests of the owners and the farmer workers in a private enterprise are not completely consistent. In recent years, there was a shortage of migrant workers in the Pearl River Delta in south China. Why? Because the wages of migrant workers were too low to match the local economic development level. Then why not increase wages? Owners and management would say – because this will put us out of business. These enterprises were small and labor-intensive, with a business model that depended entirely on low-cost labor. They had no means of adapting to rising wage costs. In the past, under a planned economy, such problems could be solved simply by issuing administrative orders. But under reform and opening-up and today's socialist market economy, excessive and abusive use of administrative orders is no longer feasible. The price of labor is mainly determined by the market, and owners of private businesses will resent being given orders to increase wages – entrepreneurs in private enterprises are builders of socialism just as migrant workers are socialist workers!

This example shows the type of conflict that can occur between emerging social strata and traditional social strata. In fact, with the changes in the society, huge differentiation has emerged inside the original social classes: A worker who rode a bicycle and carried a blue canvas bag thirty years ago might have gone on to become a powerful and influential chairman of a company driving a

Porsche and carrying an LV, or he might just as easily have become a porter riding a tricycle who has lost his job or been laid off, and had to find a job for himself. The psychological gap caused by such changes can serve as a trigger to more serious conflict and confrontation. In such a social structure and with growing divergence of interests, it is unrealistic for people to continue with the thinking of the past, expecting that everyone will respond positively whenever they give an order. But how should we address this situation? The only solution is to guarantee the interests of both the old strata and the new ones. Although it is impossible to satisfy everyone, everyone does at least need to accept and recognize the solution, namely to ensure that everyone receives his or her proper share. But things are always easier said than done – this is a really hard task even with general popular support. But it is in the nature of the CPC to press ahead, even when it is clear that the road ahead is hard or is becoming harder. No matter how difficult social construction is, it will have to be done well.

The second is that the society is experiencing an unprecedented increase in openness and mobility, and the issues caused by this situation are following the same pattern. Traditional Chinese society was a "super-stable society." Such "super-stability" was seen in the simplicity of the social structure and the relative stability of social members. Before reform and opening-up, China's residency registration system played a significant role. At the time, it was very easy to locate a person in China. It was a case of "one radish, one pit." A person would be found where his residence was registered. However, geographical mobility has become increasingly frequent since reform and opening-up. At present, there are nearly two hundred million people in Chinese mainland who travel to and fro between the northwest and the southeast, the southwest and the northeast, the inland and the coastal areas, and the countryside and the cities. This poses obvious difficulties for social management. A series of related problems have emerged involving social welfare, fairness and justice, and social governance. For example, migrant workers build the city but they can seldom settle in the city. They have to travel around like migrant birds. Mobilizing the migrant population in the construction of the places where they migrate to, and ensure their social welfare benefits there, are both testing challenges.

The flow of population is at least visible; the expansion of information is both invisible and intangible. Before reform and opening-up, the acquisition and possession of information formed a "reverse pyramid" pattern. The higher a person was at the level of decision making, the more timely and sufficient information he got. The transmission of information was conducted in the form of a "proper pyramid." Information was communicated from higher to lower levels. The lower the level, the less and later a person got information. At the time there was no Internet, no mobile phone, and no microblog. When an important event occurred, the whole story of the event and the opinions and responses of the central authorities were often communicated level by level to subordinate authorities in the form of documents distributed by central authorities. Sometimes the process could last one or two months or even longer. Ordinary citizens did not have proper channels of information and the information they did receive was often very slow. And they also had less information exchange among themselves. In such circumstances, even if there were diverging or opposing opinions between one or two regions or communities, such problems would not have a wider impact or influence on policies already determined because there was no effective communication and contact between them. Even when significant incidents occurred, it was easier to minimize their scope and their influence. After the beginning of the age of informatization, such approaches and ideas were no longer effective. The emergence of the Internet allowed an exponential spread of information. When a major incident occurred, it was often the case that "when the smoke has just started to rise offline, the online fire has already started." The emergence of Weibo, Renren and other social networking tools gives the Internet a powerful capacity for social mobilization. It can unconsciously assemble people from anywhere in the world, who have no other connection at all, in collective action.

Furthermore, in an informatized environment, the boundary between virtual society and real society becomes increasingly ambiguous. Social interaction between people is no longer only physical and face-to-face – the fact that a person stays indoors does not mean that he is totally isolated and cannot interact. Otaku (Japanese Manga obsessives) can be part of a community that has the most complicated and extensive social relations. Virtual society is different from real society but it has millions of connections with real society. All actions and behavior in virtual society have a strong orientation towards reality. Improving the governing of the virtual society is both a new requirement generated by changes in the society and a point at which breakthrough is required to improve wider social governance.

The third is that social demand constantly increases. Public expectations have expanded from material subsistence to the cultural and political. The people now have interests and expect

rights. Until the issue of subsistence was resolved, people wanted no more than to have enough to eat and something to wear. They could withstand difficult conditions because ultimately survival was the primary need. But now people have sufficient to eat and wear and also the time and energy to think about other things. They will find that their mouths are not just used for eating but also for expressing opinions and expectations. Their brains are not to be filled up with nothing more than what their leaders tell them, but also with their own thoughts. At this point, people's needs start to rise from the material level to the cultural or even political level. Their needs become more and more diversified. An honest analysis recognizes that after thirty years of reform and opening-up, the Communist Party of China has knowledge, experience and results with respect to the issue of how to resolve the material needs of the people. However, it has not worked sufficiently on how to address their cultural and political expectations. In other words, due to the limitations imposed by the current stage of development, the CPC has not had the energy and resources to deal with these issues. But this is a message that falls on deaf ears. Whenever they encounter a problem, the public come to the authorities for a solution or an explanation. In particular, as public awareness of their rights increases constantly, something that was not an issue at all in the past might become a big problem today, and something that was natural in the past might become less and less justified and self-evident.

At present, as China enters a new phase in building a comprehensively prosperous society, the CPC is accumulating the resources and the knowledge to resolve this issue. However, in order to achieve success, the people too need to remain committed to the right path. They need to exercise both determination and patience.

Building a harmonious society is also not something that can be achieved overnight.

What is the CPC's philosophy for social construction?

Words meaning "constructive" can be found in both Chinese and English. What are their meanings? Being "constructive" means that the words people say or the actions they practice will help to solve an issue rather than cause trouble or make things worse. In the face of the profound changes that have occurred in China, the CPC formerly tried to manage problems based on its old approaches and habits. But more and more conflicts began to pile up, and the situation was becoming unmanageable. However, through many years of reform and opening-up, the CPC gradually developed the ability to resolve issues with a constructive attitude and approach. There were some major changes in its ideas and philosophies. The Report to the 18th CPC National Congress documents a number of major changes that have occurred in recent years:

Firstly, the CPC does everything possible to balance social consensus while recognizing and respecting differences and distinctions. There is an ancient Chinese saying: "Harmony makes things grow but individuality makes nothing work." The key of a harmonious society lies in harmony and the key to harmony lies in the coordination of differences. The society that the CPC wants to build is "a society in which all the people fully exert their abilities, receive what they deserve, and live in harmony." "To fully exert abilities" means to bring into play the initiative of each main party and not to suppress it. "To receive what people deserve" means to let each main party enjoy the rights and interests that they deserve. "To live in harmony" means that, when each main party pursues its own interests, it should not jeopardize the interests of other main parties. But in social development, it is impossible to reach a situation where everyone is a constant winner and no-one ever loses. What should be the response if the main parties who suffer damage to their interests start to complain? The first thing is that they need a place and a channel to speak out. The second is that their issues must be resolved. This demands a coordination mechanism in which different parties involved can express their own interests in an effective and regulated manner. This is the purpose of the proposal in the Report to the 18th CPC National Congress to "complete and refine the letter-and-visit petition system and also the working system for the linkage between people's mediation, administrative mediation, and judicial mediation. There must be smooth and regulated channels for expressing public requirements, coordinating the interests of the parties involved, and guaranteeing their rights."

Secondly, while social stability must always be the top priority, this does not mean that silence and rigid conformity should prevail. In the eyes of the CPC, a harmonious society should be a society that is neither unstable nor rigid. Social management does not mean imposing suffocating control on society. Rather, there should be social dynamism and social initiative, increasing harmony as much as possible and creating a harmonious and orderly social environment. Of course, during particular periods and under particular circumstances, it is necessary to maintain "control." But such measures must be expedient, localized and individual. Where social control is omnipresent, it is impossible to realize long-term peace and order. Such control is more likely to sow the seeds of social turbulence, because the effectiveness of rigid social stability is limited, while elastic social stability is sustainable.

Thirdly, social management and social services are essential. This represents an important change and innovation in the CPC's philosophy of social management. It was pointed out in the Report to the 18th CPC National Congress that the government should "improve the way in which it provides public services. It should strengthen the system of social management and services at primary level. It should enhance the service functions of urban and rural communities, and it should reinforce the roles and responsibilities of enterprises, institutions and people's organizations in social management and the provision of services..." In this short passage, the word "service" appears four times. As far as social management is concerned, management is the means and service is the end. The positions of host and guest must not be reversed, and there must be no confusion between cause and effect. Of course, a certain degree of control, examination, and approval is genuinely necessary in the provision of social services. However, in the final analysis, management should be the generator of better services rather than the converse. Government does not exist for the purposes of control, examination, and approval, but for serving society. It is specifically proposed in the Report to the 18th CPC National Congress that government should be service-oriented, featuring scientifically-designed functions, an optimized structure, honesty, and high efficiency, and inspiring public satisfaction. In recent years, some local governments have implemented service procurement and other measures, which are practical examples of realizing management through the provision of services.

By 2013, the Nanjing Government Affairs Service Center had been in operation for 18 months. Eighty percent of 319 questions of permission, examination and approval were handled and completed on the spot. The other 20% took an average time of less than a week. This represented a significant improvement in efficiency of examination and approval.

Fourthly, "to prevent" must take priority over "to cure." During the Spring and Autumn and Warring States periods (770-221B.C.) in ancient China, there was a doctor named Bian Que who could treat and cure any serious disease. People called him a miracle-doctor. But Bian Que said his elder brother's medical skills were far superior. His patients were surprised because they had no idea that his brother could treat sickness. Bian Que explained that this was because his brother could treat a disease before it occurred. He would tell a patient how to take care of his health, practice a healthy regimen, and adjust his body systems. Such medical skills were indeed more sophisticated. But because his 'patients' never fell ill, they did not appreciate the mastery of Bian Que's brother, so he did not achieve the same repute as a great doctor.

Social management is much like the story. When people resolve a major social issue, they can be seen to have achieved a notable success. But when they take precautions in advance, their efforts are at least as valuable. Talent and ability are often seen in the effort to make preparations in advance and prevent small problems from becoming major issues. The consummate standard of social management is to follow the example of Bian Que's brother – "preventing people from falling ill rather than curing their disease." Bian Que's ability to cure diseases, once contracted, is also an acceptable solution. But we should avoid the bad doctor in a joke who cut off the protruding end of an arrow shaft in a patient's arm and claimed he had cured him. The Report to the 18th CPC National Congress proposed a complete mechanism to evaluate the risks to social stability involved in important decisions. The focus of this proposal is "to prevent rather than to cure."

Fifthly, There needs to be a change from depending on mechanisms to promoting the establishment of systems. Social construction is a dynamic systematic project which needs to be addressed through general planning. Every party involved should shoulder its own responsibilities, and all parties involved should jointly promote relevant initiatives. People cannot afford to deal with issues always in an ad hoc way. There needs to be a greater reliance on systems to provide guarantees rather than on ad hoc groups. Therefore, the Report to the 18th CPC National Congress emphasized that "in order to strengthen social construction, social system reform must be accelerated." It also proposed the thinking behind and the direction of the reform, which aims to address four main areas: The first is a social management system with the leadership of the CPC committee, the responsibility of the government, the collaboration of the whole society, the participation of the general public, and the guarantee by the rule of law. The second is a modern social organization system with the division of governmental and social functions, the clear definition of rights and responsibilities, and the autonomy in accordance with the rule of law. The third is a sustainable government-led public service system covering both the city and the countryside. The fourth is a social management mechanism that integrates control and regulation at the source with dynamic management and emergency treatment. Government functions and systems must succeed in performing the social management and public service tasks that the government undertakes. Government departments should transfer their functions to social organizations and open more public resources and areas of activity to social organizations. Attention should be given to building the emergency response capacity of government departments in order to provide effective response to and proper handling of public incidents.

How does the Communist Party of China resolve the issue of employment?

The 18th CPC National Congress reported that: "In strengthening social development, ensuring and improving standards of living must take a high priority, providing as many benefits as possible to the people, resolving as many difficulties as possible for them, and solving the most pressing real problems that concern them most. People have the right to enjoy their rights to education, employment, medical care, old-age care, and housing so that they can lead a better life."

There are many and wide-ranging problems related to standards of living. Education, medical care and housing are all factors in the equation. But the most important issues are as follows: The first is employment. No job no income. Without income, education, medical care and housing are all inaccessible. The second is social security. What can citizens do if they are jobless? What can they do if the money they earn does not pay their medical expenses? What can they do when they get old? All these and many others are issues that must be resolved through social insurance. The third is fair distribution – the income gap between the richest and the poorest must not become too large. The wealth gap produces a sense of unfairness, which becomes resentment, which can then spark social disharmony. The issue of income distribution becomes the very essence of society.

In 1993, Deng Xiaoping said: "The issue of income distribution is a very important one. A small number of people have obtained so much wealth, while the majority have very little. If this situation continues, there will be big problems coming in the future… In the past, we said we should develop first. Now we can see there will be just as many problems after we have developed as before." Precisely because it understands these issues, the Communist Party of China attaches great importance to the three issues outlined above.

The Report to the 18th CPC National Congress emphasized that employment is the basis of livelihood. In practice, security of employment is the major priority for ordinary people. Employment issues were a major source of the social turbulence that has spread throughout the Arabian world, the large-scale public protests that have broken out repeatedly in European countries with heavy debt burdens, the riots in London, and the "Occupy Wall Street" movement in the USA. While China is no exception, there are differences. China faces both employment shortages on the one hand and difficulties in recruitment on the other. Since 2010, there has been a situation where millions of people joining the working population are struggling to find jobs, while employers find it difficult to recruit suitable workers for the jobs they provide. Around the time of Spring Festival, once-crowded labor markets in many places are quiet and almost deserted. Facing the shortage of labor, many enterprises in the coastal regions in southeast China go to central and western China to recruit workers, while local enterprises are also offering favorable conditions in an attempt to keep workers in their hometowns. This knotty problem reflects a radical contradiction of supply and demand in the employment market in China: a structural imbalance.

What is structural imbalance? Let's explain it by taking the "new generation of migrant workers" as an example. The new generation of migrant workers are a labor force that consists of young adults who were born in the countryside and came to the city with parents who had migrated to work in the city. They have grown up in the city. According to the *Research Report on the New Generation of Migrant Workers in China*, published by the China Youth and Children Research Center, this new generation now account for 60% of the total of migrant workers in China. They prefer urban life. Seventy-one percent of the women and 50% of the men hope to buy an apartment and settle in the city. In terms of employment, the biggest difference between this and the previous generation of migrant workers is that the wage is not the only factor that they consider when looking for a job. They now care about the working environment, about prospects for happiness, and about the realization of personal values. They are no longer satisfied with repetitive and monotonous assembly-line jobs in large-scale workshops and factories. This happens not only to the new generation of migrant workers – common to the generations born in the 1980s and 90s, but particularly to college students of these generations. Although they have more and better choices than migrant workers, they have growing difficulties in finding a job. They would rather be jobless than work on a factory assembly line. What they are looking for is a decent office job with a good environment.

There has been no obvious change in employment structure in terms of job supply. Factories have not changed much, and there have been no significant changes in the working environment. The majority of these jobs are blue-collar positions. In developed countries, when the secondary industry cannot provide enough satisfactory work opportunities, many people choose to enter the tertiary industry. This is because the tertiary industry includes emerging sectors such as finance, consultancy, the media, education and logistics, in addition to traditional areas like catering, hotel and commercial businesses. They provide more individual service work, and offer a better working environment and higher social status. However, China has not yet fully developed its tertiary industry, and the extended businesses are still limited in number and scale, so not many job opportunities of individual service can be provided. Limited number of jobs and information asymmetry result in insufficient competition in employee recruitment.

Another reason for the imbalance in supply and demand in the jobs market is the general increase in affluence in China. Twenty years ago, when family incomes were limited, a young man had to go to work immediately after completing school even in the city. The wage he earned was of secondary importance; what was critical was that he was bringing money into the family home. Things are different now. Some young people choose to take time out for a year or two after they graduate. They first become "NEETS," and then go to work when they find a satisfactory job. Thus the attitude toward employment of both the new generation of migrant workers and today's college graduates is not determined entirely by the issue of livelihood. They give more priority to personal factors like feelings and development prospects. This is a sign of social progress.

In response to this new situation in employment, it was proposed at the 18th CPC National Congress that China should "promote the realization of employment of higher quality." There are two aspects to this. One is quantity – there should be a job available for everybody who needs one. The other is quality – everybody should be able to fully exert their talents through their work. In order to achieve this, "priority should be given to the principles of promoting self-reliant employment, market-regulated employment, and government-backed employment and entrepreneurship, to the strategy of giving top priority to employment, and to a more positive employment policy." The government has adopted a number of measures to achieve these ends.

The first is promoting employment through policy: Expanding the existing supply of high-quality positions and creating new ones amidst economic transformation. In recent years, China has given increasing emphasis on the responsibility of the government in promoting employment. The first step was to establish a legal and regulatory framework with the *Employment Promotion Law* as the core, and a complete set of policy systems to stabilize and expand employment. Against a macroscopic backdrop of global economic depression, and with the Chinese economy facing huge pressure to transform its development model and adjust its structure, the government set maximal employment as its bottom-line policy and high-quality employment as its highest goal.

The relationship between adjusting structure and ensuring employment, and the need to provide jobs to different employment groups with better-determined objectives, have both been addressed: On the one hand, there is a need for a certain number of high-end jobs in the transformation and upgrading of manufacturing industry. On the other hand, it is essential to ensure the proper and safe relocation of those whose jobs are being eliminated, and to mitigate any negative impact on them and their families. In the process of cultivating emerging industries, priority should be given to industries that have a strong ability to create high-quality employment opportunities. Of particular value are jobs of public service in industries such as environmental protection, urban landscaping, health care, and transportation, and community service to disadvantaged groups such as middle-aged redundant workers and registered disabled people. Government procurement of public interest jobs is a good way to address these needs.

The second is promoting employment through independent entrepreneurship – opening up more space for employment. The Report to the 18th CPC National Congress highlighted the need to "guide workers to change their outlook about employment, encourage employment through multiple channels and forums, and expand job opportunities by promoting entrepreneurship." An entrepreneurship business not only creates employment for the entrepreneur him/herself, but also has a multiplier effect in providing others with jobs. In recent years the Chinese government has promulgated a series of policies and measures to support independent entrepreneurship, for example the *Guiding Opinions on the Work of Promoting Entrepreneurship to Expand Job Opportunities*. Provinces and municipalities implemented a campaign to create and build a first batch of state-level "entrepreneurship cities." Various industrial and regional barriers obstructing entrepreneurship were cleared and eliminated. Financial policies to encourage entrepreneurship in areas such as loans, interest discount, and housing rental reduction and exemption were also developed or improved. More and more entrepreneurs were able to set out on a journey to realize their dreams, free of all kinds of burdens and concerns. News media also vigorously promoted model entrepreneurs, particularly those who through persistence had succeeded in establishing a second business after failing with their first attempts. A harmonious entrepreneurship environment developed, with strong public support, in which people were advocating entrepreneurship, racing to start a business, rewarding successes, and tolerating failures, with the result that more and more people are giving serious consideration to the idea of becoming an entrepreneur.

The third is promoting employment through vocational training: Giving job-seekers the strengths they need to become winners. The Chinese government has become more and more aware of the importance of employment training. During China's 11th Five-year Plan (2006-2010), RMB 23 billion was made available for funds for vocational training. In terms of form, innovative labor and employment schemes such as "placing-order-type" employment training have become more popular. In terms of policy, the Report to the 18th CPC National Congress specified the need to "strengthen vocational skills training, improve worker's ability to find jobs and start businesses, and enhance the stability of their employment."

The fourth is promoting employment through information services – smoothing the job-seeking channel. Governments

---

"Placing-order-type" employment training is also called "future-type" training. This means that employer enterprises submit job information concerning their requirements, such as the type of work, number of workers, payment, and technical requirements, to local labor departments. Labor departments integrate such information and provide it to the labor departments of the areas exporting labor. These labor departments arrange for and organize training on the basis of the skills and timing requirements in the "order." Once the training is complete, the labor departments send these trained workers to the employer enterprises as a package before the work project starts.

A vocational school in Qingdao adopted the approach of combining working with learning and provided a large number of skilled practical workers to the frontline of production.

at various levels have positively mobilized market and social resources to establish various types of public employment and human resources service agencies. They have provided people with legal and policy consultation services and carried out personal occupational qualification assessments so as to help them to understand the requirements of various jobs and know how to apply for jobs. A nation-wide network of employment information is under construction, and more open and accessible employment information provides people fairer job opportunities.

What kind of social insurance system is China to build?

The process of market reform involves major adjustments of social interests and social structure. While the social insurance model under the old planned economic system is dismantled, there is an urgent need to build a new social insurance system so as to provide safety to the whole society. During the period of economic transformation, drastic social changes are expected. So a system to prevent and relieve risks and maintain basic subsistence for the public is therefore needed. Otherwise, it may cause social instability and create obstructions to the reform. In 1993, the Third Plenary Session of the 14th CPC Central Committee adopted the *Decision on Several Issues on Building Socialist Market Economy*, which required to establish an all-covering and multilevel social insurance system. Since the beginning of the new century, the CPC has proposed a series of innovative concepts in social insurance such as the equalization of basic public services. Many important developments have achieved. The most important are as follows:

1. The establishment of relevant institutional systems. In 2003, the new-type rural cooperation medical service was set up. In 2007, the rural minimal subsistence guarantee system was established. In 2009 pilot projects on the new-type rural pension insurance was launched. In 2010, the *Social Insurance Law* was passed. After 20 years of continuous work on the public service system, China's pension, medical care, employment and housing guarantee provisions have made constant progresses. A primary framework of social security system has formed in the principle of government leadership, responsibility sharing, socialization, and multilevel structure.

2. There is a constant expansion of system coverage. By 2010, the basic medical care system will cover all urban and rural residents. This system has now covered 1.26 billion residents, making China the country providing basic medical care to the largest population. Of them, 430 million were covered by urban employee medical care insurance and urban resident medical care insurance, an increase of 213% over 2005; 830 million were covered by the new-type rural cooperative medical care insurance with a participation ratio of 96%. In the whole country, 400 million people were covered by pension insurance.

Although China has made considerable progress in social insurance, there are still many problems. The most prominent include the following: The first is the issue of fairness. In January 2013, the government decided to raise once again the standard of basic pension for enterprise retirees, making the average monthly pension reaching RMB 1,900. This was the ninth successive increase, but, however, not everyone was happy about it. There were louder calls to make change to the "dual pension system." The dual pension system refers to the system established according to the *Decision on Reforming the Pension Insurance System for Enterprise Employees* promulgated by the Central Government in 1991. The document specified that an enterprise's pension fund should come jointly from the state, enterprise and employees. Thus, pensions for enterprise retirees became the responsibility of the society, while however the pensions for retirees of government organs and institutions continued to be funded by the government, or more precisely by the taxpayers. This is the same for medical care. Enterprise employees must contribute to participate in the medical care insurance, while public servants and similar enjoy state-funded public medical care.

The second is unequalled standard of social security. There are differences in the standard for urban employees and for urban residents and rural farmers, as well as the differences between various regions. The gap is very big, some being dozen-folds. It is the same for pensions. Another unfairness is seen in the system for flowing laborers, that is, pension insurance cannot be continued between different regions. For example, Mr. Zhang works in Guangdong and participates in the local pension insurance. If one day he wants to return to his hometown in Henan to start his own business, he can only withdraw the part he has paid to the accumulation fund but not the part paid for him by the enterprise where he works, which will be regarded as his "contribution to the development of Guangdong."

The third is that the present social security structure is oversimple. Early in 1993 the goal of reform proposed in the Third Plenary Session of the 14th CPC Central Committee included building a multilevel social security institutional system. However, when the social security systems, like the basic pension insurance and basic medical care, have been established, enterprise supplementary pension insurance, enterprise annuities and occupational annuities, supplementary medical care insurance and commercial medical care insurance are developing very slowly. In fact, a multilevel institutional pension and medical care system has not yet formed.

In response to these issues, the 18th CPC National Congress has proposed some breakthrough and innovative concepts. First, on the basis of "comprehensive coverage and basic guarantee," greater stress should be put on the principle of "multilevel" and "sustainability." Second, emphasis should be laid on the "fairness, mobility, and continuity" in building the social security system. Third, it determines to "reform and improve the social security systems of enterprises, government organs and institutions, integrate the systems of basic pension insurance and basic medical care insurance for urban and rural residents, establish personal pension insurance accounts step by step, and realize the unification of basic pension system nationwide." When this has become effect, China's social security system will surely become more complete and perfect, benefiting the economic development and social harmony.

Some people said that China's incomplete social security system was due to short of money in the past. Now China becomes richer, with huge foreign exchange reserves, and it is a socialist country. Why does it still stick to "basic" guarantee? Why not build a high-level welfare society all at once? The fact is that the social security standard of any country must be in conformity with its national conditions. In China's case, it has a population of 1.3 billion, 960-square-kilometer territory, a history of only thirty years of quick growth, and the development is imbalanced. It is still in a transitional period. It looks prosperous, but money is tight in all sectors and regions. If all the reserves of several decades were put into social welfare, how could the socialist cause with Chinese characteristics be continued. In addition, we have seen the lessons of some European "welfare states" which are now in the debt crisis. With a huge population and relative fragile foundation, China might face a catastrophe if it fell into such a trap.

Will China really take action to change the current structure of interests?

In recent years, a social phenomenon has emerged in China where some monopolistic industries provide the business resources under their control to their employees or their family members, free or at reduced prices. This is a form of industrial corruption under the guise of "employee benefits." For example, employees in the public transportation system take buses and subways for free. Employees in telecommunications departments make phone calls for free. Employees in the power grid system use electricity for free. Employees in banks can get housing mortgage loans at vastly-reduced interest rates. Employees in education pay reduced or even no school fees for their children. This phenomenon is known as "benefit corruption."

In fact, there are unfair income distribution not only in monopolistic industries but also in other industries. The income gaps are now also growing in the countryside, in the city, between urban and rural areas, between different regions and trades, and between people with different social status and educational backgrounds. At the initial stage of reform and opening-up, the CPC adopted the policy of letting a part of the people become wealthy first in order to spur social productivity, and the result is that many people made the fortune to become rich. At that time, efficiency was first priority and fairness the second. However, with the time passes, the interests of these wealthy elite gradually become fixed, and a structure forms in which these people support each other to reinforce their established interests. As this network of interest relationships becomes increasingly complex, it is increasingly difficult for outsiders to break the structure. Not only will they face resistance from those who benefit from the status quo, but this may cause social instability. "It is harder to affect their interest than their soul," as observed by Premier Li Keqiang.

However, if the issue of unfair income distribution is not resolved now, it will only become harder to solve it in the future. In 2012, China's State Council promulgated *Several Opinions on Deepening the Reform of the Income Distribution System*, which emphasized that the problem of rigidity in the structure of interests can be addressed by broadening the base of expanding incomes and converging on common understanding. Additional comprehensive measures should be adopted to further improve the primary and secondary distribution systems.

The Report to the 18th CPC National Congress highlighted that "the income distribution reform must be enhanced to let the people to share the fruits of development." The general objective of this goal is to "raise the ratio of individual income in the distribution of national income, and increase the proportion of remuneration from work in primary distribution. Efficiency and fairness should be well balanced in both primary and secondary distribution, but in secondary distribution more stress should be put on fairness." Primary distribution generally refers to the process in which the results of productive output are distributed according to contribution and on the basis of productive factors like labor, capital, resource (land), technology and management. Secondary distribution refers to the process in which the state makes adjustment to the results of primary distribution through taxation, financial transfer payments, and various forms of social security and social relief. According to these definitions, China's income distribution system reform should be both beneficial to mobilizing the initiative of the participants in economic activity and to improving economic efficiency. And it should be able to offer a relatively fair guarantee of the basic life necessities of all members of society. Policy measures in the area of secondary distribution are of particular importance, with more attention paid to fairness, so as to supplement the "short board" caused by the unfairness resulting from the ownership of productive factors in primary distribution. Therefore, a mechanism with long-term impact can be formed to narrow the gaps in income distribution. Within a foreseeable future, the government will focus on the following aspects:

The first is to raise labor remuneration. With deepening of reform and opening-up and the development of the socialist market economy, people's sources of income have tended to diverge. Operating income, investment income and property income have increased steadily. But the main source of income for most ordinary people is still salary or wage in exchange for their labor. To resolve the issue of unfair distribution of income, the first priority is to raise the wages of ordinary workers, particularly workers on the front line of social production. Both China's *Compendium on the Twelfth Five-year Plan* and the Report to the 18th CPC National Congress proposed the goal of "two synchronizations," namely, synchronizing the growth of people's incomes with economic development, and synchronizing the growth of labor remuneration and labor productivity. These embody the principle of distribution according to effort and raising the income of ordinary workers. For the foreseeable future China will continue to raise the proportion of labor remuneration through multiple measures, such as increasing incomes and raising wage benefits and minimal life subsistence allowances, so as to increase the spending power of ordinary people.

The second is to regulate the order of income distribution. A Western philosopher has observed that "good order is the foundation of all things." There is also a saying in China, "No rules, no results." There are still some unregulated areas in income distribution in China, such as different remuneration for the same work, different remuneration for the same working position, other income in addition to wages, disorder in non-monetary benefits, unlawful income, and the prominent issue of "gray income." All these seriously affect the fair distribution of income. In order to resolve these issues, there is a need to complete laws and regulations, enhance government supervision and control, and speed up the formation of an open, transparent, fair and reasonable order of income distribution. Unlawful income should be banned, and measures should be taken to standardize and regularize "gray income," monopolistic income should be strictly regulated and controlled, and the income of senior executives should be regulated and limited.

The third is to strengthen regulation. Most countries generally use financial and taxation measures to adjust income gaps. For example, the UK started to levy estate tax in 1694 and personal income tax in 1799. Germany formulated its *Fiscal Budget Law* and *Fiscal Equalization Law* even earlier, and reduced the income gap through financial transfer payments. The Report to the 18th CPC National Congress proposed the rapid completion of the secondary distribution regulation mechanism in which taxation, social security and transfer payments are the main measures. The key points in this task include the following: First, strengthen the regulation of personal income tax. Second, strengthen tax collection and administration. A property taxation system will also be established that includes estate tax, gift tax and luxury consumption tax. On June 30, 2011, after two sessions of deliberation and an open solicitation of public opinion, the 21st Session of the Standing Committee of the 11th National People Congress adopted the decision on revising the *Personal Income Tax Law*, a measure which attracted widespread comment in China. The revision raises the taxable threshold on wage income from RMB 2,000 yuan to RMB 3,500 yuan, and adjusts the structure of tax rates. After the adjustment, the proportion of taxpayers among wage earners drops from 28% to about 7.7%. The taxpaying population reduces from about 84 million to 24 million. The tax burden on middle- and low-income groups is substantially reduced, while the regulation of high earner is strengthened.

The fourth is to help people in difficulties. China is rich yet poor. It is "rich" because its economic aggregate ranks the second in the world. It is "poor" because its per capita GDP ranks about the 100th in the world. In particular, China also has a huge population group living in poverty. According to the poverty line of per capita annual income of RMB 1,274 yuan, China still has a rural population of 26.88 million living in poverty. There are also more than 23 million urban residents included in the minimal subsistence program in the city. Providing better care to groups with exceptional difficulties is not only an important embodiment of the fair distribution of social wealth but also an intrinsic requirement of China's socialist system. Within a foreseeable future, the government will adopt a set of comprehensive means to set up a safety net of urban and rural subsistence allowances, build a stronger network of mul-

In July 2012, workers from the Yancheng County Power Supply Company in Shandong erected power lines over the farmlands in a poor village in the Matou Town.

During the 12th Five-year Plan, Shandong provincial authorities will invest RMB 1.514 billion to implement the "Power Grid Poverty Relief Project," in which 3,035 power grids in poor villages will be transformed and upgraded to provide guaranteed power for production in the countryside.

tilevel relief, make determined efforts to resolve difficult problems in poverty alleviation, further perfect the social security system, increase employment, and advocate mutual assistance and charity activities.

The Roadmap of the 18th CPC National Congress and The Chinese Dream

Chapter 9

How Can We Make China Beautiful?

Promoting ecological progress is a long-term task of vital importance to public wellbeing and China's future. Ecological progress must take the highest priority, incorporated into all economic, political, cultural, and social strategy. We must work hard to build a beautiful country, and achieve the lasting and sustainable development of the Chinese nation.

— Report to the 18th CPC National Congress

Since reform and opening-up, China has remained committed to the principle of socialism with Chinese characteristics, achieved notable successes, and enhanced both its economic strength and its comprehensive national strength. However, while radical change affects every aspect of life in China, the issue of the ecological environment is becoming increasingly prominent. Significant ecological damage has impacted many regions and areas in China. This has become a major bottleneck that is restricting China's comprehensive economic and social development.

In order to address the issue, the 15th CPC National Congress proposed the strategy of sustained development. Subsequently, a succession of new development concepts were proposed, including developing a new type of industrialization, creating a resource-conserving and environment-friendly society, and making ecological progress. The Report to the 17th CPC National Congress reinforced the new commitment to making ecological progress. This report set building China into a country with good ecological environment by 2020 as an important target for a well-off society. The Fifth Plenary Session of the 17th CPC National Committee required to "form a green and low-carbon development concept." In the 12th Five-year Plan, there is a special section devoted to green development, indicating China's determination and confidence to take the road of green development. The 18th CPC National Congress further included ecological development in its overall plan of building socialism with Chinese characteristics.

Will China really become beautiful from now on?

Focusing on ecological progress: no alternative or strategic choice?

Strengthening ecological civilization is a unilateral strategic choice that the CPC has made, following world development trends, based on China's prevailing national conditions and actual stage of development and on the development experience of other countries. It reflects a profound change in China's development concept, and will certainly cause a real revolution in China.

"Harmony of man and nature" reflects the general trend of the times. The history of mankind's development is a history of the relationship between man and the nature. "Unity between heaven and man" is the most representative idea in traditional Chinese culture. It emphasizes the harmonious coexistence between man and nature. However, over a very long historical period in the development of mankind, man and nature have been separated from each other. Man regards nature as the source of production and life materials rather than something that exists in organic unity with man. Particularly after mankind entered the stage of industrialization, his exploitation of and damage to nature became more and more serious. The negative consequences to mankind caused by this situation are also becoming more serious. As Friedrich Engels aptly pointed out in his book *Dialectics of Nature*, "Let us not, however, flatter ourselves overmuch on account of our human conquest over nature. For each such conquest takes its revenge on us." In the 1850s, London was a city surrounded by factories. Smog covered the sky of the city. The city modeled perfectly the characteristics of industrialization: high investment, high energy consumption and high consumption. Industrial pollution became a matter of life and death.

In the 1960s, the international community began to address issues like the "limit of growth" and "only one earth." In 1972 the United Nations published the *Declaration on the Human Environment* and declared solemnly that mankind would undertake the obligation of protecting the environment while exploiting and utilizing nature's resources. In 1987, the United Nations World Commission on Environment and Development published a long report entitled *Our Common Future* and proposed for the first time the concept of "sustainable development." Since the 1990s, a series of critical programs have been published, represented by the *Rio Declaration on Environment and Development* and *Agenda 21*. With these, the concept of ecological progress and the harmonious development of man and nature have gradually become a common international theme. Now, if you travel around Europe, you scarcely see barren land. The whole of Europe is covered with greens. In contrast, 37% of Chinese territory is afflicted with water and soil erosion; desertification accounts for 18% of its total territory; 90% of China's grassland shows varying degrees of degeneration; 325 cities' environmental and air quality exceed legal standards by 11%; and the damaged ecological system results in frequent natural disasters. It is worthless even if China becomes the first economy in the world but its people have to live in such devastated environment in the future. To rebuild the relationship between man and nature, the Report to the 18th CPC National Congress emphasized the need to "establish the concept of ecological culture by respecting nature, complying with the exigencies of nature, and protecting nature" and to "leave more space for nature to recover, provide more fine land for agriculture, and preserve a beautiful home of blue sky, green land and clear water for our future generations."

China no longer possesses "vast territory and abundant resources." The idea of "vast territory and abundant resources" is deeply-rooted in the hearts of the Chinese people. Some localities' "lavish activities" in wasting resources and energy for economic development since the reform and opening-up are caused by this mindset. The truth is that although the total volume of energy and resources in China remains abundant, per capita shares of resources like energy, farmland and water are relatively low. China's per capita territorial area is only 0.8 hectares, per capita grassland 0.33 hectare, and per capita forest area 0.128 hectare, only 29%, 50% and 20% of world's average respectively. Per capita farmland area is 0.095 hectare, less than half of the world's average. Per capita exploitable reserves of crude oil, natural gas, and coal are 2.6 tons, 1,074 cubic meters, and 90 tons respectively, only 11.1%, 4.3% and 55.4% of world's average. Among the 144 countries for statistic survey, China's per capita coal resources rank below the 50th, its fresh water reserves below the 55th, and its land, farmland and forest resources rank far below the 100th. Its per capita reserves of important mineral resources such as oil, gas, copper and aluminum are only 8.3%, 4.1%, 25.5% and 9.7% respectively of the world's average.

Since reform and opening-up, China has fed 21% of the world's population with the grain produced from 7% of the world's farmland. This is truly a remarkable achievement, but it was done at a heavy cost in resources and environment. The contradiction between economic development and resource scarcity is becoming increasingly sharp. China's consumption of foreign oil has risen to 56.7% of its total oil needs. The dependency on foreign supplies of important mineral resources is also rising quickly. The total shortage of water in China is 53.6 billion cubic meters for many consecutive years. Two thirds of its cities lack water; 110 cities are short of water "seriously." In China's seven major water systems, nearly 30% is below Grade V, which is useless. Ecological problems, such as falling underground aquifers, reducing rivers and lakes, decreasing wetlands, and deteriorating ecosystems, have already seriously restricted the development of local production and the quality of life of local people.

China's total energy consumption is increasing too fast and too intensive. The contradiction between supply and demand in natural resource consumption has already become China's Achilles' heel in its long-term economic development. This is the reason why the Report to the 18th CPC National Congress has defined "resource conservation" as a "radical policy to protect the ecological environment." This is why the report emphasized "improving the ability to exploit marine resources, develop the marine economy, and build a marine power."

The Western model cannot be copied. All the developed countries have followed the traditional route to industrialization in the middle and later stages of development: tolerating pollution at first and then carrying out prevention and control measures. From the 1930s, shocking environmental disasters appeared in capitalist countries of Europe, and in the USA and Japan. All these incidents were related to wastes – waste gas, waste water, and industrial waste, resulting in polluted air – water sources, soil, and food, and even deaths of people. The oil crisis that broke out in the 1970s posed an enormous threat to the traditional road to industrialization followed by Western countries. In mid-1970s, developed capitalist countries in the West completed industrialization and entered the post-industrial era. They started to make use of their technical strengths to update and upgrade their industry, moved some heavily-polluted industries to developing countries, with the result that environmental hazard incidents were also transferred. This causes a global environmental crisis.

With the advent of reform and opening-up, China began to make use of the industrial technologies from developed countries in a rapid drive for industrialization and modernization. Inevitably, it also became a destination to which developed Western countries transferred industrial and environmental pollution. In the three decades that followed China achieved remarkable economic results. During the same period, the same kind of environmental incidents that had frequently occurred in developed countries also appeared in China. Since the development strategies of many countries have greatly changed, it is impossible for China to follow the industrial transfer model of Western developed countries and move its outdated industries to other developing countries. Therefore China must endeavor to transform its production and consumption mode to an environmentally sustainable model, and avoid as much as possible the damage that Western industrialization caused to nature and to human society.

Building a beautiful China: lip service, or a real commitment?

Although the concept of building a beautiful China was first proposed in the Report to the 18th CPC National Congress, the CPC has for a long time attached importance to the issue of environmental protection, and this has been a basic state policy supported by a series of other strategic measures.

Firstly, China has implemented a successful family planning policy. At the time when developed Western countries were encountering environmental incidents, China mainly faced the problem of food for its fast-growing population. Early in 1957, Chinese population specialist Ma Yinchu published the *New Population Theory*, in which he pointed out that excessive population growth would offset the results of economic development, so he proposed a family planning policy in response. However, the new China, fresh from the ruins of war, still faced further military threats. "Preparations against war and natural disasters" were China's main priority at the time. Therefore Ma Yinchu's family planning policy was not implemented until it became a basic state policy in the *Constitution of the People's Republic of China* in 1982. During this period, China tried to feed its population through measures like creating farmland by destroying forests, filling in sea, and reclaiming uncultivated land. At the same time, political campaigns such as "going to work in the countryside and mountainous areas" were intended to relieve the pressure of the urban population on food supplies and employment. Although these measures temporarily eased the pressure, they caused serious ecological problems like deforestation, water and soil erosion, land desertification, and an increase in natural disasters, which in turn exacerbated the problem of food shortage. Ultimately, China had to implement Ma's family planning policy which was ignored earlier. For over 30 years, the family planning policy has been successful, reducing the number of births by at least 300 million. This effectively alleviated multiple social and environmental pressures linked to excessive population growth.

Secondly, China has formulated and promulgated a series of environmental protection laws. By early 1970s, it had already established a relatively complete industrial system. At the same time, the developed capitalist countries in the West had entered the age of informatization. In the process of industrialization, China also encountered the same environmental destruction that the Western developed countries had previously experienced.

In 1971, water quality in the Guanting Reservoir, an important source of water supply for Beijing, was showing obvious signs of deterioration, and the State Council was seriously concerned. In 1972, the State Development Planning Commission and the State Construction Commission submitted to the State Council the *Report on the Conditions on the Pollution in the Guanting Reservoir and the Suggestions for Solutions*. This report laid the political and legal foundation for China's control of pollution and protection of the environment. In 1973, China held the first national environment protection meeting and formulated *Several Provisions on Protecting and Improving the Environment (Draft for Trial Implementation)*. In 1974, the State Council promulgated the *Interim Provisions of the People's Republic of China on Preventing and Controlling the Pollution to Coastal Waters*. In 1978, the *Constitution of the People's Republic of China* for the first time made specific stipulations on environmental protection: "The state protects the environment and natural resources and prevents and controls pollution and other public hazards." Environmental protection standards, formulated and promulgated in the same period, also included the *Standards for Trial Implementation on the Discharge of the Three Wastes Produced in Industry*, the *Standards on Domestic Drinking Water*, and the *Food Hygiene Standards* setting a series of quantitative indexes for environmental management in China. In 1979, China formulated and promulgated the *Environment Protection Law of the People's*

Republic of China (For Trial Implementation). In 1989, the *Environment Protection Law of the People's Republic of China* was officially promulgated and implemented. In 2005, China promulgated the *Law of the People's Republic of China on Renewable Energy Sources*. In 2011, China's State Council officially distributed to lower levels the *National 12th Five-year Plan on Environmental Protection*.

Thirdly, China actively participates in worldwide environmental protection initiatives. Facing a serious deterioration in ecological environment, China participates actively in international cooperation in environmental protection and strengthened its legislation work related to environmental protection, while drawing the experience from developed Western countries. In 1984, China took part in drafting *Our Common Future*, the research report of the UN World Commission on Environment and Development. In 1992, the Chinese government signed the *Rio Declaration* at the environment and development conference held in Rio de Janeiro. In 1993, China took the lead in formulating a national "Agenda 21." In 1998, China signed the *Kyoto Protocol*. China participated, in 2007 and 2009, in the Bali Conference and Copenhagen Conference and promoted the *Bali Roadmap* and the *Copenhagen Protocol*.

Although measures were taken, no radical improvements have been seen. The situation remains the same: "resources becoming less, environmental pollution getting worse, and ecological system degenerating." GDP worship had a deep root in the concept for economic development. Therefore the Report to the 18th CPC National Congress proposed: on the one hand, take preventative measures as a priority to comprehensively resolve prominent environmental issues that cause damage to the public's health, and strengthen the prevention and control of water, air and soil pollution; on the other hand, address the root cause of deterioration of the ecological environment so as to reverse this trend, create a good working and living environment for the people, and contribute more to global ecological security.

In recent years, as a series of forceful measures in environment protection have been adopted, China's environment has seen a certain level of improvement. However, the prominent environmental problems that represent a threat to the public health, such as water, air and soil pollution, have not been fundamentally reversed. Some of these problems have already begun to affect social harmony and stability – environment-related mass incidents are on the rise. The government considers this issue to be a major priority – good health is an essential contributor to individual quality of life, and essential to social progress at a national level. In the view of the CPC, problems of environment quality are the biggest obstacle to China's ability to complete the task of building a comprehensively prosperous society by 2020 on schedule. If the major environment issues that threaten public health are not resolved, a human-orientated society will become an empty talk. Therefore, it is a public product to ensure the environmental rights and interests of the people and provide them a good environment. People must have clean water to drink, fresh air to breath, safe food to eat, and green surrounding to live. Modernization should promote the harmonious development of man and nature.

To fundamentally resolve these problems, we must promote green growth, recycled development, and a low-carbon economy. We must enhance the building of a system-based ecological progress that supports and promotes changes in the mode of production and in daily life. The Report to the 18th CPC National Congress emphasized the need to "include resource consumption, environmental damage and ecological benefits into the system of standards for the evaluation of economic and social development and the establishment of relevant goals, evaluation methods and reward and punishment mechanisms that embody the requirements in promoting ecological progress."

The principles of an evaluation system will have a determinant effect on policy. During three decades of reform and opening-up, the Chinese government has been successful in formulating a series of parameters for the evaluation of economic and social development. However, the current parameters place too much emphasis on economic aggregate and speed of growth. They cannot comprehensively reflect the total social balance sheet of economic growth and the resource and environment costs as a consequence. Nor can they properly reflect the efficiency, benefits and quality of economic growth. Therefore the existing principles must be expanded to form an evaluation parameter system that shows the comprehensive development of economy, society, ecology and human, and that integrates resource consumption, environmental damage and ecological benefits to guide correct choices in both value orientation and action, and to realize the organic unification of economic benefits, social benefits, and resource and environmental benefits.

In 2011, China's State Council distributed the *National 12th Five-year Plan on Environment Protection, which* specifically required the implementation of the environment objective accountability system, and included the parameter system on ecological progress in the performance evaluation of local government at various levels, targeting "local governments which have been responsible for major and catastrophic environmental incidents, or those which have failed to complete essential tasks and achieve related goals in environment protection, and requiring measures such as regional approval restrictions and analysis of the responsibilities of relevant leaders."

In the future, the Chinese government will further strengthen its work in this respect. The Report to the 18th CPC National Congress proposed a system for the development and protection of territorial space, refining and completing strict farmland protection systems, water resource management systems and environmental protection systems, and completing the accountability system for environmental protection and the environmental damage compensation system. Reform will be required on pricing and taxation of resource-intensive products, establishing measures like a pay-by-use system for key resources and an ecological compensation system

Yinjiaping Village, an ecology demonstration village in the city of Yichang in Hubei.

that can not only reflect market supply and demand, but also address such issues as resource scarcity, and integrate ecological value and cross-generational compensation. With the promulgation and implementation of these systems, China's ecological environment will have radical improvement, and a more beautiful China will be seen.

Fighting climate change: good faith or fake?

In recent years, China has been a positive and active participant in international climate negotiations. It has set independent, specific and compulsory goals to reduce carbon dioxide emissions, promoted energy conservation and emission reduction, developed renewable resources, and increased carbon sink. It has made a substantive contribution to mankind's fight against climate change. It can be said that fighting climate change has already become an important element of China's drive to build an ecological civilization. In this process, China has always been scrupulous in abiding by the principle of "common but differentiated responsibilities." At first glance, these two views might seem contradictory, but in fact, making ecological progress and adhering to the principle of common but differentiated responsibilities are two sides of a coin.

Firstly, the principle of "common but differentiated responsibilities" is not only applicable to the issue of climate change, but is also a globally-accepted basic standard in handling international affairs and a generally-recognized basic principle in international environment law. Any international progress in campaigns, such as anti-fascism, anti-terrorism, the fight against AIDS and poverty alleviation, is the result of the joint efforts of different countries working in cooperation, and the fair sharing of responsibilities. In the face of issues that affect all mankind, every country has the responsibility to take action. However, it has never been the case, and should not be the case, that all countries must share the same level of burden. With regard to the environment issue, the principle of "common but differentiated responsibility" is a generally-accepted principle for sharing responsibility. It is applied in the *United Nations Framework Convention on Climate Change* and the *Kyoto Protocol*. It is also seen in international legal documents such as the *Declaration on Human Environment*, the *Vienna Convention for the Protection of the Ozone Layer*, the *Montreal Protocol*, and the *Convention on Biological Diversity*. In June 2012, the UN Conference on Sustainable Development adopted the document *Our Common Future* and reaffirmed the principle of "common but differentiated responsibilities." It urged developed countries to meet their commitments on development assistance and to transfer environment-friendly technologies to developing countries and help them strengthen their performance. UN Secretary General Ban Ki Moon said in his speech at the 25th anniversary of the signing of the *Montreal Protocol* on September 16, 2012, that the successful experience of the *Montreal Protocol* indicated that it was beneficial to all countries to adhere to the principles of science-based decision making, prudent practice, common but differentiated responsibilities, and equality within the same generation and between different generations.

Secondly, the principle of "common but differentiated responsibilities" is a common understanding in international climate negotiation that has formed through arduous long-term efforts. It is a positive result that has been achieved by the inter-

national community in fighting climate change. Commitment to this principle is crucial in ensuring that efforts to fight climate change continue on the right path. Since the birth of the United Nations Framework Convention on Climate Change in 1992, international climate negotiations have experienced 20 years of constant change. During this period, the international community has carried out a series of negotiations centered on fighting climate change, and achieved important successes such as the *Kyoto Protocol*, the *Bali Roadmap*, the *Copenhagen Accord*, the *Cancún Agreements*, and the *Durban Platform*. These successes were achieved by remaining committed to the principle of "common but differentiated responsibilities." It is hard to see how developed and developing countries could continue negotiation and cooperation if this principle was abandoned. As was affirmed by Yvo de Boer, former executive secretary of the secretariat of the UN Framework Convention on Climate Change, the principle of "common but differentiated responsibilities" is the cornerstone of the undertakings of fighting climate change. It plays a "very important" role in the international negotiations on the issue of climate change.

Thirdly, adhering to the principle of "common but differentiated responsibilities" is an intrinsic requirement of maintaining climate justice. The idea of "common responsibilities" is that because of the universality of the earth's climate and the complex factors that cause global warming, every country shares the responsibility to protect the global climate regardless of its size, wealth, influence, and power. The idea of "differentiated responsibilities" recognizes that for historical and practical reasons, the responsibility for shouldering the burden should be differentiated. This refinement and limitation to the concept of common responsibility is necessary to ensure fairness, justice and feasibility in the assignment of responsibility. According to scientific research, current global warming is the result of excessive emission of greenhouse gases, particularly carbon dioxide, since the start of industrialization. For both historical and practical reasons, developed countries should shoulder a greater share of the burden than developing countries. According to the Carbon Dioxide Information Analysis Center in the USA, the global accumulation of carbon dioxide emission from 1751 to 2004 amounted to 1,15 trillion tons. Half of these emissions were made before developing countries had even started their industrialization process. According to the statistics of an institution in Switzerland, the accumulated carbon dioxide emissions of the USA from 1900 to 2002 amounted to 303 billion tons, and accounted for 28.3% of the world's accumulated emission in the same period. China's emissions over the same period amount to only 8% of the world's total. This means that the USA's contribution to the current CO_2 "stock" is 3.5 times that of China.

In recent years, as the industrialization process in developing countries has advanced, their carbon dioxide emissions have risen rapidly. Their share of total emissions has risen in proportion. However, the emissions from developed countries still account for the majority of the world's total. In addition, globalization and international transfer of industrial activity mean that developing countries are producing large amounts of transferred emissions. As Western economies progress from industrialization to post-industrialization, they transfer industries characterized by high energy consumption, high levels of pollution, and high carbon intensity to developing countries, thereby transferring emissions that are generated by their own consumption. According to the International Energy Agency,

China's exports in 2004 represented about 1.6 billion tons of energy-related carbon dioxide emissions, accounting for 34% of China's total emissions – one third of China's carbon dioxide emissions were generated by foreign consumption.

Although every country makes its contribution to the total emission of greenhouse gases, there are significant differences between individual countries in both total and per capita volumes. According to the USA's Carbon Dioxide Information Analysis Center, China's carbon dioxide emissions amounted to 5.007 billion tons in 2004, accounting for 17.28% of the world's total. The per capita emission was 3.85 tons. The USA's emission was 6.046 billion tons and its per capita emission was 20.56 tons. The USA's per capita carbon dioxide emissions were more than five times China's.

In this sense, developed countries have already been enjoying an affluent lifestyle, and their per capita emissions are still far higher than developing countries. Most of these emissions are generated by consumption, while the emissions of developing countries are mainly subsistence emissions and emissions generated by international transfer. It was in response to this phenomenon that former Chinese Premier Wen Jiabao pointed out at the Copenhagen Climate Conference that it is unreasonable to required developing countries, which have only recently begun industrialization and which have large populations living in absolute poverty, to commit to emission reduction targets that exceed their obligations and capacities.

Finally, adhering to the principle of "common but differentiated responsibilities" is essential to maintaining the rights and interests of the developing countries. In fighting climate change, reducing carbon dioxide emissions has to be done. However, within the scope of existing technology, reducing emissions will certainly require controlling the development of some high-emission industries, and the growth of some energy-consuming sectors. It will surely require investing more in low-carbon energy technologies and low-carbon industries. Because developing countries have low standards and backward technologies, their industries are at the low end of the international industry chain. Therefore, they are dependent on high-emission and high energy consumption industries, and at the same time they lack the funds and the qualified personnel to develop low-carbon energy technologies and low-carbon industries. From this perspective, the issue of climate change is not an environment issue but a development issue. At present, there are 1.3 billion people in the world still living below the poverty line and 1.6 billion people who still do not have electricity supply. These people are mainly in developing countries. Therefore at this juncture the primary tasks for any developing country, including China, remain to develop the economy, to eliminate poverty, and to improve their people's standard of living. Only when the world recognizes the objective reality of the difference in development between different countries, and accepts the principle of "common but differentiated responsibilities" can the legitimate development rights and interests of the developing countries, including China, be assured. As Anthony Giddens, a famous UK sociologist, said in his book *The Politics of Climate Change*: "For the poorer countries there is a development imperative. It is not only that they have the right to become richer, but that such a process has direct implications for sustainability." So, he suggested: "The developed countries must aim to make large cuts in their greenhouse gas emissions, starting now. Developing nations can increase their emissions for a period in order to permit growth, after which they must begin to reduce them. The two groups of countries will then progressively converge."

In the current situation, developed countries must take the lead in making substantial reductions to their emissions. At the same time, they must provide the funds and the technology required to help developing countries to strengthen their ability to fight climate change. Positive adaptive and alleviative measures must be taken on the basis of the prevailing conditions in individual countries which are in the process of developing their economy and eliminating poverty. In this respect, China has fulfilled its international responsibilities as a major developing country.

Firstly, China has made a positive and constructive contribution to fighting global climate change and to the UN's negotiations on climate change. In all the international negotiations on climate change, China has adhered to the dual-track negotiation mechanism proposed in the *United Nations Framework Convention on Climate Change* and the *Kyoto Protocol*. It has also followed the rules of signatory's domination, openness and transparency, active participation, and agreement by consensus. It has strengthened communication and exchanges with interested parties, encouraged divergent views to reach a common understanding, and played an important role in keeping negotiations from breaking down or straying from the matter at hand.

Before the opening of the Copenhagen Conference, China made its own solemn commitment on reducing voluntary emissions – by 2020, its carbon dioxide emissions per unit of GDP will drop by 40-45% compared with that in 2005. Non-chemical energy resources will reach about 15% of total consumption of primary energy. Forested areas will increase by 40 million hectares compared

In June 2013, a boiler was dismantled in the largest coal-burning heating plant in the area within the Fourth Ring Road in Beijing. This was part of the plan of using clean natural gas as the fuel for various facilities in the area within the Four Ring Road.

with 2005, and growing forest stock will increase by 1.3 billion cubic meters. These commitments on the part of the Chinese government contributed directly to the success of the Copenhagen Conference. In each subsequent round of negotiations, China's positive role continued to win praise from the parties involved. During the Durban Conference, the *Washington Post* published an article on November 13, 2011, observing that China's positive contribution had inspired the conference to achieve important progress. Christiana Figueres, executive secretary of the secretariat of the Framework Convention, also spoke highly of China's actions. She stated that, as a developing country, China had become a model for other countries in the fight against climate change.

Secondly, being responsible for the people of China and of the world, China has taken practical steps to fight climate change and achieved positive results. China has formulated the *National Climate Change Program* and set up a national leading group for the work of fighting climate change. It has proposed specific commitments on medium- and long-term emissions reduction, and incorporated the fight against climate change into its economic and social development plans. During the 11th Five-year Plan (2006-2010), China set for the first time energy conservation and emissions reduction as its obligatory target in national economic and social development. It was proposed that, on the basis of the figures for 2005, the energy consumption per GDP unit be lowered by 20% and the chemical oxygen demand of main pollutants and sulfur dioxide emissions each be reduced by 10%. Through the joint efforts of various regions and departments, China's energy consumption per GDP unit during the 11th Five-year Plan was lowered by 19.06%, and chemical oxygen demand and sulfur dioxide emissions dropped by 12.45% and 14.29% respectively. The targets were therefore exceeded. Comprehensive control and restoration work was conducted on an area of 230,000 square kilometer of land suffering water and soil loss. 25.29 million hectares of forest were planted, bringing national forest coverage to 20.36%. From 2001 to 2010, there was an increase of 17.6% in the water surface area achieving Grade III or better, and a drop of 14.9% in the area rated below Grade V. Main pollutant indexes such as ammonia nitrogen, five-day BOD, and permanganate showed falling trends in terms of annual concentration. The number of cities of and above prefecture level whose ambient air quality is up to the standard increased by 50.8%. The annual concentrations of main pollutants such as sulfur dioxide, nitrogen dioxide, and inhalable particles dropped respectively by 23.9%, 9.7% and 28.88%. From 2012, China started to monitor and publish information on PM 2.5 in Beijing, Tianjin, Hebei, the Yangtze River Delta, the Pearl River Delta, centrally-administered municipalities and provincial capitals. During the entire 12th Five-year Plan, China will adopt more powerful measures to promote energy conservation and emissions reduction, and make more contribution to fighting climate change.

Thirdly, China is also a vigorous promoter of South-South cooperation in sustainable development and fighting climate change. By the end of 2011, China had canceled about RMB 30 billion in debts owed by 50 heavily-indebted poor countries and least-developed countries. It had implemented zero tariffs on over 60% of products coming from 38 least-developed countries and provided concessional loans worth over RMB 100 billion to other developing countries. With respect to fighting climate change, China adheres to the principle of "common and differentiated responsibilities." It is committed to maintaining the solidarity of developing countries in international climate negotiations and defending the legitimate rights and interests of developing countries. It meets the standards of a responsible power. It provides facilities like automatic meteorological observation stations, upper-air observation stations, and forest protection equipment in the form of aid to needy countries. It allocated RMB 200 million to carry out a three-year international cooperation program to help small island states, least-developed

In April 2013, egrets in flight over Xianhe Lake in Shizi Village, Taoping Township, in Sichuan Province. Egrets were once nearly extinct in southern Sichuan. But as the environment improves, their numbers are recovering.

countries, and African countries to fight climate change. It was pointed out in the report published by International Energy Agency on May 24, 2012, that global carbon dioxide emissions in 2011 amounted to 31.6 billion tons, showing an increase of one billion tons in comparison with previous year. China's emission per unit of GDP dropped by 15% from 2005 to 2011. "China's achievements in the area of improving energy efficiency and developing clean energy are major dividends to the global environment."

In sum, the principle of "common but differentiated responsibilities" holds that developed countries and developing countries share different obligations in the fight against climate change. This fight is at the core of international cooperation and it must be continuous. In fighting climate change, sustainable development must be the goal. Developing countries must not be forced to pay the price in poverty and backwardness. As a responsible power, China will continue to make the fight against climate change a core priority in realizing economic and social development and in building an ecological civilization. It will remain committed to the principle of "common but differentiated responsibilities," and work hand in hand with the international community to build a "green and prosperous world" free of poverty and ignorance, discrimination and suppression, and excessive exploitation of and human damage to nature, and an environmentally-friendly world that has achieved balance, harmony, economic development, and social justice. Thus the fruits of modern civilization can benefit all mankind and generations yet to come.

The Roadmap of the 18th CPC National Congress and The Chinese Dream

Mankind has only one earth to live on, and countries have only one world to share. History teaches us that the law of the jungle will not lead to the coexistence of human society, and that the arbitrary use of force cannot make the world a better place. China will continue to hold high the banner of peace, development, cooperation and win-win results and strive to uphold world peace and promote common development.

— Report to the 18th CPC National Congress

PART THREE

How Should China's Relationship with the Rest of the World Progress After the 18th CPC National Congress?

Since the beginning of the new century, extensive and profound changes have taken place both in China and the wider world. With these changes, the relationship between China and the rest of world is also experiencing unprecedented historical change. Previously China's fortunes were bound to the rest of the world; now the rest of the world's fortunes are bound to China. In the past, China was at the edge of the international arena; now it has moved to the center stage. It has developed from a participant in the international system to a builder of the system. It has evolved from a learner of the West to a provider of development experience. China's status in the world is growing, its role is becoming more prominent, and its influence is increasing.

As China gradually achieves its development goals, and as the China Dream starts to come true, the international community has begun to ask itself what functions, roles, and responsibilities China will take on in the international community, and whether China's development will lead to tensions in the relationship between China and the rest of the world.

In response to this concern, the Report to the 18th CPC National Congress emphasized that the country will continue to hold high the banner of peace, development, cooperation and win-win efforts, and firmly devote itself to maintaining world peace and promoting joint development. The four terms above reveal the true essence of China's foreign policy. Careful readers might notice that, in comparison with the Report to the 17th CPC National Congress, this report has added the term "win-win efforts" to China's diplomatic banner. In the eyes of the CPC, cooperation is not the ultimate goal of China's diplomacy because cooperation can be either active or passive and either voluntary or forced. If the result of cooperation is a win-lose situation rather than a win-win situation, can such cooperation truly "maintain world peace and promote joint development"? China has included "win-win efforts" in its own aims. This reflects a deepening understanding of the relationship between China and the world in changing times. It is a solemn commitment to the international community and also a sincere expectation of the new international order.

The Roadmap of the 18th CPC National Congress and The Chinese Dream

Chapter 10

How Should China Advance on Its Road of Peaceful Development?

> *China will unswervingly follow the path of peaceful development and firmly pursue an independent foreign policy of peace. We are firm in our resolve to uphold China's sovereignty, security, and development interests, and will never yield to any outside pressure.*
>
> — Report to the 18th CPC National Congress

The rise and fall of great powers is a topic that has been discussed from ancient times. China is a major developing country with a population of 1.3 billion that remains committed to the socialist path, and that is experiencing a major transitional period. How will China achieve its rise and how will this influence the international order? The response of the international community is a mixture of both expectation and doubt. In response to this, China has repeatedly emphasized that it will take the road of peaceful development. This statement was also reaffirmed in the Report to the 18th CPC National Congress. The report also elevated China's commitment to peaceful development to the status of an essential component of socialism with Chinese characteristics. Notwithstanding, the international debate on "China's rise" continues, centering in particular on whether China will challenge the USA's current hegemony. In fact, any adjustment in the balance of major powers – any change in the international configuration – will inevitably lead to some uncertainty. A range of deliberations and predictions on China's development path and its prospects is to be expected and welcomed. But the issues at hand must not be misinterpreted, particularly if this leads to the conclusion that China's commitment to peaceful development is a matter of expediency, or conceals ulterior motives.

Will China genuinely take the road of peaceful development?

The thinking behind these questions lies in the traditional logic that "whenever a country becomes a power it will seek hegemony." Many do not believe that China will be an exception. This traditional logic has been a feature of Western power politics for centuries. It is a key element of the "realistic" theory of international relations. It is accompanied by a belief that this competition for hegemony will be accompanied by conflict or even war.

Over the course of human history, the development of the modern international system has featured a number of hegemonic powers – Rome, Portugal, Spain, the Netherlands, the UK, France, Austro-Hungary, Germany, Japan and Russia. Major countries on the rise regularly challenged the dominant country in the existing international system. In the 20th century, the USA rose to become a major global power exercising unprecedented influence and control. Since the beginning of the 21st century, China's international strength, status and influence have grown rapidly. On the basis of traditional logic, some have started to worry that China cannot avoid straying from the path of peace. Either it will challenge the USA's hegemonic status at global level, or it will provoke conflict with its neighbors at regional level. Such reasoning seems logically sound, but it makes a dogmatic mistake in failing to understand the differences between countries and consider the prevailing conditions of the time.

The logic of power-hegemony is to a large extent a conclusion drawn on the basis of the historical experience of Western countries. Western culture tends to focus on the external, and this determines its tendency to lay stress on personal values and competition. It cultivates a worship of "force." With the rise of the nation-state, this awareness has evolved into armed competition and a drive for expansionism. Ever since the international system with the nation-state as its basic unit was established in Europe, the rise of a power has been accompanied by wars. The drive to establish a colonial system, fight for a sphere of influence, and engage in armed external expansion represents the traditional pathway to power in modern history. However, any theory or logic applies only under certain conditions. There is no such thing as a universally applicable truth. The logic of power-hegemony might have applied in the past, but it is not applicable to the present, and not at all applicable to China. This is an era of globalization. The most important characteristic of this era is the growth of increasingly close connections between countries, which coexist, integrate, and share common interests. In the face of confrontation or conflict of interests, hegemonic approaches, in which the bigger countries bully the smaller, the powerful oppress the weak, and all seek solutions through the use of force, will risk making turbulent situations become chaotic. While this approach might resolve an individual issue, it will result in escalating disputes and wider threats. In a world of global issues and common challenges facing all mankind, countries can survive only through cooperating towards shared goals and seeking joint development on the basis of peaceful coexistence. Multi-polarization and economic globalization are on the increase, bringing new opportunities for international peace and development. This situation represents a solid foundation for harmonious coexistence between countries, for the harmonious development of the global economy, and for the harmonious progress of diverse civilizations.

Against such a background, a country can realize its own rejuvenation through participating in equal, orderly and mutually beneficial international competition and cooperation, and seizing development opportunities. No country needs or can afford to try the old path of expansionism and colonialism. The traditional model is no longer appropriate or even feasible to the present. But there is now an opportunity for a major country to achieve its rise through peaceful development. Evidence for this idea is offered by the rise of emerging market countries, represented by the BRICS countries including China. China's path of peaceful development is consistent with this general trend, and in the context of the country's rapid development, both practical and sound. China can achieve a peaceful rise not because it is an exceptional case or because it operates according to some principles that violate existing rules, but because the world today has changed and the rules for the rise of a country have changed.

Of course, a proper understanding of the logic behind China's commitment to peaceful development requires a proper understanding of China's historical and cultural traditions and ways of thinking. The path a country chooses for its development or rise is undoubtedly influenced by objective conditions and factors, but it is even more dependent on subjective choices. In this age of globalization, there are still some countries that engage in hegemony, some that engage in power politics, and some that are keen to overthrow the legitimate regimes of other countries by means of force. The reason for this is that these countries make a subjective choice to do so. But the reason that China's road of peaceful development is credible is because this is a strategic choice that China has made on the basis of the conditions that prevail in China and in the rest of the world. It is a choice that is consistent with China's own interests, and with those of the world. It is not an expedient measure.

The following are the main factors that China has taken into consideration in making its choice:

The first is that it is not in China's nature to seek hegemony. It is often said that character determines destiny. The character of a country or a nation is mainly determined by its cultural traits. China is a country that does not have a religion in the strict sense, so it does not have the religious impulse to outward expansion. China does have Taoism, which is a form of religion. But Taoism advocates following nature in the Great Way and ruling through inactivity. China is also a country with long history and a profound cultural tradition. The Chinese civilization has strong continuity, and is inclusive and open. China is a nation that loves peace. "To prepare for war is to prevent war and to take up arms is to stop violence" – this ancient teaching is deep-rooted in the hearts of the people of China, along with traditional ideas and thoughts like "cherish peace, wage war with restraint, advocate charity, and exchange interests," and "never impose on others what you would not choose for yourself." In its foreign exchanges, China has always stressed the principles of cementing peaceful relations by upholding good faith, advocating benevolence and good-neighborliness, coexisting in harmony and diversity, and building up profound virtues and shouldering important responsibilities. This consistent theme in China's five-thousand-year-long civilization, or the so-called "path dependence," imposes a radical restraint that prevents modern China from competing for hegemony. During the period of more than a century following the Opium War of 1840, China suffered endless bouts of foreign invasion and colonization. The Chinese people have seen their fill of war and poverty, and they sense all the more deeply how precious is peace and how desirable is development. They fear turbulence, pursue stability, and hope for world peace. They will never impose the sufferings that they have experienced on others or realize their own development by jeopardizing the interests of other countries.

The second is that China's system does not allow it to seek hegemony. China is a socialist country under the leadership of a communist party. The nature of its system requires that China must take the road of peaceful development. As Deng Xiaoping pointed out: "We are building socialism with Chinese characteristics. It is the socialism that constantly develops social productivity and also the socialism that advocates peace." Successive generations of CPC leadership since the founding of new China have all consistently followed the basic national policy of never seeking hegemony or engaging in expansionism. The sincere and solemn commitment that China will "work hard to maintain world peace and promote the undertakings of human progress" is recorded in both the *Constitution of the People's Republic of China* and the *Constitution of the Communist Party of China*. It operates as a sign to the world and as a principle of self-discipline for the Chinese people. China is also the only nuclear-armed state that has committed itself to non-first-use of nuclear weapons.

The third is that the pursuit of hegemony is an invitation to one's own destruction. This is a lesson that history teaches us: No power that has sought hegemony has come to a good end. Germany and Japan launched a world war but were finally defeated. The disintegration of the former Soviet Union was related to a large extent to the policy of expansionism that it advocated. Although the

USA remains the only superpower, the decline of its soft and hard strengths is a hard fact, certainly related to the wars it has launched since the end of the Cold War. China is a country that attaches great importance to historical experience. It is impossible for it to follow in the misguided footsteps of these countries. In addition, China is still in the initial stage of socialism. It does not have the ability to seek hegemony, and even in a future where it is fully developed, China will not seek it. Why would China jeopardize the progress it has made and invite its own downfall by seeking hegemony?

The fourth is that China can achieve development without seeking hegemony. There are precedents for peaceful development. Modern Germany is a good example. After World War II it found renewal because it conducted a profound introspection on its mistakes and chose the road of peaceful development. China's reasoning is as follows:

The country has large domestic demand and relatively abundant resources. It does not need outward expansion – China is capable of independent development.

China is committed to reform and opening-up. It makes constant adjustments to the various factors that affect development through reform. It is a committed participant in the process of economic globalization. It tries to capture development opportunities through competition and cooperation, particularly opportunities brought about by scientific and technological revolution. It can catch up with and establish itself in the front ranks of the world by relying on its own strengths. Although minor war and conflict are common in the present world, a large-scale world war that could affect the global situation of China's development seems unlikely. Therefore China can pursue its development in a relatively stable international environment and drive international development with its own development. Practice has proven that this road is not only a workable one but also the only correct one for China. It is consistent with the mutual interests of the Chinese and of the people in other countries. There is no reason for China to seek any alternative path. It must maintain firm confidence in its chosen alternative, and sufficient patience to advance with perseverance.

In sum, adhering to the road of peaceful development is not some kind of whim. It is a strategic decision that China has made on the basis of a profound understanding of the characteristics of the present age and international trends, by accurately judging historical evidence and prevailing national conditions, by thoroughly summarizing its development process since reform and opening-up, and by sagely drawing from the experiences and lessons in the rise and fall of other powers.

China has a sincere desire and a resolute determination to follow the path of peaceful development. This is a brand new road that satisfies the interests of all members of the international community. It takes advantage of a peaceful international environment to realize the joint prosperity of countries throughout the world. Key to the drive for peaceful development is that countries strive to move towards each other. China's path of peaceful development is not a matter for China alone. Its success needs both the ongoing efforts of the Chinese people and the understanding, support, and cooperation of the international community. The international community must understand China's commitment to peaceful development. China is a country with a vast territory and a huge population. If it cannot free itself from poverty and backwardness, there is a risk that it might become a major source of instability. China is a responsible and important member of the international community, a constructive force and a reliable partner. China's development will bring blessings rather than misfortune and opportunities rather than threats. China sincerely hopes that the international community can learn to understand China's tradition of civilization, developed over thousands of years, and to appreciate the historical evolution of its social system, political system, and values.

The world should respect the feelings of the Chinese people, who have suffered much in recent history, understanding that they cherish state sovereignty, national security, territorial integrity and social stability. It should respect China's core interests and concerns and understand the difficulties that China needs to resolve step by step as the world's biggest developing country. It should believe in the sincerity and determination of the Chinese people in taking the road of peaceful development, and support rather than obstruct, and promote rather than disturb China on its way. Even if people do not understand or accept China's own "explanations," they could, at least, behave in a more open-minded way and allow China to try to present its case, rather than clinging tightly to worn-out doctrines of dogmatic ideology, cold war mentality, and zero-sum game.

Will China continue its commitment to a non-aggressive national defense policy?

When China talks of the road of peaceful development, some people in the international community make the mistake of thinking that China will stand by and concede anything to achieve this goal. In truth, the first requirement of peaceful development is guaranteed security. This can be compared to the living conditions of a person. If a man lacks the bare necessities of life or is constantly sick, how is it possible that he can have any career or future? The same is true of a country. If a country lacks the most basic sense of security and is constantly surrounded by threats, how can it achieve any development? Therefore, security is the basic premise for and guarantee of peaceful development. In order to achieve this, armed forces and a national defense strategy are required. In addition, the more a country develops, the broader the interests it needs to protect, and the higher the demands on its forces and national defense.

Thus the Report to the 18th CPC National Congress proposes that: "It is a strategic task in China's modernization to build a solid national defense strategy and strong armed forces appropriate to China's international status and adapted to the needs of national security and development. China faces security issues that extend across the areas of survival and development and between traditional and non-traditional security threats. This requires a modern national defense strategy and armed forces."

However, China's reasonable stance has often been subject to misinterpretation by the outside world. Many people believe that China does not increase its defense spending and strengthen its military forces only for the purpose of self-defense but with the objective of seeking hegemony. In fact, China adheres to a defensive national defense policy. Its principal aims are to defend state sovereignty, national security, and territorial integrity, to guarantee the peaceful development of the country, and to maintain world peace and stability. China has absolutely no intentions other than these.

Firstly, China's investment in national defense always remains at a reasonable and proper level. China has a population of 1.3 billion spread over a vast territory with long borders and coastlines. Compared with other countries, China's investment in national defense has historically been at a relatively low level. In recent years, it has accounted for a relatively stable proportion of the gross domestic product, amounting to around 1.4%. Other major countries spend as much as 3-4% of their GDP. In 2012, China's spending accounted for only 1.3% of total GDP, while the USA, the UK, and India all spent over 2%. China's limited military forces are retained exclusively for maintaining state sovereignty, national security and territorial integrity.

According to data provided by the Stockholm International Peace Research Institute in Sweden and other foreign research institutions, China's military spending has doubled over the past decade, making it the country with the highest growth rate in defense spending. Nevertheless, what must be emphasized is that when examining a country's defense budget, both the absolute and the relative values must be considered, and China's spending is still far lower than that of the USA in absolute terms. In comparison with other countries, China's total and its per capita military spending are still very low. China poses no threat to the outside world. For many years, China has addressed attention to the coordinated development of both national defense and the economy. When determining the specific increment in defense spending, China always follows the reasonable principle that it should be synchronized with and adapted to the growth in comprehensive national strength. For example, in 2010, due to the impact of the financial crisis, the growth in China's defense spending was adjusted to 7.5%. In 2011, it was increased to 12.7%, as the country's economic sectors gradually recovered. But it is important to understand that the relatively rapid growth in China's national defense spending has compensated for the fact that economic construction took priority over defense spending during the early period of reform and opening-up. As the country was starting from a low base, the actual value of the increase is still limited even when the rate of increase reaches two digits.

Besides, China manages national defense spending in accordance with its relevant laws and regulations such as the national defense law and the fiscal law. Every year, the defense budget is incorporated into the draft national budget. It is reviewed and approved by the National People's Congress and then circulated to lower levels and implemented according to stipulated procedures. The process is also under the supervision of national and military auditing departments. The so-called "hidden military spending" that attracts so much Western media hype does not exist.

In military spending, China always follows two guidelines. One is the test of "appropriateness". It will never engage in an arms race with any country. It will never develop weaponry that exceeds its economic strength. It will never pursue sophisticated arms or growth in the size of its forces. History offers numerous examples where a country has been weakened due to excessive investment in military forces. China will never follow that path to self-destruction. The other is the test of "sufficiency". China's military spending must guarantee the minimal requirements for national defense, otherwise the country will be in danger.

Secondly, military modernization is a response to the new calls upon the forces in a new historical era. China's forces must be able to respond positively to diverse security threats, and must have the capacity to perform a range of diversified military tasks. In times of peace the army plays an increasingly important role in safeguarding national security interests and development, protecting the people's interests, and maintaining world peace and promoting joint development. For example, the army has undertaken several arduous non-combat military operations in recent years. Domestically, they participated in the key earthquake disaster relief operations in Wenchuan and Ya'an, and the emergency rescue operation following the landslip in Zhouqu, Gansu. In the international theater of operations, among the five permanent members of the UN Security Council China is the country that dispatches the largest number of peacekeeping personnel. To date, the Chinese army has taken part in 22 UN peacekeeping missions. Over 20,000 military officers and soldiers have been dispatched on peacekeeping missions. Nine Chinese soldiers have died in the cause of world peace. The Chinese army has also carried out 30 foreign humanitarian missions. On December 26, 2008, the Chinese navy patrolled the Gulf of Aden and the seas off Somalia for the first time, as an escort to passing merchant ships. To date, 13 sailings have conducted 474 escort missions accompanying 4,727 Chinese and foreign vessels. To be capable of responding to such diverse demands, it is reasonable and necessary to increase military spending year by year.

In addition, China's defense modernization must "advance with the time" to keep pace with accelerating military transformation in the present world. In order to further narrow the gap with developed countries in military technology, the Chinese army has applied a reasonable increase in the funds allocated to high-tech weaponry and auxiliary projects in recent years. As China strengthens in economy and science and technology, the pace of military modernization will see further acceleration. China neither

Chapter 10
How Should China Advance on Its Road of Peaceful Development? | 297

On January 6, 2009, the Chinese fleet arrived in the seas off Somalia to conduct its first escort mission.

needs nor seeks to conceal its reasonable and legitimate increases in defense spending. It is only when China is fully developed that it will have the power to contain any forces seeking or competing for hegemony. And by that point China will have the strength to promote the growth of world peace and realize the goal of building a harmonious world. Some voices in the international community use various pretexts to play up the "China Threat" theory and regularly claim that China's military and national defense arrangements lack transparency. Such people need to understand this issue from three perspectives: First, the military transparency of any country is always relative. There is no such thing as absolute transparency in this area. Second, so-called military transparency is a dynamic development process in itself. Higher transparency depends on both the constant improvement of technology in fields such as measurement standards and information communication, and on improvements in the international environment. In particular, the transparency of strategic military intentions is directly related to the degree of mutual trust. Third, China is nevertheless constantly trying to increase its military transparency.

Since 1998, China has published eight white papers on national defense. Three of their consistent themes are a commitment to peaceful development, an independent foreign policy of peace, and a non-aggressive national defense strategy. The white paper on national defense published in 2011 proposed for the first time basic goals such as the construction of an equal, effective, and mutually beneficial military mutual trust mechanism. In 2013, the *Diversified Employment of China's Armed Forces* appeared – the first white paper on national defense devoted to a specific topic. This white paper published for the first time the designations of the 18 group armies in China's land force, the number of troops in mobile operational units in the land force and in the navy, and the code names for the types of missiles deployed by the second artillery force. In order to improve communication on China's national defense policy to the world, a spokesperson for China's Ministry of National Defense made his first appearance on May 18, 2008. From April 2011, an official regular press conference system was established in the Ministry of National Defense. On August 20, 2009, the Ministry of National Defense website ran an online pilot. On August 1, 2011, after nearly two years of stable operation, the website was officially launched on the 84th anniversary of the founding of the People's Liberation Army.

Also worthy of note is that in recent years China has several times issued information on the development and testing of sophisticated national defense technology and equipment. For example, on January 11, 2010, China carried out a successful trial of ground-based in-flight missile interception technology. In 2011, its first stealth combat aircraft, the J-20, made a successful maiden flight. In August 2011, China carried out a successful sea trial of its first aircraft carrier. In November 2012 its first carrier-based fighter, the J-15, made a successful take-off from and landing on the carrier. In January 2013 it completed its first independently-developed large transport aircraft, the Y-20. Also in this month, it conducted a second successful test of its ground-based in-flight missile interception technology. The development and testing of this sophisticated military technology and equipment is consistent with China's declared defense policy and security strategy.

In the context of foreign interactions, the Chinese government participated in 2007 in the *United Nations Report on Military Ex-*

penditures, which aims to increase military transparency. Since then it has lodged an annual report with the United Nations on its military expenditure. China also lodges returns with the UN Register of Conventional Arms. The armed forces are also involved in regular, diverse, and in-depth foreign exchanges. For example, Robert Gates, then US Secretary of Defense, visited the Second Artillery Force Command in January 2011. Six months later, Michael Mullen, the Chairman of the Joint Chiefs of Staff of the US Naval Operation, also visited the Second Artillery Force Command. He boarded a third-generation fighter from China's air force and inspected a PLA unit anti-terrorism exercise. He conducted field visits to the composite mobile command and control system of China's land force and a new-type navy submarine. Joint exercise and training maneuvers between Chinese and foreign forces have become a regular event and an important element of transnational communication and cooperation. These new developments all indicate that China's military diplomacy has become increasingly open, practical and active. These consistent efforts above all highlight China's sincerity in its declared intention to improve military transparency.

Does China's peaceful development have a "bottom line principle"?

For China, peaceful development is never a simple matter. There will always be pressure and obstruction from various quarters. In a complex environment of conflict in which some countries still maintain or covet hegemony, it is essential to remain firmly committed to the declared national policy, and to address in full the practical issue of defending national interests with multiple means. China has always advocated and practiced the principle that all countries are equal members of the international community regardless of size, power and wealth, and they should respect each other and treat each other with equality. China advocates understanding and tolerating the world's diversity with an open heart. All parties should respect the values of other countries and the development road that they have chosen. They should respect the core concerns of other countries and should not interfere in the internal affairs of other countries.

Of course, concerning China's core interests and important concerns, China will adhere to the same principles and defend its own right of equality and respected for its legitimate and hard-earned rights and interests. A country's choice of development road should never be made at the cost of sacrificing its core interests. No one should imagine that China will compromise on any issue involving its fundamental principles for the sake of "peaceful development".

The white paper *China's Peaceful Development*, published in 2011, defines six core interests: "state sovereignty, national security, territorial integrity, national unification, stable state political system and general social situation as established in China's *Constitution*, and basic guarantee for sustainable economic and social development." These core interests represent the supreme principles of the Chinese government and the Chinese people which brook no compromise, concession or infringement. They are of fundamental importance to maintaining national security and formulating and improving national security strategy. While China will adhere to the road of peaceful development and will never seek hegemony in the present or in the future, this will not be done at the price of giving up legitimate rights and interests, sacrificing core national interests, or jeopardizing Chinese sovereignty, security and development interests. Like every other country, China has its own principles and its own bottom line, and no threat or intimidation of any kind will ever place these in jeopardy.

This is particularly true on the issue of Taiwan. In recent years, the Chinese government has adopted various measures to promote the peaceful development of cross-straits relations with Taiwan. It firmly believes that peaceful unification ultimately conforms to the best interests of the Chinese nation, including the Taiwan people. The Report to the 18th CPC National Congress also proposed a series of important measures on continuing to promote communication and cooperation. For example: "Discussions on political relations across the Taiwan Straits should take place recognizing that the nation has not yet been unified, and making proper and reasonable arrangements accordingly... Consultations should take place on establishing a mutual trust mechanism on military security across the Taiwan Straits and stabilizing the situation across the Taiwan Straits... Consultations should take place on concluding a peace agreement across the Taiwan Straits and opening up a new future for the peaceful development of the relations across the Taiwan Straits."

It was emphasized at the same time in the report: "The fact has never changed that the territories across the Taiwan Straits belong to one China. The nation's territory and sovereignty have never been severed and are not to be severed." The Chinese government "resolutely opposes any schemes for 'Taiwan Independence'." The Chinese people absolutely will not allow any person or force to separate Taiwan from the motherland by any means.

Because China has not promised to give up the use of force over the Taiwan issue, some in the international community have questioned the sincerity of China's commitment to peaceful development. In fact, maintaining national unity and territorial integrity is the sacred right of any sovereign state and also a basic principle in international law. For a variety of historical reasons, Taiwan is currently in a state of separation from the mainland. To resolve the Taiwan issue and realize the unification of the country is the solemn mission of all the Chinese people.

The declared basic policy of the Chinese government in resolving the Taiwan issue is to unify the motherland by peaceful means. It advocates that any disagreement and confrontation across the Taiwan Straits can and should be resolved by peaceful means. The Chinese people across the Taiwan Straits should do everything to avoid a situation where the people of a single nation make war against each other. They should work hand in hand in an atmosphere of peace to build a bright future together for the Chinese nation. This is the policy and the aspiration of the Chinese government. However, such matters cannot be handled on the basis of wishful thinking. If Taiwan independence emerges, resolute and bold measures may be called for in response, including the use of force. This is the fundamental principle on the basis of which peaceful reunification and the resolution of the Taiwan issue will be achieved. Its principal targets are foreign forces, separatists, and the force for Taiwan independence. If the Chinese government commits to the non-use of force, this may incite independence protagonists into radical and imprudent actions which could cause the problem to escalate.

In practice, the mainland policy towards Taiwan is always people-oriented. It emphasizes that the mainland people and the

On May 17, 2011, the "ECFA Practice Workshop" – a themed forum at the 13th Cross-strait Fair for Economy and Trade – was held in Fuzhou, Fujian Province. Experts, scholars, and individuals from industry and business across the Taiwan Straits gathered together to discuss the new conditions and issues that have emerged since the implementation of ECFA, and proposed improvements and ideas.

people of Taiwan form a community of shared interests with connected blood lines, and that the fruits of peaceful development across the Straits should be shared by the people of both the mainland and Taiwan. In 2010, both sides concluded the *Economic Cooperation Framework Agreement* (ECFA). This agreement plays a positive and fruitful role in expanding economic and trade exchanges across the Straits, promoting economic development on both sides. It also generates positive economic and social benefits in Taiwan. It was proposed in China's defense white paper of 2011 that the Taiwan authorities may engage in contact and communication on military issues at any appropriate time, and discuss the issue of establishing a mutual trust mechanism on military security. In the *Compendium on the 12th Five-year Plan* published in 2012, a specific chapter is devoted to relations with Taiwan. All of the above serves to demonstrate that the relationship across the Straits is now presented with important and unprecedented opportunities. It is believed that the Chinese people on both sides of the Taiwan Straits have the ability and wisdom to be open to a future that foresees the prospect of national rejuvenation. They will hold the fate of Taiwan in their own hands.

In addition to the Taiwan issue, China has had a number of other disputes with neighboring countries in recent years, centering around island ownership and marine rights and interests. Such frictions and conflicts have recently showed a tendency to increase in number and intensity. Some international opinion criticizes China for taking a hard-line position and straying from the path of peaceful development. What must be pointed out is that China's path of peaceful development means that China will not seek development by means of war. But it does not mean that China is afraid of waging war to defend its national interests. If China's strategic commitment to peaceful development is regarded as a block that will prevent China from maintaining its rights and interests, including its marine interests, encouraging adversaries to try to act as they please, this is most unwise and they are likely to pay a heavy price.

China is neither proud nor arrogant, but it will not hesitate to defend its own core interests. The Report to the 18th CPC National Congress requires accelerating the modernization of the defense forces. The CPC leadership has also told the army to bear in mind that "to be capable of waging war and to be able to secure victory are the key to a strong army." This does not signify that China is engaging in wars of words. History has proven that, if a country wants to avoid war, it should be prepared for war. The more diligent the preparation, the less likely the prospects of war breaking out. Of course, peaceful negotiation should be the first resort in resolving disputes in preference to threats of force or actual use of force. This will always be China's approach to maintaining the integrity of its territory and its other national interests.

In sum, China's intentions towards the rest of the world are good. It takes responsibility for its own actions and respects other countries. It seeks to treat others equally, coexist in peace, achieve mutual benefits and win-win results, and develop jointly. At the same time, it is a country that does not accept willful offense or humiliation. After over 60 years of arduous and tortuous effort, particularly through three hard decades of reform and opening-up, China has truly found the confidence to build the country and defend its own legitimate national interests. Its stance is also firmer. But this is not any kind of "arrogance" or "hard-line position". It is the normal reaction and behavior of a major country that is developing towards maturity and becoming increasingly integrated into the international community. China's peaceful development is the dream of the century of the Chinese people. It is also the goal of the struggle of several generations who have continued the march of their fallen predecessors. It will continue to be the noble responsibility of the generations to come. China will not let its commitment to its chosen road of peaceful development be shaken by the doubts and misunderstandings of external forces.

The Roadmap of the 18th CPC National Congress and The Chinese Dream

Chapter 11

Can China Really Achieve Win-Win Results with Other Countries?

China will unwaveringly adhere to an opening-up strategy of mutual benefits and win-win results. It will promote robust, sustainable and balanced growth of the global economy through deepening cooperation.

— Report to the 18th CPC National Congress

When China acceded into the WTO in 2001, many people both in China and abroad worried that the need to adapt to its international trading rules might have a negative impact on China's development. But continued growth in the decade that followed proved that such concern was unnecessary. Indeed China's success has caused another concern – namely, once it is fully-developed, will China share its good fortune and win-win results with other countries in the world? Particularly in the present situation where many countries are still suffering from the impact of the global financial crisis, the international community has deep concerns on such issues as whether China will slow down the pace of reform and opening-up, whether China will engage in trade protectionism, and how China will address trade friction with other countries. They are also wary of whether China's foreign aid will come with political strings attached, like that of the West.

To these questions, the Report to the 18th CPC National Congress gave the following answer: "China will unwaveringly adhere to an opening-up strategy of mutual benefit and win-win results. It will promote robust, sustainable and balanced growth of the global economy through strengthening cooperation. China is committed to reducing the South-North Gap and helping developing countries to enhance their capacity for independent development. China will strengthen its coordination with major economies in macroscopic economic policies. It will properly resolve economic and trade frictions through negotiation. China adheres to the principle of the balance between rights and obligations. It participates positively in the governing of the global economy and promotes the liberalization and facilitation of trade and investment. It opposes various forms of protectionism."

On December 31, 2012, General Secretary Xi Jinping emphasized at the second collective learning session of the Political Bureau of the 18th CPC Central Committee that China will remain committed to an opening-up strategy of mutual benefit and win-win results. It will expand and deepen the convergence points with the interests of various parties. It will refine and improve the relevant systems and mechanisms and take effective action against potential risks so as to promote development, reform, and innovation with opening-up.

Has China slowed down the pace of opening up to the outside world?

Opening up to the outside world is a basic national policy determined by the CPC at the Third Plenary Session of the 11th CPC National Congress held in 1978. For over 30 years, opening up to the outside world helped China quickly realize the transformation from a low-income country to a major economic and trading power. It promoted the establishment, improvement, and completion of a socialist market economic system. It accelerated the process of industrialization and greatly improved the living standards of its people. In addition, the open economy in China also makes an increasing contribution to world economic growth and has become the strongest engine of economic growth in the world today. However, since the outbreak of the international financial crisis, there have been noticeable changes to China's opening-up. The international economic structure is in a period of transition. Global governance regimes have embarked upon a process of transformation, industrial and technical innovation is in a phase of incubation, and the forces of emerging market countries are on the rise.

In the domestic environment, China is speeding up the adjustment of the industrial structure and the transformation of the mode of economic development. In consequence, China has adjusted some of its industrial and regional focuses in opening up to the outside world in recent years. But this does not represent any radical change in policy. It would be more accurate to say that China is aiming for a more solid base, and higher quality and standards, as is emphasized in the Report to the 18th CPC National Congress, with its commitment to "comprehensively improving the standards of an open economy." After the close of the 18th CPC National Congress, General Secretary Xi Jinping chose first to inspect Shenzhen, a city located at China's frontier to the outside world. The signal he intended to send out is that "reform will not be suspended, and opening-up will not come to a halt."

In the following sections we would like to offer an analysis of some of the elements that have caused misunderstandings in the international community.

On the issue of consistency in the treatment of domestic and foreign-funded enterprises. Positive treatment of foreign investors was a key element in China's opening-up. At the beginning of reform and opening-up, China urgently needed foreign investment to make up for the twin shortage of both foreign exchange and technology. At the time, China did not have a complete market economic system. Foreign-funded enterprises faced additional costs as well as administrative problems. Because of this, China provided a tax exemption guarantee known as "super-national treatment." But as reform and opening-up advanced and China joined the WTO, profound changes occurred in China's foreign investment strategy. In 2010, FDI into China exceeded USD 100 billion. China has become the country with the second largest foreign investment inflow in the world. China's market economic system is now approaching maturity. When a foreign enterprise invests in China, it benefits from lower administrative costs. The resulting competitive advantage to foreign investors has a significant impact on domestically-funded enterprises. Such treatment also distorts the decision-making process for foreign investors. It has therefore become necessary to remove the advantages offered to foreign investors. Such measures are entirely consistent with the relevant provisions of the World Trade Organization.

During the "11th Five-year Plan" (2006-2010), the advantages and the special treatment available to foreign-funded enterprises in areas such as taxation and land use were gradually eliminated. In 2008, the new *Law on Corporate Income Tax* and the new *Anti-monopoly Law* were officially implemented. They signified a substantive adjustment to China's inward investment policy, designed to create an environment for fair competition between domestic and foreign investments. In the same year, China integrated income tax provisions, imposing a unified 25% income tax rate on state-owned, private and foreign enterprises. By the end of 2010 urban maintenance and construction tax, and additional education charges were extended to foreign-funded enterprises. Since then, taxation policies for domestic and foreign-funded enterprises in China have been the same. Currently, the majority of countries impose standard tax rates on all enterprises in their territory. Foreign-funded enterprises who have become accustomed to enjoying preferential treatment may have some difficulty in adapting to the new regime, but China's measures represent a further step in falling into line with standard international practice.

On the withdrawal from China of some foreign-funded enterprises. Any business entering an unfamiliar foreign market will face a variety of risks. It is quite normal that some foreign-funded enterprises experience problems in adapting to local conditions and ultimately decide to withdraw from China. There have been several such cases in recent years. The main reason for their problems is not the deterioration of China's investment environment, but their own shortcomings in terms of outlook and decision-making. For example, some foreign-funded enterprises have attempted to mount a challenge to China's laws and regulations. When Google, for example, applied to enter China in 2006, it made commitments that accorded with the relevant laws and regulations in China. This included a provision that it should filter certain information in its search content. Four years later, Google threatened to withdraw from China in protest against the requirement. The fact is that Internet censorship was not invented by China. Governments have the right to supervise and regulate Internet service providers in accordance with the law of their lands. After the 911 Terrorist Attack, the USA passed the *Patriot Act,* which specifically provided that the police authorities had the right to access the email traffic of private citizens. Many states in the USA have also passed legislation on filtering and screening Internet content.

Google's threat to withdraw from the Chinese market, intending to establish extraterritorial rights in China, violated fundamental international principles. In response to this, China's State Council Information Office and the ministries of Foreign Affairs, Commerce and Industry, and Information Technology, all categorically reaffirmed the primacy of Chinese law. They took the view that foreign-funded enterprises in China should abide by Chinese law and act in accordance with relevant regulations, and they opposed the politicization of business issues.

Other foreign enterprises fail to conduct the necessary research into the Chinese market. The Barbie doll is a case in point. Although it was a relatively upmarket doll brand, its proprietors failed to carry out a proper investigation of Chinese market and the purchasing behavior of Chinese consumers. They did not have a proper understanding of the competition in China's doll market. As a result, their marketing strategies were ineffective and their plans were flawed. A brand which has enjoyed huge success in the West failed to communicate its core brand values to its target customer groups in China.

On the supposed "deterioration" of the investment environment for foreign businesses in China. The changes brought about by more than 30 years of reform and opening-up have had a profound impact on the investment environment. In terms of market access, China has constantly increased its openness to foreign investment. The *Catalog for the Guidance of Foreign Investment Industries* promulgated in 2011 showed that, far from reducing the areas in which foreign investment was permitted, China was greatly expanding them. The catalog specified five areas where foreign investment was prohibited, but added 94 items where foreign investment was encouraged. High-end manufacturing was a key example of such an area. The catalog also added nine service industries, and included foreign-funded medical institutions and financial leasing companies in the list of approved areas. However, China's own private and state-owned enterprises are developing and growing rapidly, and the number of transnational companies in the Chinese market is also increasing constantly. All of this serves to intensify competition. The steady rise of wages in China applies cost pressure to foreign investors. China's consumer market is maturing, increasing expectations in terms of the quality of the products and services provided by foreign-funded enterprises. The result is greater pressure on foreign-funded enterprise than in the past, and such changes do have a degree of influence on the investment strategy of transnational companies. Some companies have relocated from China back to their homeland, or moved their operation to other countries. This is a fact, but it should not lead to the conclusion that China's investment environment is deteriorating. Data shows that foreign-funded enterprises in China generally perform well, and foreign investors register a high degree of satisfaction with China's investment environment.

According to statistics from the Ministry of Commerce, China absorbed USD 90 billion in FDI in 2009, showing a drop of only 2.6% in circumstances where global transnational direct investment had dropped by nearly 40%. China remained the country that attracted the second largest volume of foreign investment on the globe. In 2010, China attracted over USD 100 billion in foreign investment, with a year-on-year increase of 17.4%. The *Global Investment Trends Monitor* published by the United Nations Conference on Trade and Development indicates that, in the first half of 2012, China absorbed USD 59.1 billion in FDI and became the world's largest FDI destination. In terms of popularity as an investment destination for transnational companies, China ranked first, followed by the USA and India in second and third places. The *2012 China Business Climate Survey Report*, published by the American Chamber of Commerce in the People's Republic of China (AmCham China), shows that 39% of the US enterprises interviewed indicated that their profit rates in China are still higher than in any other region.

Change is happening in China's investment environment. But while this change discouraged some investors, it is still attractive to others. For example, Coca Cola plans to invest USD 4 billion in China by 2015. Other well-known transnational enterprises like Siemens and BASF are also strengthening their investment in the Chinese market.

In the past, the main attraction for foreign companies was China's low labor cost. Now, they are starting to move towards the high-end of their industry. Statistics indicate that by the end of 2011 there were already over 1,600 foreign-funded R&D centers in China. Of these, nearly 50% were engaged in research on pioneering technologies. Over 60% of these R&D centers have as their principal target the global market. In addition, new-type service sectors like tourism, transportation, communication, insurance, consultation and advertisement are becoming new growth areas for attracting foreign investment.

What is China's view of trade liberalization?

After the international financial crisis in 2008, there was a resurgence of protectionism. In fact, history teaches us that protectionism is the inevitable consequence of any major economic or financial crisis. Against the background of this international financial crisis, various governments adopted measures to stimulate their own economy. At the same time, they began to create trade barriers. Protectionism emerged in various forms – some of them new – such as strengthening the protection of manufacturing industries, employing extensive non-tariff barriers, restricting the international flow of labor, and expanding protectionism into the area of investment. China's attitude to all this is clear. The Report to the 18th CPC National Congress emphasized that: "China adheres to the balance between rights and obligations. It participates positively in global economic governance and promotes the liberalization and facilitation of trade and investment. It opposes all forms of protectionism."

Trade is the engine of economic growth. Trade liberalization helps to optimize the trade and economic structure of a country. Trade liberalization promotes competition. It can lower the power of monopoly in an industrial area in which competition is suboptimal. It can increase the effect of scale economies and promote increased labor productivity. Trade liberalization can help to create a positive international distribution of work. Different countries can concentrate on the manufacture of the most profitable or relatively more profitable products on the basis of their national conditions and comparative strengths. This helps to achieve the optimal configuration of productive factors and increases productivity. Trade liberalization can increase the volume of product in circulation. It can expand markets, promote scale economies, and lower production cost and product price.

For China, trade liberalization is an important institutional factor in its economic success. Reliable research shows that following the 1990s, every 10% increment of export growth in China drove an additional 1% growth in GDP. Trade liberalization not only promotes China's technical progress but also generates significant competitive pressure among its businesses, which promotes efficiency and favors selection of the strong and elimination of the weak. In addition, under the propulsion of trade, China's surplus rural labor is gradually transferred towards manufacturing industry. Manufacturing industry is also experiencing an internal structural transformation and upgrading. Overall production efficiency in industry is on the increase. As opening-up impacts on goods and services, factors such as operational philosophies, flow of personnel and capital, and new concepts, techniques and technology all flow into China and inject dynamism into China's economy.

When China started to implement free trade policies, and particularly following its accession to the WTO in 2001, its comparative strengths were liberated. In the areas of international trade, foreign investment in China and China's investment overseas, China achieved win-win development together with other countries. Article 4 in the first chapter of the General Provisions in the *Foreign Trade Law of the People's Republic of China*, revised, promulgated and put into effect in 2004, stipulated that: "The state implements a centralized foreign trade system, encourages the development of foreign trade, and maintains the fair and free order of foreign trade." In the ten years since accession to the WTO, China's average tariff has dropped from 15.3% to 9.8%. It has opened over 100 service trade sectors to the world. It has also carried out the largest rationalization of laws and regulations in its history, involving more than 3,000 items. The opening-up of its service sector has been a major step forward in China's opening-up to the outside world. China is committed to implementing the WTO principles of non-discrimination, transparency, and fair competition in its economic system, and to enhancing market awareness, consciousness of the rule of law, and respect for intellectual property right protection. Imports have grown by a factor of almost five, and China has become the second largest importing country in the world. China's trade volume accounts for one tenth of the world total, and it has therefore become an important driver and power source for international economic growth.

China attaches great importance to building free trade zones with suitable partner countries and considers this to be an important means to promote trade liberalization. In 2007, China proposed for the first time that it would "implement the strategy of free trade zones and strengthen bilateral and multilateral economic and trade cooperation." At present, China is building 16 free trade zones with 29 countries and regions on the five major continents. Twelve of these have already been signed and put into effect, comprising the free trade agreements with ASEAN, Singapore, Pakistan, New Zealand, Chile, Peru, Switzerland, Iceland, and Costa Rica, the closer economic partnership arrangements with Hong Kong and Macao, and the Cross-Strait Economic Cooperation Framework Agreement with Taiwan. The four free trade zones under negotiation are those with the Gulf Cooperation Council, Australia, Norway, and South Korea. In addition, China has already completed joint studies on regional trade arrangements with India and on a free trade zone with Japan and South Korea with the participation of representatives from government, industry, and education. China has also acceded to the *Asia-Pacific Trade Agreement*.

In the process of implementing its free trade zone strategy, China's approach is that of "taking neighbors as basic partners while

Chapter 11
Can China Really Achieve Win-Win Results with Other Countries?

On July 6, 2013, Gao Hucheng, Minister of Commerce of China, and Johann Schneider-Ammann, member of the Swiss Federal Council and head of the Federal Department of Economic Affairs, Education and Research, officially signed the Sino-Swiss Free Trade Agreement, the first FTA that China has signed with a European country.

extending its gaze towards the wider world." Its policies are characterized by principles such as openness, equality, substance, step-by-step progress, and inclusion.

The principle of openness means that China adheres to open regionalism and takes the position that it can discuss the possibility of building free trade zones with all economies that are willing to cooperate. The principle of equality means that the parties participating in the negotiations have equal status and set mutual benefit and win-win results as their basic objectives. The principle of substance means that China advocates "high-quality" free trade agreements involving substantive liberalization standards. The principle of step-by-step progress means that China advocates that people should adopt a progressive approach that proceeds in an orderly manner starting with the easy tasks before moving on to the more difficult ones, and working in phases dealing first with scope of membership, then areas to be negotiated, and on to the extent of liberalization and the realization of predetermined objectives. The principle of inclusion means that people should take into consideration the particularity of different economies and be flexible in making arrangements with underdeveloped and smaller countries.

Implementing its free trade zone strategy plays a very important role in promoting the rapid development of trade and investment between China and its trade partners, promoting China's domestic economic growth and structural adjustment, and enhancing the economic partnership between the members with mutual benefits and win-win results. It also embodies China's positive attitude in peaceful development and opening up to the outside world. For example, after the China-ASEAN free trade zone came into full effect on January 1, 2010, it had a remarkable impact on driving the growth of bilateral trade. From 2008 to 2010, imports and exports between China and the ASEAN showed an average annual increase noticeably higher than the average growth of China's foreign trade in general over the same period. Also noteworthy was that imports grew faster than exports. Obvious changes also occurred in the structure of bilateral trade. Growth was faster in technology-intensive products such as transportation equipment, electric and electronic products, and precision machinery.

In 2012, trade cooperation with ASEAN became even closer under the framework of the free trade zone. From January to November of 2012, bilateral trade between China and ASEAN grow steadily. The total value reached USD 360 billion, showing year-on-year growth of 9.3%. At present, ASEAN is China's third largest trade partner, its fourth largest export market, and its second largest source of imports. Bilateral investment between China and ASEAN is also increasing steadily. By the end of October 2012, cumulative bilateral investment was already approaching USD 100 billion. Chinese enterprises had invested in and built five economic and trade cooperation zones in Cambodia, Thailand, Vietnam and Indonesia. These zones continue to develop, with the number of enterprises and the output value both increasing. Such developments drive local employment and tax income.

The impact of China's free trade zone strategy is undeniable, but the gap between China and some of the other major world economies remains. In the 12th Five-year Plan, the Chinese government specifically proposed the basic goal of "implementing an opening-up strategy of mutual benefit and win-win results, and increasing opening-up to the outside world." China would take "guiding and promoting the process of regional cooperation and accelerating the free trade zone strategy" as a strategic task in the development of foreign economic relations over the next five years. China possesses tremendous market capacity and huge development potential. As its total trade volume and economic strength continue to increase, China will continue to conclude appropriate free trade agreements with more countries. Beyond the scope of the current five-year plan, more and broader free trade zones will develop as a new channel and platform for China's reform and opening-up. This will provide new dynamism to the economic growth of China and its trade partners.

What would happen in the case of trade friction with other countries?

Trade friction and disputes are the inevitable consequences of economic globalization and trade liberalization. This is particularly the case when a country is in a phase of rapid foreign trade growth. History provides examples such as the USA, Japan and Germany, which all underwent a long period of trade surplus accompanied by rising trade friction. Presently, trade friction and disputes exist at several levels – between China and other countries, among developed countries, and among developing countries. For a variety of reasons, as China's foreign trade grows rapidly and the economy merges with the rest of the world, trade disputes between China and its trading partners are on the increase. The main reasons for this situation are as follows:

First, trade protectionism against China has been rising. The economic depression due to the impact of the international financial crisis has resulted in some countries turning to protectionism as a response. In developed countries such as Europe and the USA, some traditional labor-intensive products have gradually lost their competitive advantages in world markets. Manufacturers and trade unions in relevant industries in these countries have exerted pressure on their governments to implement policies to encourage exports or restrict imports, causing regular friction with China. Following the example and under the influence of the developed countries, and in order to protect their own industries, some developing countries have also employed trade protection measures against China in order to compete for the markets in developed countries. The steel and iron industry is a good example. As China's steel exports grew, its products became a focus of charges related to the anti-dumping and anti-subsidy sanctions of other countries. According to the "Global Trade Alert" project run by the Center for Economic Policy Research, a UK think tank, 40% of world protectionist measures since the international financial crisis of 2008 have been directed against China.

Second, China still has "non-market economic status". When China acceded to the WTO, it accepted some restrictive terms like "non-market economic status" and "special safeguard measures". Some of China's major trade partners still do not accept China's "full market economy status." This makes it easier for them to initiate trade investigations against imports from China. When carrying out anti-dumping investigations, they classify China as a "non-market economy" in order to justify taking discriminatory measures. Chinese exporters are therefore disadvantaged when they try to determine a reasonable pricing strategy. Developing countries like India, Mexico and Brazil also follow the example of developed countries in Europe and the USA. When they carry out anti-dumping investigations, they treat China as a "non-market economy".

Third, China's economy and trade have grown consistently and rapidly, and this is exerting serious pressure on some countries. In 1978, China's total volume of imports and exports amounted to only USD 20.6 billion. It ranked 32nd in terms of trade, accounting for less than 1% of the world total. In 2010, this figure had reached USD 2,974 billion – multiplied by a factor of 143 in comparison with 1978 – and representing an annual increase of 16.8%. After 1990, China's foreign trade turned from an overall deficit to overall surplus. In contrast, developed economies like the USA, Japan and Europe were suffering slowdowns or even recession in economic growth. Even developing countries with faster economic growth have erected trade barriers to Chinese products in order to protect domestic industries and local employment. Some blame China for self-inflicted economic problems and propagate the "China Threat" theory. All of this serves to intensify their trade friction with China.

Fourth, there are still certain defects in China's economic and trade system. After reform and opening-up, China's foreign trade system gradually aligned itself with international trade rules. A centralized and open foreign trade system that conforms to multilateral trade rules gradually formed. However, China is still a developing country. It suffers from a weakness in scientific and technological innovation, a sub-optimal industrial structure, and a weak agricultural base. There are also certain system defects in the process of economic transformation. There is still a gap between China's prevailing systems and the requirements of the WTO rules. For example, China's legal system lags behind its economic development. Protection of intellectual property rights is still unsatisfactory. Relevant government departments and industry associations lack effective coordination mechanisms. Exporting enterprises sometimes get into a price war to win orders, bringing chaos to the export system. All these factors can very easily trigger trade disputes, and cause countries to erect trade barriers against China.

In this respect, the Chinese government takes the view that trade friction and disputes should be avoided as much as possible, responded to positively, handled prudently, and resolved properly.

The basic principle that China follows in addressing its trade disputes with other countries is the principle of "peaceful settlement of disputes" specifically proposed in the *United Nations Charter of Economic Rights and Duties of States*. That is to say, when trade disputes arise, the countries involved should respect each other's rights and adopt peaceful measures to settle them. They should avoid unilateral measures and refrain from using force or threatening the use of force. The Report to the 18th CPC National Congress pointed out that China "will strengthen the coordination of macroscopic economic policies with major economies and properly resolve economic and trade friction through negotiation." The main measures through which this is achieved are as follows:

First, by strengthening communication and exchange with the parties involved and making use of bilateral dialogue and cooperation mechanisms to resolve conflicts. China always maintains that dialogue is better than confrontation and cooperation is better than exerting pressure. Disputes between trade partners should be settled through consultation and negotiation. Over the years, China has established a large number of bilateral dialogue and consultation mechanisms with relevant countries. It makes full use of a variety of platforms, such as high-level economic consultation and dialogue, and joint committees and joint commissions. Through these measures, China can properly settle its disagreements and disputes with third parties and address their concerns in a reasonable manner so as to avoid the politicization of economic issues and the intensification of conflict. The Department of International Economic Affairs of the Ministry of Foreign Affairs of the People's Republic of China was officially established in October 2012. Its main function is to carry out economic communication with other countries, including coordinating and handling international economic disputes. The Ministry of Commerce has already established trade remedy cooperation mechanisms with the investigation organs of 16 trade partners, including the USA, the EU, Russia, India, Korea and Australia.

Second, all parties should abide by the WTO rules and make effective use of multilateral trade mechanisms. China diligently fulfills the commitments it made on accession to the WTO and observes WTO rules. It argues strongly on just grounds in accordance with WTO rules. In cases where negotiation cannot resolve a dispute, China will handle trade disputes and maintain the stability of multilateral trade systems through the proper use of the WTO dispute settlement mechanism. In the multilateral system, China is not only a passive "respondent," but also an active "plaintiff." For example, the World Trade Organization responded to a Chinese complaint in 2010 and decided that U.S. restrictions on poultry imports from China violated the WTO rules. In a trade dispute between China and the EU concerning fasteners, the WTO Appellate Body also supported China's position.

Third, reform of foreign economic and trade systems should be strengthened, to create a fair and transparent market environment. In order to decrease economic and trade friction, China is constantly striving to improve its foreign trade regulations, and to build a relatively comprehensive legal system to deal with foreign trade. This promotes the opening-up of China's domestic market and eliminates internal regional barriers and industrial monopolies. China is also increasing transparency and setting up the required import promotion system and policies, with a view to easing external pressure and conflict. It is strengthening the protection of intellectual property rights and maintaining the interests of the investments of transnational companies in China in accordance with the law. It is adjusting and optimizing its industrial structure and ensuring orderly competition. It is steadily refining and completing an early warning mechanism for trade disputes so as to ensure that potential disputes are identified as early as possible, and can be resolved through negotiation.

Fourth, import controls designed to protect domestic industries should always be implemented in accordance with the law. The WTO stipulates that in order to maintain fair trade and orderly competition, its members are allowed to adopt remedial measures such as anti-dumping, anti-subsidy, and protective measures for domestic industry, in cases where imports threaten their domestic industries. To these ends, China has formulated relevant laws and regulations like the *Foreign Trade Law* and the *Anti-Dumping and Anti-Subsidy Regulations*. China has always taken a very prudent attitude on remedial investigations as its relevant measures are intended to correct unfair trade practices rather than to engage in protectionism.

Why does China attach no conditions to its foreign aid?

New China began its foreign aid program in the 1950s. Even when it was itself experiencing the most difficult times, China still provided generous aid to many countries in Asia, Africa and Latin America. According to the white paper *China's Foreign Aid* published in 2011, the cumulative value of China's foreign aid over the past 60 years exceeds RMB 250 billion yuan. China has helped developing countries complete over 2,000 projects. About 80% of its foreign aid has gone to countries in Asia and Africa. In the course of its foreign aid program, China has gradually formed a set of guiding principles with Chinese characteristics. Of these, the most prominent is that Chinese aid has no political strings attached. At the Asian-African Conference held in 1955, Premier Zhou Enlai proposed the Five Principles of Peaceful Coexistence. Non-interference in internal affairs is a fundamental principle in China's handling of foreign relations, and is the root of the principle of having no political strings attached to foreign aid.

Early in 1964, when Premier Zhou Enlai visited 14 countries in Asia and Africa, he proposed the "Eight Principles for Economic Aid and Technical Assistance to Other Countries" with its core principles being "pursuing equality and mutual benefit, respecting the sovereignty of recipient countries, and having absolutely no strings attached." Having no conditions attached, and particularly no political conditions attached, became a basic guiding principle in China's foreign aid program, and successive governments in China have always adhered to this principle. In November 2009, when he participated in the Fourth Ministerial Meeting of the Forum on China-Africa Cooperation, Premier Wen Jiabao once again solemnly declared to the world that China's support and assistance to Africa did not have in the past and will never have in the future any political strings attached. China always respects the equal status of aid giver and recipient. The relation between the countries is the relation of friends and partners rather than the relation of teacher and pupil. It follows the pattern of South-South Cooperation rather than the relation of unilateral alms.

Chapter 11
Can China Really Achieve Win-Win Results with Other Countries? | 331

China's Eight Principles for Economic Aid and Technical Assistance to Other Countries are: 1. The Chinese government always works from the principle of equality and mutual benefit in providing aid to other countries. It never regards such aid as a kind of unilateral alms but as a mutual exchange. 2. In providing aid to other countries, the Chinese government strictly respects the sovereignty of recipient countries and never attaches any conditions or asks for any privileges. 3. China provides economic aid in the form of interest-free or low-interest loans and extends the time limit for the repayment when necessary so as to ease the burden on recipient countries as far as possible. 4. In providing aid to other countries, the objective of the Chinese government is not to make recipient countries dependent on China but to help them embark on the road to self-reliance and independent economic development. 5. The Chinese government does its best to help recipient countries complete projects which require less investment but yield quicker results so that the latter may increase their income and accumulate capital. 6. The Chinese government provides the best-quality equipment and materials manufactured by China at international market prices. If the equipment and materials provided by the Chinese government are not up to the agreed specifications and quality, the Chinese government undertakes to replace them or refund the payment. 7. In giving any particular technical assistance, the Chinese government will see to it that the personnel of the recipient country fully master the technology. 8. The experts dispatched by China to recipient countries will accept the same standard of living as the experts of the recipient countries. The Chinese experts are not allowed to make any special demands or enjoy any special amenities.

However, some Western countries and their media disapprove of or even condemn China's practice of foreign aid without political strings attached. This stems from the fact that China and the West both differ and compete in their philosophy and approach to foreign aid, resulting in the deepening of the misunderstandings and concerns of the West.

Since the end of the Cold War, Western countries have addressed more and more attention to issues such as human rights, democracy, and the governance of the recipient country in the exercise of their foreign aid programs. They require that aid funds promote political, economic, and social progress in the recipient countries. In practice, Western countries often attach political conditions to their aid so that they can influence and change the development process and direction of the recipient countries. Western countries do not consider the attachment of political conditions as being a negative phenomenon. Rather, they believe that the attachment of political strings is helpful in regulating and guiding the use of aid funds, and in monitoring the aid process so that the goals of foreign aid can be better reached.

But China believes that the attachment of political conditions is equivalent to interfering in the internal affairs of other countries and seeking political privilege. It holds that such practice violates the Five Principles of Peaceful Coexistence. China does not accept that any other country impose its ideology, values and development model on China, and it will absolutely not impose its own ideology, values and development model on other countries. China's aid, free of political strings, provides a new option for many countries that were previously dependent on Western aid. Some of these countries reject aid from Western countries that comes with extensive political conditions attached, and it thereby weakens the influence of the West that has traditionally been exerted on these countries through aid and assistance. In addition, as China quickly emerges as a major source of foreign aid, Western countries see China's foreign aid as a disturbance to the order of international development assistance which the West is accustomed to dominate.

At present, China's foreign aid strategy attracts criticism from some elements of the international community. Some of this comes from a misunderstanding of the fundamental differences between Chinese and Western aid philosophies. However, another part stems from ulterior motives. It is argued in some quarters that the objective of China's aid, free of political strings, is to acquire the energy resources of the recipient countries and to facilitate access to their markets. In fact, oil exported to China accounts for less than 30% of the total exports from Africa. In 2009, China's investment in the mining industry accounted for about 29% of its total investment in Africa. In contrast, U.S. investment in the mining industry accounted for 60% of its total direct investment in Africa. China has also helped Mali, a country with few resources to offer, to build bridges and roads.

Similarly, China's foreign aid strategy is accused of ignoring corruption and human rights abuses by the governments of recipient countries. In fact, the Chinese government and the governments of the recipient countries jointly participate in the development and implementation of aid projects, and in the entire process of aid provision and supervision. Additionally, China's foreign aid is generally provided in kind or though initiatives such as construction project implementation. China avoids providing aid in cash as much as possible, so as to limit the risk of government corruption. One thing that must be emphasized is that although China does not attach political strings to its foreign aid, this does not mean that China neglects humanitarian issues in recipient countries. On the contrary, the Chinese government focuses its aid on infrastructure projects that are helpful to improving the life of ordinary people precisely because of the importance that it attaches to human rights. Through providing aid in the type of projects that are closely related to the living conditions of ordinary people, such as schools, hospitals, stadiums, gymnasiums, highways, bridges, railways, power stations, docks, ports, airports, and postal and telecommunications facilities, China brings practical help to recipient countries in improving their living standards and strengthening their capacity for independent development.

China's approach has been widely welcomed in the recipient countries. Abdoulaye Wade, president of Senegal, pointed out that: "Through various fair and reasonable contracts, China has already helped African countries build many infrastructure projects and improve the living standards of millions of African people. Compared with those in the West who criticize China, the Chinese people are more competitive and less bureaucratic, and China is more suitable to Africa as a partner." In July 2008 the World Bank issued a research report entitled "Building Bridges: China's Growing Role as Infrastructure Financier for Sub-Saharan Africa." The report said that China had invested a lot of money and built many bridges, railways and highways in Sub-Saharan Africa, where the natural conditions are extremely harsh. The improvement of infrastructure has made a significant contribution to economic development in Africa, and helped to create a much-improved investment environment.

In contrast with Western aid, which comes with political strings attached, actually restrains the initiative of recipient countries and is limited in impact. In Africa, for example, since the 1980s Western countries and international institutions have provided structured loans with conditions attached in an attempt to promote policy change in Africa. But this approach has not been successful in bringing fundamental change to Africa. Since the 1990s, the West has attached extensive political conditions to its aid with the aim of furthering the democratic process in African countries. But its efforts have failed to reduce the corruption rate there. On the contrary, many African state heads have had to get close to the Washington Consensus in word and deed in order to secure assistance from the West. Such practice directly narrows their space for regulatory action in many areas such as financial policy, monetary policy, exchange rate policy and trade and industry policy, and lowers their capacity for development.

In addition, attaching political strings implies that aid-giving countries know better than recipient countries how to achieve economic development and social progress. This condescending attitude is inconsistent with the principles in international law. It also departs from the endogenous laws of economic development, and has invited criticism from both governments and the public in recipient countries. African state heads such as Ugandan President Yoweri Museveni and Botswanan President Festus G. Mogae have demanded that the West cease interfering with the decision-making processes of African countries, asserting that Africa's development choices must not be determined according to the will of the West.

Is China engaging in neo-colonialism in Africa?

According to the Oxford Dictionary and the Merriam-Webster Dictionary, 'neo-colonialism' refers to the practice where a power controls or influences other countries through economic or political pressure. For many years, China has adopted a policy of equality, mutual benefit, and win-win cooperation with Africa, and it has never engaged in control, intervention or plundering of resources. In politics, China has established a relationship of equality and mutual trust. In military sphere, China has never built any military bases or stationed any troops in Africa. In terms of economic and trade cooperation, China has always adhered to the principles of mutual benefit, win-win results, and giving more while taking less, or giving without taking. To date, China has implemented over 900 aid projects in Africa and trained over 40,000 skilled workers. In 2012, trade between China and Africa approached USD 200 billion, and personnel exchanges between China and Africa exceeded 1.5 million people. In 2013, Chinese President Xi Jinping set foot on the soil of Africa on his first foreign trip. This confirms that China cherishes its traditional friendship with Africa. During his visit, China and Africa concluded over 40 cooperation agreements, including a group of major projects beneficial to the national interests and the ordinary people of African countries. China also declared a series of measures to support Africa, including strengthening China's aid to Africa, cooperation in investment and financing, and training of professional talent. China emphasized that it will fulfill its practical commitments without any political strings attached. China will focus on helping African countries to turn their resourc-

In May 2009, the Gotera Overpass, an aid project build by China in Ethiopia, was completed. The flyover, 8,281 meter long, greatly improved the traffic flow in the urban area of Addis Ababa.

es into development strengths and realize diversified, independent and sustainable development. It will encourage Chinese-funded enterprises to be socially responsible and bring positive benefits to local people. All of this serves to prove that China is helping rather than colonizing Africa.

First, China's investment in Africa has a sound structure. Under the old unequal international economic order, despite its comparative wealth of natural resources Africa spent many years at the low end of the international industry chain. As they became independent states, African countries regained their ownership of their resources. But in the wave of democratization that followed, state-owned enterprises were once more privatized. Because the countries involved lacked capital, their main industries fell back into the grip of Western capital. It can be said that this was true "neo-colonialism."

In contrast, China's investment in Africa is different. At present, China's share still accounts for a very small proportion of foreign investment in Africa. By the end of 2011, the value of China's investment in Africa amounted to USD 16.25 billion, accounting for 3.8% of China's foreign investment and 2.9% of foreign investment in Africa. However, China invests large amounts of funds in industries other than raw resources. By June 2012, China's investment in Africa amounted to USD 45 billion. Of this total, investments in manufacture, finance and construction accounted for 60%, while mining accounted for about 25%. The majority of China's investments are beneficial to the development of Africa's industry chain and infrastructure.

Careful analysis will show that in Africa, Chinese enterprises are mining the poorest grades of resources, hiring the least-skilled workers, and engaging in the industries with the hardest conditions. It is not that Chinese enterprises take pleasure in operating at the lowest level of industry, but that China believes that economic and social development has to be achieved through improving the lowest stratum of society. Western countries have been investing in Africa for centuries. They have created a few affluent industries and a small number of high earners, but the divide between the rich and the poor is becoming increasingly pronounced. What Africa really lacks is the kind of foreign investment that can bring prosperity to those people at the lowest levels of society, and China's investments bridge this gap. Chinese companies actively invest in infrastructure, and in initiatives to improve local investment and local living conditions. Through partnerships in infrastructure, Chinese enterprises help their host countries build communications networks, telecommunications facilities, urban water supply and drainage systems, schools, and hospitals. Partial statistics show that since 2000, Chinese enterprises have completed housing projects of about 70 million square meters, laid about 60,000 kilometers of roads, and built power stations with an installed capacity about 3.5 million kilowatts. PetroChina's positive actions have helped local people to build schools and provide basic education facilities in Africa. It has donated or built 35 schools in Sudan alone, providing schooling opportunities to over 70,000 school-age children.

Second, Africa's exports to China are growing rapidly. In its economic interactions with Africa, China adopts a policy of encouraging imports form Africa. Since 2009, China has been Africa's biggest trade partner. In these three years, Africa's exports to China have doubled. There has been a notable expansion in the range of goods exported from Africa to China. These include both African agricultural products and manufactured goods like steel, copper and fertilizers. In order to promote balanced trade development between China and Africa, in 2012 China promulgated a series of stimulation polices, for example, the "special plans on trade with Africa." China also dispatched investment and trade promotion delegations to Africa to expand its import of African products, and supported exhibitions on African goods to provide opportunities for African enterprises to promote their leading products. It increased openings in the Chinese market for African countries, and raised the number of items classified as zero tariff from the least developed countries in Africa. With the encouragement of these policies, African products have won access to a wider market in China. In addition, as the majority of the African countries are not rich, China helps ordinary African people by exporting products to Africa at reduced prices.

Third, China is firmly committed to resolving the grain issue in Africa. The Chinese government has often indicated that agriculture and secure food supplies should be priority areas in Sino-African cooperation so as to provide a fundamental support to Africa's economic and social development. Over a long period of time, China has carried out a variety of agricultural initiatives with African countries. Through a variety of measures such as trade expansion, investment, aid, and technical cooperation, China has helped African countries improve their capacity to produce and process food. Through Africa-aid agriculture demonstration centers, China continues to send agricultural technology teams to African countries to teach agricultural production technology and expertise. Through providing emergency food assistance to African countries, China helps African countries to survive food crises. In the *Beijing*

Action Plan (2013-2015), the Chinese government declared a series of Sino-African agricultural cooperation plans. China will continue with its efforts to alleviate Africa's food problems in the future.

Fourth, China attaches high importance to human rights in Africa. China has always believed that the right to life is the most essential human right, and the most urgent problem to be solved in Africa is first and foremost the issue of survival and development. Therefore, China will concentrate its aid to Africa on improving and coordinating basic survival and development conditions. It will put more weight on living conditions, development, poverty alleviation and relief, disaster prevention and reduction, and building expertise. It builds new schools, hospitals, bridges, roads and water supply projects. It dispatches large medical teams. It has trained nearly 40,000 Africans in various skills. It provides over 20,000 government scholarship opportunities to students in African countries. These efforts provide precious human resources for the construction and development of Africa.

In sum, the economic interaction between China and Africa is the interaction of mutual benefit and win-win results built on the basis of traditional friendship. The "neo-colonialism" argument of the West does not hold water. On this matter, the state heads of African countries are best qualified to speak. When President Xi Jinping visited three African countries in March 2013, President of the Republic of Congo Denis Sassou-Nguesso confirmed that China respects and helps Africa, and does not interfere in the internal affairs of African countries. He pointed out that accusations of Chinese neo-colonialism in Africa stem from ulterior motives. African people had experienced colonialism and knew what it was. They would not be misled on the subject. African people support Sino-African

Chapter 11
Can China Really Achieve Win-Win Results with Other Countries? 341

Chinese agricultural experts in discussions with agricultural technicians on practical issues of high-yield rice production in the farmlands of Sierra Leone.

Since 1996, China and the UN Food and Agriculture Organization have been involved in South-South Cooperation under the framework of the Special Program for Food Security. China has sent more than 800 agricultural experts and technicians to over 20 developing countries.

cooperation and hope that China will play a bigger role in promoting peace, stability and development in Africa.

President Obiang Nguema Mbasogo of the Republic of Equatorial Guinea indicated his indignation about the hype surrounding accusations of "neo-colonialism." He stated: "This is an absurd and groundless accusation. Africa has confidence and trust in China. China sincerely hopes that Africa will achieve development!" Chadian President Idriss Deby Itno repeatedly told President Xi that African friends greatly welcome the Chinese people and companies from China. The British magazine *The Economist* published an article acknowledging that China's image had been damaged as a result of Western criticism, but was now recovering. More and more Africans see that the Chinese create jobs, transfer technology and inject funds into the local economy. Such change was particularly obvious in small countries that had once feared this Asian giant. A CNN report said that the infrastructure built by China in Ghana in a decade was more than that built by the UK in a century. Deborah Brautigam, a professor at Johns Hopkins University and a recognized Sino-African expert, pointed out in her book *The Dragon's Gift: The Real Story of China in Africa* that what China brought to Africa was trade and investment projects that could truly promote the development of Africa.

The Roadmap of the 18th CPC National Congress and The Chinese Dream

Chapter 12

What Role Will China Play as a New Power?

China will firmly pursue an independent foreign policy of peace. China is committed to developing friendship and cooperation in all fields with other countries on the basis of the Five Principles of Peaceful Coexistence.

— Report of the 18th CPC National Congress

On diplomacy, the Report to the 18th CPC National Congress emphasized that China would resolutely adhere to an independent foreign policy of peace. In addition, it used the "four opposes" to clarify its attitude in resolving international disputes and issues. (Namely, China opposes the unnecessary resort to force or threat to use force; opposes any foreign attempt to subvert the legitimate government of another country; opposes terrorism in all its manifestations; and opposes hegemony and power politics in all their forms.) It proposed: "China will continue to focus on both the interests of the Chinese people and the common interests of the peoples of all countries, become more actively involved in international affairs, play its due role as a major responsible country, and work jointly with other countries to meet global challenges."

The idea of China as a "major responsible country" was not invented by China. It originally appeared in the speeches of some state heads in the West. It arose from the hope that China would shoulder international responsibilities appropriate to its own strength and not concentrate only on its own development. But when China took on board this term and included it in the report to the CPC congress, it still triggered much discussion in the international community. Some questioned whether it meant that China was planning to make significant adjustments to its long-standing foreign policy of "keeping a low profile and making some contribution," and turning to more positive or active – or even more hard-line – policies. Did China regard itself as a power rather than a developing country? Did China want to use its strength and influence to change the current international order and international rules? All in all, what kind of international role will China play?

All these questions are understandable, but cannot reflect the whole picture of China's foreign policy. With the developments and changes on both the domestic and international stages, China cannot maintain an unchanged foreign policy. But any adjustment must be beneficial to both China's development and the world's development, because on the banner of China's foreign policy there are written the four words: peace, development, cooperation, and win-win results, because China plays its role of a major responsible country on the basis of combining the interests of the Chinese people and the interests of the rest of the international community, and because China plays this role with an aim to respond to global challenges in harmony with other countries.

Will China adjust its policies of "non-interference" and "non-alignment"?

Since the start of the Syria crisis in 2011, China has twice vetoed draft resolutions on the issue proposed by Western countries at the Security Council. China opposed the proposal to exert pressure on Syria and threatening to use sanctions, and advocated resolving the dispute through political dialogue. This action caused resentment in some Western countries. In the eyes of many Western politicians and media, China's principle of not interfering in other countries' internal affairs is no longer appropriate in an age of increasing globalization. This is obviously not helpful to resolving many international issues and to establishing China's international image as a responsible country.

In fact, Western countries have criticized China's non-interference policy since the end of the Cold War. Their main reasons are that the principle contravenes international norms on human rights, particularly the "responsibility to protect." The "responsibility to protect" is a concept proposed in a report submitted to the United Nations by the Canadian International Commission of Intervention and State Sovereignty in 2001. The term was used to replace the concept of humanitarian intervention that had caused much controversy. Later, it was written into the final communiqué of the 2005 World Summit on the 60th anniversary of the establishment of the United Nations. Western scholars and politicians who advocate "the responsibility to protect" claim that where a certain community is suffering serious impairment due to civil war, insurrection, suppression or state dysfunction, and the state does not want to, or cannot stop or redress the situation, the principle of non-interference should give way to a responsibility on the part of the international community to protect.

Superficially, this argument appears to occupy the moral high ground and demonstrate "concern" for developing countries. In reality it becomes a pretext to practice hegemony, power politics and neo-interventionism under the guise of humanitarianism. It is typical of the behavior through which the West tries to shape the world according to its own standards. If China's principle of not interfering in the internal affairs of other countries is examined from this perspective, it is natural that it will be labeled as "contravening international norms." It is not only the West that questions this policy, there are differences of opinion inside China too. Some suggest that as its overseas interests expand, China should adjust its non-interference policy as a means to protect its own economic interests. For example, during the unrest in West Asia and North Africa, the rights and interests of localized Chinese citizens and corporations suffered considerable damages due to the non-interference policy of the Chinese government. Thus the principle prevents China from making some contribution to international and local affairs. Why does China maintain such a policy in the face of so many doubts and opposing views?

Not interfering in other countries' internal affairs is one of the core principles in the *United Nations Charter*. It is also the main element in the Five Principles of Peaceful Coexistence. It is a powerful weapon with which small and weak countries can protect their independence and sovereignty and oppose hegemony and power politics. In its modern history, China suffered much oppression and humiliation by various world powers. It knows all too well the pain of losing sovereignty and being oppressed by others. Therefore, new China has always resolutely opposed any interference in China's internal affairs by external forces. It has fought with great determination against numerous attempts to interfere in China's internal affairs.

As the saying goes, "Never impose on others what you would not choose for yourself." China will never interfere in the internal affairs of other countries. It opposes interference in the internal affairs of other countries, on whatever pretext. It advocates that all countries, no matter how large or small, are equal and that the affairs of every country should be determined by its people. It was solemnly promised in the Report to the 18th CPC National Congress that China would not interfere in the internal affairs of other countries and that it opposed the overthrow of the legitimate regimes of other countries. Whatever the reaction of the major Western powers, China's policy is popular in the wider international community, particularly among the small and medium-sized developing countries.

The principle of non-interference does not conflict with China's international responsibilities. The "responsibility to protect" in the final communiqué of the UN World Summit has at least three pillars. First, it remains the case that the sovereign state is considered to have the key role in protecting the citizens of a country. Second, the role of the international community lies only in providing support to the government of a sovereign state to help it meet the responsibility to protect its citizens. Third, if the international community really needs to take collective action, including military intervention, such actions must be taken under the framework of the United Nations Charter.

Therefore, it is incorrect to believe that the "responsibility to protect" entitles external forces to carry out arbitrary interventions to other countries where humanitarian disasters are. China has always advocated resolving international conflicts peacefully by means of negotiation, but it does not simplistically object to any and all international intervention. It opposes forcible and illegitimate interventions. The premises of a legitimate international intervention are that it must have the authorization of the United Nations and that it must have the consent of the target country. If the will of the target country and the international community are neglected or violated, if the United Nations are circumvented, then any resulting intervention is more likely to exacerbate the situation and cause a humanitarian disaster than to solve the problem. The first exercise of this new "responsibility to protect" was the military campaign launched by the NATO coalition force on Libya. In fact, the NATO air strikes caused significant civilian casualties, and the "responsibility to protect" was a sham.

China's non-interference policy does not mean that it is indifferent to international affairs. The Report to the 18th CPC National Congress emphasized that China "decides its position and policy on the basis of specific rights and wrongs. It will pursue fairness and uphold justice." It will work together with the international community to "jointly maintain international fairness and justice." As to the conduct that violates human rights, China insists that relevant problems be resolved within the framework of the United Nations. As a permanent member of the UN Security Council, China will not shirk from its duties in resolving international disputes. In recent years, China has participated positively in addressing and resolving a series of major regional issues like the Korean Peninsula nuclear issue, the Iran nuclear issue, and the issues in Libya, Sudan and Afghanistan. China won the trust and respect of these countries by taking a clear-cut stand, sticking firmly to its principles, and adopting flexible strategies. On these occasions, China's contribution to maintaining peace and stability was an important one.

Non-alignment is an important element of China's independent foreign policy of peace. It is also an important means of maintaining China's own independence and peaceful development. The policy took shape in the early 1980s, and has since been regularly restated in the important literature of the Communist Party of China, in sections dealing with foreign affairs in government work reports, in the white papers on national defense, and in the important speeches of state heads on foreign policy. It was specifically pointed out in the Report to the 14th CPC National Congress that "China will not enter into alliance with any country or group of countries and it will not participate in any military bloc." It was reaffirmed in the Report to the 15th CPC National Congress that "China will not enter into alliance with any country or group of countries and it will not engage in any military bloc, participate in any arms race, or engage in military expansionism." It was emphasized in the white paper *China's Peaceful Development* published in 2011 that China "remains committed to developing friendly cooperation with all countries on the basis of the Five Principles of Peaceful Coexistence, and it will not enter into alliance with any country or group of countries." All of this confirms that the non-alignment policy is core to China's state will. It is one of China's long-term policies.

However, non-alignment does not equate to isolationism. An important feature of China's diplomatic relations after the end of the Cold War is that China has formed an extensive range of partnerships with major countries around the world and with key countries in various regions. Such partnerships, particularly the China-Russia comprehensive strategic partnership of coordination and the related Shanghai Cooperation Organization, are often misinterpreted by the outside world as a de facto alliance or a new type of alliance. In fact, such partnerships are substantively different from alliances.

First, partnership is the means by which China strengthens its cooperation with other major countries and with key regional countries. This does not necessarily involve the strengthening of security or military cooperation. Second, partnership is a new form of interstate relationship whose general popularity is growing in today's world. It is not a model unique to China. Third, China has established partnership relations not only with individual countries, but also with some important regional organizations like the EU, Africa, the ASEAN, and central and eastern Europe. The partnership with the latter involves no security considerations. Fourth, the security element in China's partnership relations is generally designed to increase communication, strengthen cooperation, and enhance mutual trust in military matters. It lacks the substantive security cooperation terms that an alliance entails. In sum, the partnerships that China establishes with other countries and regions are characterized by non-alignment and non-confrontation, and they are not directed against any third country. This is both the inheritance and the legacy bequeathed by the independent non-alignment policy.

Will all-out confrontation occur between China and the USA?

China and the USA are respectively the largest developing country and the largest developed country in the world. The relationship between them goes far beyond bilateral scope and possesses growing global influence and strategic significance. China and the USA will benefit from peaceful coexistence and will lose from any conflict. How to address such a relationship is inevitably a headache to the leaders of the two countries. It is hard to foresee how the two countries can become close, as their social systems and ideologies are too different. But if they become too far estranged, there are reasonable grounds to fear that these differences might cause misunderstandings and misjudgment.

When Xi Jinping, the then vice president of China, visited the USA in February 2012, he proposed that the two sides should work hard to "build a cooperative partnership of the two coun-

On June 7 and 8, 2013, Chinese President Xi Jinping and US President Barack Obama met at the Annenberg Estate in California, USA.

tries into a new form of relationship between great powers." The Report to the 18th CPC National Congress further proposed: "We will improve and develop our relationship with developed countries. We will expand areas of cooperation, properly handle disagreements, and promote a new form of relationship between great powers manifesting long-term, stable, and healthy development." The CPC therefore advocates that China needs to extend this new form of relationship with the USA and beyond to other major countries.

This new form of relationship between great powers is defined in contrast to traditional relationships between great powers. History provides too many painful lessons where great powers fought for hegemony and brought disaster upon themselves and the wider world. From the Hundred Years War between Britain and France in the 14th and 15th centuries, through the two World Wars, to the confrontation and the Cold War between the USA and the Soviet Union in the 20th century, relationships between great powers have never managed to escape the "historical trap" in which a rising power challenges an established power and the established power tries to contain the rising power. It is inevitable that the rise of new power will squeeze out the interests of an established power, and that the established power will go to great lengths to suppress any rising power. Historically, such conflicts were almost invariably resolved through war. Changing the existing order through war has been considered an iron law of international relations. Based on such traditional mindset, many Western politicians and academics believe that the rise of China will inevitably trigger new conflicts. Early in the 1990s, the "China Threat" theory began to emerge in the international community, particularly in the West. When its economic aggregate exceeded that of Japan and China became the No. 2 economy in the world, the outcry against China became even harsher and louder.

The CPC proposes building a new form of relationship between great powers. This is to be done on the basis of both drawing from the lessons of traditional relationships between great powers, and observing the changing and developing trends of the present age and the current international situation. Today, multi-polarization, economic globalization, cultural diversification, and social informatization are on the rise. Countries around the world have increasing mutual connections and interdependence. There are growing numbers of issues of global importance, such as the financial crisis, climate change, energy and food security, and terrorism.

No country can now achieve development entirely under its own steam. Nor can it settle conflict and address challenge on its own initiative. The world is gradually becoming a "global village" in which "there is a bit of me in you and a bit of you in me" applies to all countries. The world forms a community of common interests with a destiny in which all countries have a shared stake. The right way to address mutual relations between countries is that they should work together towards the same aims and cooperate to achieve win-win results. World trends march inexorably onward. Those who follow the trends will prosper, and those who try to oppose them will perish. Worn-out tricks like cold war thinking, the zero-sum game, dividing according to ideology, and cliques and factionalism can no longer work. Building a new form of relationship between great powers characterized by non-alignment, non-conflict, non-confrontation, mutual respect, peaceful coexistence, cooperation, and win-win results is both the sensible choice that will function in the best interests of all concerned parties, and the strong call of the times.

But what should the new form of relationship between great powers that the CPC advocates be like? The Report to the 18th CPC National Congress gave an answer to this question. It contains three phrases: "Equality and mutual trust, tolerance and learning from each other, and cooperation and win-win results."

Equality and mutual trust means that people should follow the purposes and principles of the United Nations Charter. They should respect the principle that all countries are equal regardless of size, power and wealth. They should promote the democratization of international relations, respect other countries' sovereignty, enjoy mutual security, and maintain the peace and stability of the world.

Tolerance and learning from each other means that people should respect the diversity of civilization and the diversification of paths to development. They should respect and maintain the right of different countries to choose their own social system and their own path to development. They should learn from each other and draw on the strong points of others to make up for their own weak points so as to promote the progress of human civilization.

Cooperation and win-win results means that people should promote the awareness of a human community of shared fate. When a country pursues its own interests, it should take into consideration the reasonable concerns of other countries. When a country strives for its own development, it should promote the joint development of others. It should establish a more equal and balanced form of global development partnership. Countries should cooperate in pursuit of the same aims, and share rights and responsibilities so as to enhance the common interests of humanity.

Among these three elements, tolerance and learning from each other play the role of a touchstone that functions as a connection between the first and the third phrases. If people cannot practice tolerance and learning from each other, any commitment to equality and mutual trust will be nothing more than lip service. If people cannot practice tolerance and learning from each other, it is unlikely that they will achieve cooperation and win-win results.

Only when the principle of tolerance and learning from each other is respected and practiced, can the ideological roots of contradictions and conflicts be eliminated, and lasting peace in the world be achieved. And only in this way can the ties and bridges for a new form of relationship between great powers be built. Human history is full of contradictions and conflicts related to culture, civilization, religion, values and ideology. Behind the breakout of World War II was the haunting presence of the theory of racial superiority. Ideological differences made a major contribution to the confrontation between the USA and the Soviet Union in the decades following World War II. The role that religion has played in the Israeli-Palestinian conflict is widely known. The numerous wars that the USA has launched since the end of the Cold War have much to do with the worldwide "democratization" strategy it promotes.

All these examples indicate that instability and insecurity in the world inevitably follow where one culture or set of values repels or rejects another culture or set of values, or treats it as an enemy. In fairness, the emergence of individual strains of thought and ideologies have their roots in relevant historical conditions and specific environments. There is no strain of thought or ideology that is absolutely good or absolutely evil. If people follow the philosophy that "those who are not with us are against us," there will be no peace in this world.

In foreign relations, China advocates that differences in ideology must be transcended, that political positions related to social systems should not become political banners, and that Cold War thinking must be abandoned. This is because these thoughts violate the fundamental spirit and principle of tolerance and learning from each other. They are harmful both to establishing a new form of relationship between great powers and to building a fairer and more reasonable world order. If the USA can be more tolerant of China's systems, and learn something from China's development experience, there will be fewer issues between China and the USA. And the USA might get out of its financial crisis sooner.

Does China intend to "keep friendly relations with distant states and attack its neighbors"?

China has the largest number of neighboring countries in the world. It has more than 22,000 kilometers of terrestrial boundary and over 18,000 kilometers of coastline. China has 29 neighboring countries, 14 of which have shared borders with China. As the Chinese saying goes, "A far-off relative is not as close as a near neighbor." It is always a priority task in China's foreign affairs to strengthen relations with its neighbors. Since the start of the new century, China has devoted a greater effort to building a harmonious neighboring environment with lasting peace and joint prosperity. In 2002, the 16th CPC National Congress defined "being a good neighbor and partner" as the guiding policy in China's diplomacy with regard to its neighbors. After that, the Chinese government further proposed the policy of "bringing harmony, security and prosperity to neighbors." In April 2011, Hu Jintao, the then state president, proposed the joint initiative of "Harmonious Asia" for which he obtained extensive support from various countries in Asia. The Report to the 18th CPC National Congress once again emphasized: "We will adhere to the principle of being a good neighbor and partner, consolidate friendly relations with our neighbors, strengthen mutually beneficial cooperation with them, and ensure that China's development will be of benefit to them."

It is precisely under the guidance of these policies that China is steadily developing its relations with neighboring countries. They engage in frequent bilateral high-level interactions, harmonious coexistence in politics, mutual benefits and reciprocity in economy, mutual trust and collaboration in security, and mutual learning and borrowing in culture. These efforts promote joint development, prosperity, and progress, and bring practical benefits and interests to their own people. They also promote the peace, stability and development of the entire region. It should be said that Asia's rise as a whole is closely related to China's policies and practices. If China had adopted a policy of self-interest and depreciated the Renminbi when the Asian financial crisis erupted in 1998, it is unlikely that Asia would enjoy its current strong momentum of economic growth, and the attention of the international community might now be focused elsewhere.

It is undeniable that there are conflicts and disagreements in the relations between China and its neighbors. The biggest problem is disputes over territory and marine rights and interests. Certain countries constantly stir up trouble over issues concerning the South China Sea and the Diaoyu Islands. They have used their naval vessels and police forces to illegally attack and harass Chinese fishermen and detain Chinese citizens. Such actions represent a serious infringement of China's sovereignty. The CPC and the Chinese government has had to take corresponding measures to maintain state sovereignty and territorial integrity, and protect the safety and the lives and property of Chinese citizens. Some have accused China of taking a hard-line position in these disputes, and returning to its historical tradition of keeping friendly relations with distant states and attacking those nearby. This view is unreasonable. China's position on issues related to its territory and territorial seas has been consistent and unequivocal. China possesses indisputable sovereignty over the Nansha Islands and surrounding seas, and over Diaoyu Island and its associated islands. There is extensive historical and jurisprudential evidence to back this up.

Although the countries concerned are both provocative and hostile in their attitude, China consistently exercises restraint. It maintains its approach of developing friendly bilateral relations. It continues to advocate the amicable settlement of disagreements through dialogue, negotiation and bilateral diplomatic consultation. It retains normal communications with the countries in question, and at the same time resolutely opposes any intervention by any third party. It can be said that China is "in the right" in its conduct over these matters. But China does not take advantage of this to become intolerant. Chinese state leaders repeatedly emphasize that when China handles its relations with the outside world, particularly with its neighbors, it needs to maintain a stance of modesty and prudence and must not resort to arrogance. But this does not mean that China will allow its forbearance to be abused. Both large and small countries should respect each other. A large country should not abuse or bully a small country. And a small country in return should not go out of its way to provoke a large country.

China's policy on disagreements with its neighbors not only reflects the proper and responsible attitude that a major country should have, but also shows that China values the relations with its neighbors in Asia. In the future, China will continue to follow the diplomatic policies of "being a good neighbor and partner" and "bringing harmony, peace and wealth to its neighbors." It will vigorously advocate a new security outlook characterized by mutual trust, mutual benefit, equality and collaboration. It will try to find major points in common, and try to set aside minor differences. It will take into consideration the security concerns of all parties and exhibit goodwill, wisdom and patience to the best of its ability. It will remain committed to settling conflicts through dialogue and negotiation. It will positively promote regional cooperation on matters of security. It will work hard to maintain a peaceful and stable regional environment.

In sum, China will work together with its neighbors to seize opportunities and respond to challenges. It will make every effort to ensure that China's development successes are of benefit to its neighbors, so as to promote joint development and build a harmonious Asia together with them.

Will China continue to speak for developing countries?

In 2010, China's economic aggregate exceeded that of Japan and it became the second largest economy in the world. Voices appeared in the international community suggesting that China could no longer be considered a "developing country." Some academics in the USA have proposed the concept of a "G2" under which China and the USA would rule the world together. There are even people who have started to talk about "China ruling the world." It seems that China has become a superpower overnight. So is China still a developing country?

When judging the true development standard of a country, people should not examine its economic aggregate alone, or draw conclusions from only one or a few indices. China has achieved continuous and rapid growth through reform and opening-up. This is true. There is a tendency to exaggerate China's size and growth speed with words like "huge" and "fast." But this overlooks the reality that China also has a large population and a limited economic foundation. Although China is second only to the USA in terms of the total size of its economy, it still is a developing country when examined from the standpoint of per capita development. According to the statistics of the World Bank, China's per capita GDP in 2011 amounted to around USD 5,500, and ranked 87th on the globe. Per capita annual income was about USD 1,100 and ranked 133rd. There are 150 million people in China whose income falls below the UN standard of one dollar per day.

These are only seen from the data. What lies deeper is that the quality of China's economic development needs to be further improved. China cannot be compared with developed countries in terms of its standard of living, its science and technology, or its environmental protection. Other hard facts that must be taken into account are China's sub-optimal industrial structure, and its comprehensive development capacities that lag seriously behind developed countries. China has followed an intensive development model for many years. There are discrepancies in both economic structure and industrial structure. In addition, there are large gaps between China and developed countries in both the standards of science and technology and the capacity to introduce scientific and technological innovation. Because of this, Chinese products are often poor in quality and inferior in technology. The reality is that China is extensively involved in low-end manufacture and processing in the international economic chain, and still features low consumption, urbanization, education and management standards, showing how easily China's economic strength can be exaggerated.

In addition, although China has substantially enhanced its economic power since reform and opening-up, its soft power lags far behind its economy. Academics in China have made quantitative comparisons on the level of soft power between China and the USA. They believe that, if compared across the three combined metrics of international appeal, international mobilization, and domestic mobilization, China's soft power is about one third of America's. The maturity of the USA's culture industry, college education and civil society, its awareness of democracy, human rights and law in the area of social politics, and its ability to set and dominate the agenda, all exhibit the strength of its soft power. In contrast, China still has a long way to go in terms of the attraction of its culture, the emotional appeal of its values, the power of its development model, and the influence of its diplomatic philosophy and image. China still faces decades or more of hard work to achieve significant gains in these areas.

In sum, per capita indices and comprehensive development capacity are the best measures of the development level of a country and the actual living conditions of its citizens. When judging whether a country is a developing country, economic aggregate or even per capita GDP can be misleading. Comprehensive development capacity must also be taken into account. Just as then Premier Wen Jiabao pointed out at the UN high-level plenary meeting on the millennium development goals, although China had achieved enormous steps forward in moving from a subsistence economy to a generally prosperous society, it would remain for a considerable period of time a developing country in terms of numerous per capita indices, imbalanced development conditions, and the total population of those living in poverty. The Report to the 18th CPC National Congress also emphasized that China's international status as the largest developing country in the world had not changed.

China is a developing country. This is not merely the affirmation of a fact. It also signifies a commitment in politics. It means that China will continue to take the side of the extensive community of developing countries in international affairs. Deng Xiaoping emphasized repeatedly during his lifetime that "China is very much part of the third world. It belongs to the third world now. In the future, when it has achieved development and prosperity, it will still be part of the third world. China will always take the side of the third world."

From the founding of new China to the present day, the Chinese government has always insisted and repeated that its relations with other developing countries are the basis of China's foreign policy. Strengthening solidarity and cooperation with other developing countries is a fundamental principle of China's foreign relations. China's improving international status today is closely related to the support and cooperation of the extensive community of developing countries. At many critical points in recent history, it is the developing countries that have truly supported China. Although China's national strength has grown, no essential change has occurred to the interests and aspirations it shares with other developing countries in international political and economic matters. In particular, with the overall strengthening of emerging market countries and developing countries, solidarity and cooperation between China and other developing countries must be enhanced. This is why the Report to the 18th CPC National Congress emphasized: "We will strengthen solidarity and cooperation with other developing countries, jointly uphold the legitimate rights and interests of developing countries, and support efforts to increase their representation and voice in international affairs. China will always be a reliable friend and sincere partner of other developing countries."

What kind of international order does China advocate?

Many foreign friends are concerned about the influence a rejuvenated China will exert on the world. Will China observe the current international order or seek to replace it with a new order? What kind of world does China want?

China has already offered answers to these questions. It was also emphasized repeatedly in the Report to the 18th CPC National Congress that China would "promote a harmonious world of lasting peace and joint prosperity." This proposal was welcomed by many countries in the international community. However, some have expressed the opinion that a harmonious world is a utopia that can never be realized. Others see China's proposals as a surreptitious means of seeking hegemony. On May 31, 2012, a dialogue between Chinese and Western academics was held at the foot of the Great Wall in Beijing. Peter J. Katzenstein, former president of the American Political Science Association and professor of international studies at Cornell University, observed that many Americans did not like the word "harmony" that China proposed because they felt some sense of "hegemony" in it. At the time, Katzenstein did not explain where this feeling came from. But what people can be sure of is that it is a clear misunderstanding of traditional Chinese culture to consider that "harmony" is in any way associated with "hegemony."

Part of the unique spiritual wealth of the Chinese nation, the concept and culture of "concord and unity" has a specific meaning. Neither "concord" nor "unity" stresses on absolute "identity" but on "coexistence in harmony and diversity." "People should appreciate what they have in common and respect what they have in difference" is an apt way to express the idea. It refers to a harmonious coexistence that incorporates differences and distinctive features. "Concord" relates to harmony, amicability, peace and geniality. "Unity" relates to convergence, combination, coalition and merging. "Concord and unity" is a concept under which people recognize the nature of harmony of the world, further their interests by peaceful and cooperative means, and achieve concord and the Great Unity. The embodiment of the culture of "concord and unity" in international relations incorporates the idea that people should take "harmony" as the dominant value and appreciate its worth. No-one should support the idea that a powerful country may bully a weaker one or that one country may interfere in the internal affairs of another. As a saying goes, "Never impose on others what you would not choose for yourself." Chinese culture emphasizes that the achievement of mutual trust between large and small countries lies in the humility of a large country to a small country and the respect of a small country to a large country, and advocates the "non-aggression" philosophy under which the countries "appreciate each other and work to each other's mutual benefit." They should treat other countries like themselves, and establish a reputation for justice in the world. It is in the profound roots of China's traditional philosophy of "concord and unity" that the ultimate core goals of "bringing peace to the world" and "attaining the Great Unity" are to be found.

On the basis of such concepts and ideas, the Chinese people believe that the key to building a harmonious world is to welcome the diversity of the world, the differences in interests, and the plurality of civilization, and on such foundations coordinate interests, resolve conflicts, and pursue win-win results by peaceful and cooperative means. The process of building a harmonious world is a continuous process of resolving conflicts and increasing the contribution of harmony, and a process of constantly opposing hegemony and power politics and jointly maintaining international fairness and justice. So the harmonious world that the Chinese people promote is definitely not a world that allows the choice only between black and white. It is not a world that admires power and in which the strong bully the weak. It is not a world in which one is entitled to steal a horse while another has no right to look over a hedge. It is not a world of zero-sum game and life-or-death struggle. It is a world in which all countries are equal regardless of size, power and wealth. It is a world in which different civilizations and different development models learn from each other and offset their weaknesses by learning from the strong points of others. It is a world in which countries cooperate to achieve the same aims, share rights and responsibilities, and develop together. And it is a world in which people choose peace rather than war, development rather than poverty, cooperation rather than confrontation, and win-win results rather than zero-sum results.

This philosophy is precisely the reason why China never imposes its ideas on others and has no inclination to overthrow the existing framework and build a new one, although it has already become the second largest economy in the world and is beginning to play a decisive role in international affairs. China plays a constructive rather than destructive role in the international community. It shoulders the international burden of a responsible major country rather than turning away when its direct interests are not concerned. It plays the role of a leading member of the international community, but does not seek to become a dominant one. "We will positively participate in multilateral affairs, support the United Nations, G20, the Shanghai Cooperation Organization, BRICS and other multilateral organizations in playing a positive role in international affairs, and promote the development of the international order towards more just and equitable future."

Afterword

The chief compilers of this book are Huang Huaguang and Luan Jianzhang; its authors include: Cai Zhiqiang, Cao Rongxiang, Chen Li, Gai Ning, Gao Xiang, Guo Hongyu, Hao Honghai, He Shuping, He Zengke, Hu Changshuan, Huang Huaguang, Kou Liyan, Lai Hairong, Li Jinyan, Liang Bihan, Liang Guining, Lin Xiaobo, Ling Shengli, Liu Rensheng, Liu Ronggang, Lu Jing, Lü Pin, Lü Bo, Lü Ruijin, Luan Jianzhang, Nadira, Pan Haoyu, Pei Tiejun and Qü Bo, Ren Guixiang, Ren Hongbin, Shi Jianguo, Song Wei, Sun Haiyan, Sun Jingxin, Sun Yinan, Wang Dongqi, Wang Jun, Wang Li, Wang Wenqing, Wang Xiangping, Wang Xiao Ying, Wang Zhigang, Wu Zhijun, Xu Pengtang, Yang Jinhai, Yang Song, Yang Xuedong, Yu Yunquan, Yuan Lin, Zhang Changjiang, Zhang Dongming, Zhang Guifeng, Zhang Huijun, Zhang Kai, Zhang Mingjie, Zhao Xusheng, Zheng Zhaohong, Zhou Lin, Zhu Caihua; coordinators for liaison work are Yang Song and Li Jinyan.

The writing and editing of this book, starting in August, 2012, lasted for about a year, with the support of the Information Office of the State Council, and the assistance from the Publicity Department of the CPC Central Committee, the Party History Research Center of the CPC Central Committee, the Party Literature Research Office of the CPC Central Committee, Party School of the CPC Central Committee, Central Compilation and Translation Bureau, China Foreign Languages Publishing Administration (China International Publishing Group), Chinese Academy of International Trade and Economic Cooperation of Ministry of Commerce, Institute of International Relations of China Foreign Affairs University, and School of International Studies of Renmin University of China. Chen Baosheng, Ye Xiaowen, Chen Jin, Gao Yongzhong, Zhang Hongzhi, Huang Youyi, Wei Haisheng, Sun Yeli, Wang Changjiang, Li Jingzhi, Xing Houyuan and Wang Fan offered valuable suggestions about the conception and revision of this book, and also participated in the writing. The book also includes the recent research results by some domestic institutions. The editors hereby extend their gratitude to all the contributors.

The Editors

图书在版编目（CIP）数据

中共十八大：中国梦与世界：英文 / 黄华光主编.
—北京：外文出版社, 2013
ISBN 978-7-119-08647-7

Ⅰ.①中… Ⅱ.①黄… Ⅲ.①中共十八大（2012）—报告—学习参考资料—英文 Ⅳ.①D229
中国版本图书馆CIP数据核字(2013)第310276号

策　　划：	张燕彬　黄华光　黄友义
出版统筹：	栾建章　孙海燕
出版指导：	徐　步　胡开敏

英文翻译：	孙洪山　解圣哲
英文改稿：	David Ferguson
英文核定：	徐明强
责任编辑：	杨春燕　杨　璐
特约编辑：	李金艳　杨　淞
印刷监制：	张国祥

中共十八大：中国梦与世界

黄华光　栾建章　主编

ⓒ 2013 外文出版社有限责任公司

出 版 人：徐　步
出版发行：外文出版社有限责任公司
地　　址：中国北京百万庄大街24号　　邮政编码：100037
网　　址：www.flp.com.cn　　电子邮箱：flp@cipg.org.cn
电　　话：008610-68320579（总编室）　008610-68995852（发行部）
　　　　　008610-68327750（版权部）
印　　刷：北京朝阳印刷厂有限责任公司
经　　销：新华书店/外文书店
开　　本：787mm×1092mm　1/16
印　　张：24.5
字　　数：180千字
版　　次：2013年12月第1版　2013年12月第1版第1次印刷
（英）
ISBN 978-7-119-08647-7
07800（平）

版权所有　侵权必究　如有印装问题本社负责调换（电话：68995960）